LIVING UJA HISTORY

"Irving Bernstein was without question one of the most thoughtful, gutsy, and independent American Jewish leaders of his generation. Future generations can benefit enormously from the wisdom in this book."

- TOM FRIEDMAN, Former Middle
East Correspondent for The New York Times

LIVING UJA HISTORY

by

IRVING BERNSTEIN

As Told Through the Personal Stories
of Founders of Israel and
Leaders of the United Jewish Appeal

Jewish Publication Society
Philadelphia • Jerusalem
1997/5757

Manufactured in the United States of America

Designed by Book Design Studio II

Typeset by The Wordsmithy

Library of Congress Cataloging-in-Publication Data

Bernstein, Irving, 1921–
    Living UJA history / by Irving Bernstein.
      p.   cm.
    "As told through the personal stories of founders of Israel and
leaders of the United Jewish Appeal."
    Includes index.
    ISBN 0–8276–0648–6
    1. United Jewish Appeal—History. 2. Jews—United States—
—Politics and government. 3. United Jewish Appeal—Interviews.
4. Jews—Interviews. 5. Oral history.   I. Title.
HV3191.B427   1997
362.84'924073—dc21   97-37382
                                                    CIP
                                                        r97

In memory and in honor of Professor Moshe Davis of the Hebrew University, who inspired this history and edited the first two chapters before his untimely death in 1996.

ACKNOWLEDGMENTS

I am indebted to Jeanette Friedman, who completed the editing of this manuscript. Without her encouragement and wise counsel it could not have been done.

I am grateful to Chaim Vinitzky, the former director of the UJA office in Israel, for his invaluable memories—spanning five decades of watching American Jews and Israelis build bridges to each other. His encyclopedic mind helped me immeasurably by bringing my own memories back to life.

I extend my gratitude to Rabbi Brian L. Lurie, former UJA executive vice chairman of UJA, and to Bernard Moscovitz, the current executive vice president of UJA* for their full and complete support while I worked on this project.

*The title of executive vice chairman was changed to executive vice president in 1997.

"UJA is neither an organization nor an institution. It is a movement of passion and emotion, a link to our awareness as Jews and the meaning of Jerusalem to Jews, wherever they may be in the world."

Abba Eban

TABLE OF CONTENTS

Foreword by Prof. Moshe Davis		x
Irving Bernstein		xv
Preface by Dr. Howard Sachar		xxiii
1.	Introducing the UJA Family	1
2.	A Group Interview	7
3.	Project Renewal: An Interview with Yigael Yadin	23
4.	Project Renewal: Retrospective	35
5.	The Yom Kippur War: Frank Lautenberg with Irving Bernstein	49
6.	Frank Lautenberg: Retrospective	61
7.	Golda Meir	75
8.	Golda Meir: Retrospective	95
9.	Max M. Fisher	107
10.	Shimon Peres	129
11.	Max M. Fisher/Shimon Peres: Retrospective	147
12.	The Women's Division: Sylvia Hassenfeld	165
13.	Teddy Kollek	185
14.	Sylvia Hassenfeld/Teddy Kollek: Retrospective	201
15.	Young Leadership: Irwin S. Field	209
16.	Young Leadership: Yael Dayan	229
17.	Irwin Field/Yael Dayan: Retrospective	245
18.	Elie Wiesel	255
19.	Epilogue by Irving Bernstein	279
20.	Appendix A: Letter from Moshe Dyan	286
	Appendix B: The "We Are One" Speech	288
	Appendix C: Doctoral Citation from Yeshiva University	294
	Appendix D: Eulogy for Edward Ginsberg	295
	Appendix E: List of UJA Officers 1939–1997	298
	Index	305

FOREWORD

In his prefatory comments, the late Moshe Davis has fittingly described the role of the United Jewish Appeal (UJA) from the Israeli perspective. The function was hardly less than that of a blood transfusion, indeed, an ongoing series of blood transfusions, from the moment of the little republic's birth through all its ensuing traumas of immigration and perennial warfare. It is appropriate, therefore, that the impact of this life support system should be portrayed in these pages by those best qualified to discern its impact on their own homeland—such protean figures as Yigael Yadin, Golda Meir, Shimon Peres, Moshe Dayan, Yael Dayan, and Teddy Kollek.

It may be argued, nevertheless, that the UJA has exerted a possibly even more decisive impact upon the givers—that is, upon the Jews of the United States—than upon the recipients. The UJA was the principal vehicle, first of all, through which American Jews could give tangible expression to their identification with an ancestral homeland and with its new settlers. If American Jews themselves lived in a free and democratic nation, few of them, realistically, could have been expected to uproot themselves and replicate their own still vivid pioneering ordeal of building a new life in a new land. But they would not be found lacking in providing a concomitant opportunity for their co-religionists in Israel. The unresolved question in the 1940s was simply one of scope. What were the outer limits of American Jewish commitment and generosity?

That answer was provided almost immediately, and thereafter all but uninterruptedly. From 1947–1948 on, it became evident that there were no limits whatever to the bone marrow this tiny community was prepared to share with the Israeli republic. In 1946, a combined UJA-Federation campaign raised $100 million; in 1947, $158 million; in 1948, $205 million. Altogether, from 1946 through 1962 alone,

American Jews raised $2.3 billion in these drives, with more than half the sum going to the UJA—that is, predominantly to Israel. During the crisis of the 1967 Six-Day War, the UJA raised $311 million exclusively for Israel. In the crisis of the 1973 Yom Kippur War, the UJA alone raised $675 million. And that does not include funds raised by other organizations, including Israel Bonds.

Indeed, in 1973, as the funds poured in from both those of wealth and those of modest resources, the *Washington Post* began displaying a graph of American-Jewish largesse to Israel measured against the contributions of Arab oil-producing states to Israel's adversaries. The contrast was not invidious. In 1982, the *Wall Street Journal* observed that the year's UJA budget of $567 million equaled one-third of the nationwide United Way budget. By the same token, it was a generosity that dwarfed the contribution of any other ethnic group to any other philanthropic cause, domestic or overseas. Little wonder, then, that the effulgence of contributions should have evoked the attention and awe of the public media.

Much has been made not only of the scale of these UJA campaigns but of their folklore; of the phone calling and card calling, the door knocking and the heart tugging, the savings accounts and life insurance plans emptied by Jews of all circumstances. It is a moving story. But for better or worse, an organization's history is not made principally by majority emotion. It is sculpted by imaginative leadership. And it is here, in these pages, that we learn firsthand of the manner in which that leadership was mobilized, and then itself functioned as the mobilizing locomotive of American Jewry at large. The extraordinary figures who tell the tale in their own words, or who have the tale told of them by others, include Max Fisher, Henry Morgenthau, Jr., Sam Rothberg, Frank Lautenberg, Sylvia Hassenfeld, Irwin Field, and other dynamos of Jewish communal leadership. One can only read with fascination of the philosophies, the techniques, even the ruses by which these forceful personalities charted, and then executed, campaigns that rivaled the battle strategies of political and military commanders. In their own way, in their own skills and fortitude of talent and character, they were the Roosevelts, Churchills, and Ben-Gurions of American Jewry.

But in the end, their success could not be attributed simply to their own resources or to those of their constituents, or even to the available mechanism of a powerfully honed philanthropy. Ultimately, the UJA signified more than a functional, pragmatic conduit of American Jewish loyalty to an ancestral *heimat*, to a hearth and talisman of ethnic memory. Over the years, these massive campaigns began to serve a more specifically American purpose. In an increasingly secular society, and in the midst of an overwhelmingly non-Jewish population, UJA drives came to function as an indispensable focus of Jewish communal identity altogether. "Does anyone think that there is a separation between Jewish fund-raising and Jewish identity?" asked a speaker at one of the annual assemblies of the Council of Jewish Federations. "Fund-raising *is* a profound Jewish expression. It *is* Jewish culture."

In fact, there was a time when not every Jew could have accepted this paradigm, or at least would have hesitated to equate fund-raising for Israel with the wider ambit of Jewish culture. Were there not other, specifically American Jewish institutions—schools, synagogues, community centers, hospitals, and universities—that deserved priority in the scale of philanthropic loyalty? This question, too, eventually was resolved.

By the late 1960s and early 1970s, it became evident that a people that historically had rejected an ecclesiastical hierarchy similarly rejected the very notion of a philanthropic hierarchy. Every Jewish cause, Israeli and non-Israeli, deserved priority. None deserved pride of place over the other. None dared be neglected in favor of another. One learned to give to all. And in significant measure, it was the UJA/Federation campaigns that taught this irrefutable fact of Jewish existence. By the time Israel achieved its own third decade of life, leaders of federations and of other national and local Jewish causes were obliged to acknowledge that American Jewish cultural and educational institutions were not, after all, penalized by the "diversion" of vast sums to Israel. They were enhanced by the *omnium gatherum* of a mighty collective engine.

Recognition came in 1974—a watershed year—as the New York Federation of Jewish Philanthropies, the nation's largest, belatedly effected a merger with the UJA. Soon the evidence was overwhelming that, as local Jewish causes linked their campaigns to those of the UJA, the enlarged scale of contributions in a single drive benefited each of the component members. Perhaps of greater significance yet, individual campaigns for specifically American-Jewish institutions—universities, seminaries, hospitals, and senior citizens' homes—were raising funds at record levels. Manifestly, it was not the UJA alone that was enhancing other Jewish causes. Rather, the sunburst of identification and creativity awakened by the State of Israel itself was energizing virtually every facet of Jewish life in the United States, as elsewhere in the Diaspora. It was the genius of the Fishers, Hassenfelds, Lautenbergs, and the other giants of communal leadership to have grasped this fact from the beginning. Indeed, they themselves had stepped into their UJA command posts logically and seamlessly from the host of other public causes in which they had earlier—and often simultaneously—participated.

Not least of all, it was Irving Bernstein who shared this vision of blended Jewish communal destiny. As one reads the pages of the volume he conceived and assembled, one cannot but recall Maurice Samuel's introduction to Louis Lipsky's *A Gallery of Zionist Profiles*. "What," asked Samuel in mock incredulity, "a biography of Zionist giants with virtually nothing in the book of Lipsky himself?" To be sure, Bernstein offers us a few skeletal reminiscences of his own participation and rise to leadership in the UJA enterprise—but then, typically, focuses on the inspiration and example he derived from others. Let it be said here and now, however, that it was Bernstein, more than any of his executive predecessors, possibly more even than the legendary Joseph Schwartz, who discerned early on the intimate interrelationship between an Israel-oriented philanthropy and the wider ambit of Jewish culture.

To teach that lesson, Bernstein accordingly was the first UJA executive vice chairman consciously to reject the glamour and hoopla of public extravaganza in favor of "quality control." Upgrading his staff, he sought out personnel with advanced degrees in the humanities and the behavioral and social sciences. Indeed, Bernstein's new emphasis on education was manifest not only in seminars on community organization and solicitation, but in a wider series of lectures on Jewish history and culture, most of them conducted by trained Jewish scholars. Under Bernstein's leadership, UJA volunteers and executive staff alike were encouraged to acquaint themselves with the broader texture of Jewish social and religious traditions and to grasp that Israeli statehood related intimately to a denser context of Jewish civilization. For their part, Jewish cultural and religious figures were touched by this sophisticated new appreciation of their values.

It was no coincidence, then, that Irving Bernstein periodically has served as a respected guest professor representing Jewish communal leadership at Brandeis University, and that an institute on that campus endowed by Max Fisher also bears Bernstein's name. With equal appropriateness, Yeshiva University, in conferring an honorary doctorate upon Irving in 1987, noted in its citation that his "concern for the quality of Jewish life throughout the world has been the guiding principle of his leadership in the international Jewish community."

These pages admirably relate the chronicle of a unique galaxy of American Jewish leaders. But it is a measure of the author's characteristic diffidence and self-effacement that the story of Irving Bernstein himself has yet to be written.

Dr. Howard M. Sachar
Professor of History
George Washington University
Washington, D.C.
April 1997

IRVING BERNSTEIN

In 1961 I visited Kolno, Poland, to find nothing left of the once-thriving Jewish community from which my parents had emigrated forty years earlier—except the trace of a Star of David on the foundation of a building that had been a synagogue. The only other remnants of my forebears were crushed bits of gravestones with Hebrew lettering on them—scattered in a cow pasture that for generations had been the town's Jewish cemetery.

When we returned to Warsaw, Sam Haber of the Joint Distribution Committee (JDC)—who was with me in Kolno—led me to the former concentration camp of Treblinka. That is where my parents' *mishpocha*—their hapless family and their once neighbors and friends—perished in the ovens while the world remained silent. At that moment, as I wept openly, I resolved never to be silent again and to dedicate my life to the preservation of Jewish continuity, to protect Jews in danger, wherever they might be.

I was born in the Bronx on August 9, 1921, two years after my parents arrived at Ellis Island. In 1926 my family moved to Ellenville, New York, a small village in the Catskill Mountains—a resort area approximately one hundred miles northwest of New York City. My father had become part owner of a bakery serving the five hundred Jewish souls in Ellenville and supplying the surrounding Jewish hotels. In those early days, antisemitism in the region was overt. Non-Jewish Catskill hotels didn't accept Jews and some even posted signs, "No dogs or Jews allowed."

The Jewish area hotels attracted guests by hiring entertainers and thus created the "borscht circuit," later known as the "Borscht Belt"—the theatrical hinterlands where so many stars, Jewish and non-Jewish, honed their acts. Those of us who worked as waiters, busboys, and bellhops served as their foils. Their names read like a "who's who" of film and television history. Some of the stars I recall were Sophie Tucker, Dan Daily, George Jessel, Danny Kaye, Eddie Cantor, Jerry Lewis, George Burns, Milton Berle, and Sid Caesar. I was to meet some of them later in my life, under very different circumstances.

Our language at home, my first language, was Yiddish. When I enrolled in Ellenville's two-room Pine Grove schoolhouse, it was my WASP teacher, Miss Newkirk, who first told me that my name wasn't Itzik but Irving. [Twenty years later, when I returned home from World War II, I met her. With a twinkle in her eye she greeted me with, "Hello, Itzik! How are your brothers Abie and Mutty and your sister Faigy?"]

When I was fourteen, we moved back to the Bronx, and I became the leader of a group of boys my age—fourteen Jewish, one Italian Catholic, and one Polish Catholic. Our interests were primarily athletic—baseball and football—and we are still in touch with each other to this very day.

The impact of our association was best summed up in a letter I wrote to *The New York Times* identifying such groups as "the unifying experience in the lives of our generation. As . . . immigrants who struggled to feed, clothe, and house their children while trying to close the gap between their European experience and the American dream, our parents had little time left for us. In our athletic activities we found the kinship, security, and confidence to reach beyond the physical horizons of our neighborhood to join the mainstream of American life." [As grandparents, our most common concern now is wondering whether or not our grandchildren will share our values.]

Peter Levine, in his book *Ellis Island to Ebbets Field*, quotes my letter to support his thesis that "it was sports that played a major role in transforming Jewish immigrants into American Jews."

In 1938, like so many ghetto children, my only choice for higher education was City College of New York, where I majored in history and social studies and minored in lacrosse and football. Graduating in 1942, I enlisted in the Air Corps, and spent the next three years maintaining Flying Fortresses in Bury St. Edmunds, just north of Cambridge, England. While there, I contacted the Jewish community in London and, together with other airmen, visited Jewish and Christian children's and senior citizens' homes to share our fruits and candies, which were not available to them, especially on holidays.

In early 1945, we were offered a month's furlough in the United States if we volunteered to serve in the Pacific. After three years away from home, many of us did just that. But as we were being shipped across the Atlantic Ocean, atom bombs were dropped on Japan, the Emperor surrendered, and we were diverted to Kelly Air Force Base in Texas and discharged.

Since I had always wanted to teach, I enrolled at Columbia Teachers College, received my master's degree, and taught, or tried to teach, in a New York City ghetto school. But I found conditions beyond my abilities—even worse than the stories in Bel Kaufman's book, *Up the Down Staircase*, a satire about the New York City school system.

Since I was committed to serving the community, I left to do social work in Harlem, where I was assigned ninety-seven cases— ninety-five African American families and two elderly Jews left over from earlier migrations—far more than any individual could cope with. But I loved the work and felt I was making a difference in their lives.

At the end of 1946, my supervisor, Fannie Meirowitz of blessed memory, called me in, told me I was the best social worker in her unit of twenty, and, in the same breath, fired me. Startled, gasping, I finally asked her, "How could you?"

I'll never forget her reply. "Because you will end up like the rest of us," she said, "overwhelmed, overworked, and frustrated. You are always talking about the Holocaust and the meaning of a Jewish State. I urge you to go to the UJA or another agency that needs you more than we do." She directed me to the UJA national office, then situated at 165 West 46th Street in Manhattan.

After several interviews, I met the legendary Henry Montor. Everyone had warned me about his impatience and sharp questions, so I turned the meeting around and asked him questions before he could query me. What would my role be? What degree of support would I get from him and his staff? How much encouragement and patience would those of us in the field receive for attempting to develop innovative programs?

After two days of meetings, my forty-year odyssey with UJA

began with the keys to a car in Columbus, Ohio, and a list of small towns I was to visit. The challenge was to organize UJA campaigns and raise funds for the refugees and survivors in Eastern Europe who needed to be transported to what was then Palestine and absorbed into a new life.

In January 1948, I visited one of these small Jewish communities in Marietta, Ohio. The report I filed back then was typical of the many small towns on my itinerary in America's heartland:

January 15, 1948

Marietta's Jewish community consists of 15 Jewish families. At least 10 of the 15 families follow Orthodoxy, both in the synagogue and at home. The remaining families, although not strict conformists, follow the line of the majority. The synagogue is maintained without a rabbi, as almost everyone in the community is able to conduct services. The Sabbath is strictly observed. Every *shliach* [messenger] is warmly welcomed and personally conducted through Marietta.

The community contributes heavily to Orthodox causes. They feel that since few others do so, it is therefore their obligation. For the most part, members of the Jewish community are well-educated, Americanized individuals who follow and are concerned with the problems of Palestine and the Displaced Persons (DP) camps and are aware of, and alert to, national and international Jewish affairs.

The campaign in the community is a one-man affair with little organization. Henry LeVette, the largest individual contributor, runs the campaign. Mr. LeVette is one of those who do not strictly conform to Orthodoxy. However, he is an excellent chairman and respected by the community. The community has allowed him to run the UJA drive alone, so that they would not be diverted from their interests in Orthodox causes.

Most of these small Jewish communities are gone today—their children have left to pursue greater opportunities in America's larger cities. But I've never forgotten the small towns where I learned lifelong lessons.

In Ludington, Michigan, I met a man in the lumber industry who had never given to UJA. He received me warmly, took me to lunch, asked many questions. When I asked him about his pledge, he shocked me by saying he did not plan to give anything.

"But," I said, "you seem interested, you asked many knowledgeable questions, we spent a lot of time together, why don't you want to give?" And his answer was, "Because I don't like applesauce." More startled than ever, I asked him what applesauce had to do with saving lives. And he said: "Look kid, you'd better learn that if someone doesn't want to give, one answer is as good as another"— a lesson that has helped me beyond measure over the years, not only in fund-raising but in life.

After two years as a "traveling salesman," I realized that I would never be able to marry, settle down, and raise a family—so I decided to resign. But in the fall of 1950 I was called to New York and asked to become an executive assistant to supervise other field representatives. One of them introduced me to my future wife, Judy, in 1951. After a whirlwind courtship, Rabbi Jonah B. Wise, of the JDC, officiated at our wedding ceremony. We were then married a second time at the Jewish Theological Seminary, as my parents wanted us to have a more traditional ceremony.

When our first son, Bob, was born in 1953, we realized we could not have stability in our lives if I continued to travel as much as I did. I therefore lobbied for the position of UJA West Coast director in Los Angeles, though friends urged me not to leave the national office. Rabbi Herbert A. Friedman, then the incoming executive vice chairman, agreed to my leaving for the West Coast, but asked me to promise to return if he ever needed me.

From 1952 to 1961, I grew personally and professionally. Distance permitted me to make my own decisions and to plan new programs without being held back by superiors. During that time, I again met many of Hollywood's stars and was able to persuade a number of them to volunteer their time on behalf of UJA [see the Field-Dayan retrospective]. Judy and I also became integral members of the Los Angeles Jewish community.

Then, in 1961, Rabbi Friedman, who was a friend as well as a colleague, called and told me he needed me to be the associate vice chairman of national UJA.

Our second son, Joe, was born in Los Angeles in 1956, and we were happily settled in the community, so Judy and I really did not want to leave the West Coast. However, I kept my promise and we moved back to New York. [We had bought our house in

Beverly Hills for $23,000 and sold it for $36,000. Twelve years later the same house, with no renovations, went for $1 million—but except for a twinge every now and then, we had no lasting regrets.]

From 1961 to 1971, I worked very closely with Friedman, who developed many novel programs, including Young Leadership and the Israel Education Fund. In 1971, Friedman left to spend more time in Israel, and I was elected as UJA's executive vice chairman, the CEO of the largest Jewish fund-raising agency, providing assistance to the community through the Jewish community federations and to Israel and thirty-three other nations.

My term in office was highlighted by the 1974 campaign following the Yom Kippur War—the largest UJA campaign ever held to that date. There were the *Koach* [strength] missions in 1975 and 1976, the largest Young Leadership missions ever, with more than one thousand participants in each year. Another highlight was the three-thousand-strong "This Year in Jerusalem Mission," the largest ever to visit Israel. There was also a special UJA supplement in *The New York Times* celebrating that momentous event in 1977. At a Prime Minister's Mission with Menachem Begin in 1977, he announced the inception of Project Renewal, which in 1978-79 began twinning American Jewish communities with towns and cities in Israel.

In 1984 I resigned from my professional duties to serve as a volunteer in Jewish affairs in the United States and abroad, and to meet with and speak to Jewish communities in Australia, South Africa, Europe, and North and South America. My resignation was one result of the UJA changing its philosophy from a "leadership" orientation to a "management" orientation. After retiring, I became a member of the executive committees and the boards of governors of the American Jewish Committee, the Joint Distribution Committee (JDC) and the United Israel Appeal (UIA). I also chaired the communications committees of all three of these organizations at the same time.

This outreach enabled me to learn and understand the dynamics of Jewish communities and their relationships to each other and to Israel from far more than just the American point of view—increasing my effectiveness as a volunteer.

During President Jimmy Carter's term, Frank Lautenberg, now the senior U.S. senator from New Jersey, and I were appointed by the President to the board of the U.S. Holocaust Memorial Council, headed by Elie Wiesel. We continued as board members during President Ronald Reagan's terms in office. Then Wiesel appointed me chairman of the U.S. Holocaust Memorial Council's Museum Committee, an interfaith committee that, under Wiesel's leadership, created a museum that has become a powerful voice against prejudice wherever it may exist.

I, like others, have had my share of irreconcilable differences that develop at times between lay leadership and professionals. However, I am proud of the growth and development of the majority of leaders with whom I was associated as a mentor. They allowed me to play a not insignificant role in guiding them to become the creative forces they have been and still are in other areas of communal and political activities at the local, national, and international levels.

I also take pride in many of the professionals I recruited and trained who are now outstanding philanthropic leaders in their own right.

Among them are Ernest Michel, the Auschwitz survivor who became Executive Vice Chairman of UJA/Federation and conceived of the World Gathering of Holocaust Survivors, held in 1981; Melvyn H. Bloom, Executive President of the American Society for Technion-Israel Institute of Technology; Robert A. Pearlman, formerly CEO of the American Friends of the Hebrew University and today CEO of the Diabetes Research Institute; Eve Weiss, Executive Director of the Hasbro Children's Foundation; and Milton Shorr and Joel S. Friedman, presidents of two successful private consulting firms that plan and create campaigns for agencies unable to do so on their own.

In 1987, I was appointed national vice chairman of Yeshiva University's centennial campaign and was invited to join the boards of the Hebrew Arts School in New York City, the Friends of the Hebrew University, and the Jerusalem College of Technology. I continue to serve on the board of the Schneider Children's Medical Center in Israel; the International Center for University Teaching of Jewish Civilization; the Hebrew University's Institute of Contemporary Jewry, the Israel Academy of Arts and Science [for gifted children], and the American Society for Technion.

Jewish education has always been my top personal priority,

whether it is in the pursuit of Talmudic studies, the arts, or the sciences. I believe that when Rabbi Hillel told the stranger who stood on one leg to go and study, he meant for him to study Torah and then to go beyond it, to do *tikkun olam*, to make the world a better place.

Today, I am a visiting professor at Brandeis University and a chairman of the Board of Advisers to the university's Hornstein Program for Graduate Studies in Jewish Communal Service. I was also their 1980 Milender Fellow in Jewish Communal Leadership. The university has given me the opportunity to come full circle and return to my very first love, teaching.

In 1987, I received the first Distinguished Service Award presented by the Association for Jewish Community Organizational Professionals, and that same year I was awarded an honorary degree of doctor of humane letters by Yeshiva University.

My one regret, then and now, has been that my parents didn't live to see all that I and my generation have accomplished in rescuing Jews and rebuilding Jewish lives at home, overseas, and in the free State of Israel. I truly believe that my generation, and our children's generation, will keep the promise to fulfill the commitment I swore to uphold on that day, more than thirty-six years ago, when I visited the remains of Kolno. We will never be silent again.

Irving Bernstein
New York City/Scarsdale
Passover 5757
April 1997

PREFACE

One of the great contributors to contemporary historiography is the living witness who helps us amplify written documentation as we study the events of our time. These interviews are designed to introduce a previously untapped source for understanding the development of the UJA in the context of world Jewish history.

Among other considerations, the use of oral testimony acknowledges the value of human memory, which makes available information and interpretation not necessarily contained in written documents. Most records, especially those of corporate bodies, are carefully pruned to exclude the human factor from events that take place in the corridors of history. Consequently, through the careful use of oral testimony as well as documentation, historians of the contemporary era are able to convey the interplay of cardinal events with the lives of those involved. A review of the Oral History Division collection in the Avraham Harman Institute of Contemporary Jewry points to a substantial body of hitherto unavailable source materials relating to recent history, especially that of the past three generations.

These reflections were the substance of many conversations during the early 1970s with Irving Bernstein, then the imaginative executive vice chairman of the UJA. In those years I served as head of the Hebrew University's Institute of Contemporary Jewry, and my field of research and teaching was American Jewry. I saw in the UJA, during the cataclysmic years of the mid-twentieth century, an evolving Jewish force, a microcosm of Jewish history and destiny, whose magnetic lay and professional leadership Irving Bernstein exemplified. I felt that it was imperative to create a solid research base by recording the ongoing problems and progress of the UJA as it reshaped American Jewish communal life and the relationship between American Jewry and the people and State of Israel—even as it concentrated on providing substantial support for development in Israel.

From the very outset of our conversations, I detected that Irving Bernstein, in addition to his many other talents, possessed educational discernment and, as an executive, was not deterred by "impossibilities." A partnership between our institutions was rapidly established, and the creative team consisted of Menahem Kaufman of the institute, Issachar Miron of the UJA, and archival consultant Shalom J. Pomerenze. Flowing from the newly organized UJA Archives in both research centers, two important studies were published: Abraham J. Karp's *To Give Life: The UJA in the Shaping of the American Jewish Community* (Schocken Books, 1981); and Marc Lee Raphael's *A History of the UJA 1939-1982* (Brown Judaic Studies, 1982).

One of the vital outgrowths of this combined effort was the creation of a library of some 150 oral interviews, now deposited at the Institute of Contemporary Jewry in Jerusalem and in the UJA Archival Center in New York. These make up a treasury of information and insights available only from those who have been the history makers within the twentieth-century Jewish community. Here we have not institutional catalogues but grassroots experience, representative of the earnest commitment of these individuals.

This publication, drawn from a trove of human experience, exemplifies the union of two kinds of memory. There are the actors, each speaking in his or her own time with subjective views, and the commentary of Irving Bernstein, a keen interpreter of American life and institutions and a key participant in and observer of world Jewish communal affairs.

Bernstein joined the staff of the UJA in 1947, serving first with Henry Montor, a Reform rabbi who was the organization's first executive vice president from 1939 to 1950. [As Executive Vice President and CEO of the American Financial Development Corporation for Israel, 1951-55, Montor was instrumental in founding the Israel Bond campaign].

The first two chapters offer two examples: a group interview that illustrates the workings of the UJA in its early formative years, and a discussion with Yigael Yadin on Project Renewal, which represents another milestone in the UJA response to Israel's needs. In the former case, Bernstein's essay sets the stage for the interview; and in the latter, he contemplates the project retrospectively.

A key concept of my own early Zionist education was *kiyyum ha-umah* [survival of the people]. In these interviews, Golda Meir speaks of "continuation," anticipating the current use of the term "continuity"; Senator Lautenberg emphasizes content; and Irving Bernstein concentrates on leadership. All three motivating ideas are entwined in the UJA *am Yisrael* [the people of Israel] family as guarantors of a creative Jewish future.

The unifying theme of the Meir, Lautenberg, and Bernstein credos is that when a community faces a crisis in authenticity—as is the case of our present generation—the corrective choice is not to dilute but to intensify. In our times, such reinforcement cannot be achieved on native ground alone. To recast existing Jewish institutions in the wake of radically altered historical events requires extraterritorial, qualitative connections. In the pre-emancipated past, Jews lived transcendentally in *Eretz Yisrael* [the land of Israel] even when they actually resided in their various diasporas.

The gift of our generation is that Jews who live by choice or necessity in an actual *golah* [Diaspora] can be fortified by the very real State of Israel. Although Israel is not the whole, it is the nuclear center of the Jewish people. There is hardly any aspect of contemporary Jewish life that does not relate in some way to Israel; and certainly whatever Israel is—and continues to be— affects Jews everywhere.

This vision explains how the UJA succeeded, in the course of several decades, in metamorphosing from a body engaged almost exclusively in *hatzalah* [saving Jewish lives abroad] to a vibrant educational force involved in uplifting the Jewish lives of its members. UJA moved from one level of responsibility to the higher level of Jewish identity, thus helping to reshape the inner American Jewish being.

This evolutionary pattern emerges from the corpus of some several hundred UJA oral testimonies in the archives of the Avraham Harman Institute of Contemporary Jewry's Oral History Division. Regrettably, the main fund of evidence still remains in a virtual *genizah* [a synagogue attic that contains scraps of Jewish books]—

open to scholars and students to be sure, but not within the knowledge and research of the wider public. To begin to bring this treasury to light, the institute's America-Holy Land Project determined to publish edited portions as interpreted by Irving Bernstein, a participant-creator of the UJA program for some forty years and its executive leader. The retrospective analyses and insights of Irving Bernstein enlighten the original interviews. Thus, we are creating a new form of documentary.

Reading these crisp accounts, the human figures emerge, the past meshes with the present, and all together say hallelujah to those who never faltered when the challenge was greatest.

Moshe Davis
Stephen S. Wise Professor [Emeritus],
Jewish Life and Institutions
Founding Head, Avraham Harman Institute of Contemporary Jewry
The Hebrew University of Jerusalem

LIVING UJA HISTORY

1

INTRODUCING THE UJA FAMILY

T he decade extending from the UJA's birth in 1939 to the eve of Israel's War of Independence in 1948 was the most difficult and frustrating in all of its history. The fledgling entity struggled to keep its divided elements together and, at the same time, tried to raise the dimensions of fund-raising in a disunited and often antagonistic community.

The American Jewish community did not exist as an organized force, despite the devastation of Jewish life in Europe, the horrors of the Holocaust, or the new phenomenon of Jews as Displaced Persons across Europe. Even the unfolding drama of Israel's existence in the United Nations and Palestine did not unify American Jews. Jewish communal structures were in their infancy, response was divided, leadership hesitant. Many opposed the creation of a Jewish State. The majority of American Jews were just beginning to emerge from Jewish inner-city neighborhoods as their sons and daughters returned from service in World War II.

The sharp division in Jewish life at that time is best exemplified by the sons of the patrician Julius Rosenwald [president and later chairman of Sears, Roebuck]. In the 1930s, he gave $50 million to Negro colleges in the American South and built more than one thousand rural schools for Negro children. His eldest son, Lessing Rosenwald, founded and chaired the virulently anti-Zionist American Council for Judaism. The younger brother, William [or Bill, as he preferred to be called], was one of the three signatories to the founding of the UJA in 1939 and later served as chairman. He succeeded Henry Morgenthau, Jr., who had been Secretary of the Treasury under President Franklin Delano Roosevelt. [Morgenthau influenced Roosevelt to establish the War Refugee Board and was first national chairman of the UJA].

Bill Rosenwald's position, publicly and privately, was that Israel's independence as a democratic state was in the best interest of America and American Jews. Lessing, on the other hand, used his public platform to issue statements to newspapers and in the halls of Congress, warning that a Jewish state would jeopardize American Jews by prompting other Americans to question Jews' loyalty. His efforts continued until 1967, the watershed year of the Six-Day War, which radically changed the American Jewish community and irrevocably destroyed the credibility of Jewish anti-Israel propaganda.

Before 1967, besides splitting families, the sharp, and at times vitriolic, debate about Israel also divided communities—especially those dominated by the scions and descendants of German Jewish immigrants. They represented old wealth, social status, and political power, whereas American Jews of Eastern European heritage were only beginning their financial growth. Despite the fact that the communal and financial odds were against Israel's supporters, they were strengthened by the depth of their commitment to Israel. They, and not their antagonists, had suffered in relative silence as their families and former communities disappeared from the face of the earth in the fire and smoke of the Holocaust.

In this climate of confusion and division, a few men and women were able to influence American Jewish communities, which were neither strongly structured nor blessed with outstanding leadership. The public display of courage of conviction from ordinary people, inspired and motivated by a few leaders, stemmed the tide of negativism. These leaders went out and, individual by individual, community by community, convinced the grass roots to listen to the story of the unfolding drama in Israel—and got them to respond to their appeals to a greater degree than ever before.

The UJA came into being in 1939 through the forced union of three separate entities. The first was the United Palestine Appeal (UPA) [UIA after 1948], the equivalent of today's Keren Hayesod, which operates in Jewish communities throughout the world. It was a fund-raising unit for the *Yishuv* [the Jewish settlement in Palestine before the creation of the State of Israel]. The second was the American Jewish Joint Distribution Committee (JDC), a social service agency operating in Jewish communities outside the United States. The third was the National Refugee Service (NRS), which settled the flood of refugees from Europe in the United States.

Serving as the midwife in this difficult birth was the Council of Jewish Federations (CJF) then known as the Council of Jewish Federations and Welfare Funds. The signatories were Rabbi Abba Hillel Silver for the UPA, Rabbi Jonah B. Wise for the JDC, and William Rosenwald for the NRS. It is worth noting that during the pre-World War II period until the early 1950s, Zionist leadership stemmed from rabbinical ranks, while the community lay leadership—in the Federation and the then pre-eminent American Jewish Committee—came mainly from German Jewish stock.

By the late 1950s, and especially in the 1960s, leadership passed from rabbinic to lay volunteers, who gradually became prominent in the UJA, the Federation, and the national Jewish agencies that were developed to meet social and communal needs in the United States and overseas.

When forming the UJA, the UPA and JDC were suspicious of each other and insisted on equal co-executive directors. Those chosen were Henry Montor for UPA and Isador Coons for JDC. Montor's creativity and strength of purpose soon dominated and changed the equation. As a result, the two agencies grew together, and the redundancy of leadership was eliminated.

It is no accident that in the following group interview, Joseph Mazer, Avis Shulman, and Sam Abramson all refer to Montor. He was a Reform rabbi, a Zionist who worked in public relations before becoming the executive director of UPA. He was short, slim, and shy, with a thin reedy voice and piercing eyes that never left your eyes and face. Decisive and adamant in achieving his goals, and possessed of indomitable will and courage, Montor forced the American Jewish community to accept the first $100 million campaign in 1946—and to meet that goal. He was determined at all times to keep his promises to the Israeli authorities, particularly David Ben-Gurion and Golda Meir.

In a divided community, and with UJA's low profile, Montor could not find leadership who shared his views and goals. He went outside the organized communities, finding his pioneers primarily in the smaller cities of America.[1]

---

[1] Their names and cities reflect that period, its problems and challenges: Mathilda Brailove, Elizabeth, New Jersey; Morris Berenstein, Syracuse, New York; Louis Boyar, Los Angeles, California; Mel Dubinsky, St. Louis, Missouri; Fred Forman, Rochester, New York; Harold Goldman, Des Moines, Iowa; Zeke Grueskin, Sioux

Under Montor's domineering pressure, this small group traveled across America, its members forcing their way into resistant communities, tearing up pledge cards they thought were inadequate, locking doors to rooms so that no one could leave. They pounded on tables until they splintered, arguing and fighting to make their fellow Jews realize that the fate of the new Jewish State and the lives of its people were at stake. Those pioneers proclaimed that they would not in any way tolerate the continuing apathy, indifference, and powerlessness prevalent during the years of the Holocaust.

The end result was a fund-raising success story which had tremendous impact on the growth of American Jewish community federations and the State of Israel.

Montor reached out to men who determined the amounts to be contributed, but he also reached out to women from disparate social settings—lay and professional, Jewish and Christian. Among them were Mathilda Brailove, a housewife married to a dentist in Elizabeth, New Jersey; Avis Shulman, the articulate wife of a leading Reform rabbi; Lea Horne, the wife of a prominent New Yorker; and Jeanne Daman, a "righteous Gentile" from Belgium. Women thereafter became a central focus of the campaign.

As the Women's Division leaders grew in stature and played prominent roles in the UJA/Federation, on the national agenda they became an integral part of the fund-raising structure. Outstanding officers were Mathilda Brailove, chair of the UJA national Women's Division; Sylvia Hassenfeld, president of JDC; Shoshana Cardin, president of CJF and UIA and Chairman of the Board of Governors of the Jewish Agency; Wilma Tisch and Peggy Tishman, presidents of the New York City Federation; Barbara Weinberg, president of the Los Angeles Federation; and Elaine Winik, president of the New York UJA.

Montor's aggressive campaigning expressed itself in other ways. He threatened to run independent campaigns in Allentown, Chicago, and Los Angeles outside of their local federations. He based his threat on UJA's perennial problem of how local federations divided

City, Iowa; Lea Horne, New York City; Sol Luckman, Cincinnati, Ohio; Joseph Mazer, New York City; William Mazer, New York City; Joseph Meyerhoff, Baltimore, Maryland; William Rosenwald, New York City; Sam Rothberg, Peoria, Illinois; Dewey Stone, Brockton, Massachusetts; Jack D. Weiler, New York City.

funds. Until 1939, campaigns had all been independent of federations. The signatories to the 1939 agreement, together with those who led their respective agencies, decided that the national UJA campaign would be conducted through the local federations.

Although there are those who still lament this decision, I believe that despite recurring problems, those who made it were visionaries. This unity of campaign for overseas and domestic needs played major and primary roles in "Zionizing" the American Jewish community. It accelerated and expanded the growth of Jewish communities. From these growing communities they were able to raise the funds needed to meet the overwhelming needs of the Jewish communities in Europe and newly born Israel.

Changing needs in Israel and countries where Jewish communities were threatened, brought changes in UJA's outreach programs. Its role has undergone many changes since its inception in 1939. From its primary purpose of raising funds for immigrants and resettlement, it is now instrumental in developing leadership and strengthening local federations.

Through UJA in the United States and Keren Hayesod [which for all intents and purposes can be defined as the international UJA] contributors of all ages in communities throughout the world can see the results of their fund-raising and become involved in Jewish life outside of their personal communities. Such involvement helps UJA and the Jewish Agency create fresh programs to meet growing needs in Israel—from helping immigrants settle and adjust to Israeli society to dealing with drug abuse and domestic violence. Programs like Project Renewal and the Living Bridge [which brings thousands of young people to visit Israel] are designed to create links between individual Israelis and American Jews, to develop relationships that lead to caring and understanding.

Mathilda Brailove is right to describe UJA as the "motive force" for Jewish unity in America. Abba Eban is right too in calling the UJA both an organization and a cause.

2

A GROUP INTERVIEW

MATHILDE BRAILOVE
JEANNE DAMAN
HERBERT KATZKI
LEA HORNE
AVIS SHULMAN
JOSEPH MAZER
GOTTLIEB HAMMER
SAMUEL ABRAMSON
RALPH WECHSLER
SIDNEY LEIWANT

Interview by Moshe Davis and Menahem Kaufman March, 1975

M.D.: This roundtable gathering is quite special. *Haverim* [friends], in commitment, you are reunited, this time not to reach urgent decisions, but to describe your decisions in those critical days of twentieth-century Jewish history.

I wish to concentrate on your involvement in some of the outstanding events during the founding period of the State of Israel. For example, I should like to know where you were and what you were doing during the period the state was established. I am eager to learn if you were present or had anything to do with Chaim Weizmann's [Israel's first president] visit and with Golda Meir's dramatic fund-raising assignment. We are interested to know your role in the historical UJA process.

But first, I turn to ask a general question about 1947–1949. What was the most poignant moment in your UJA experience during that period? Mrs. Brailove, when you were in Cyprus, was that one of your great experiences?

[Mathilda Brailove was from Elizabeth, New Jersey. She was active in Jewish national organizations from 1938 as a member of the Advisory Council of the JDC, the Israel Education Fund, and the UJA. In 1948, she was a member of the first UJA survey mission to Israel and chaired the UJA National Women's Division from 1949 to 1952.]

M.B.: No, I was in Europe. You ask what was the greatest moment for me. It's funny, but I never think of the memory of those years. Prior to '46, I had been involved in community programs and worked very hard as state chairman of the United Service Organization [USO], an organization that assists American servicemen. Then the news of what happened in the Holocaust came out. When I went to one of my board meetings, I looked around the room and saw that it was as if nothing had happened in the world; so I resigned from all the boards on which I was sitting and said, "My people need me."

I think the greatest thing for me in the UJA, from 1946 until this very day, is that it is an organization that has cared very deeply about the whole Jewish people, not just a part here or there.

When I went to Europe, between the vote on partition [November 29, 1947] and statehood [May 14, 1948], I saw Jews locked in the camps of Germany and Italy; I saw our JDC program in France where the orphans, the sole survivors of their families, were being trained and given some dignity. I saw the same inside the camps— where I couldn't believe the beautiful programs, the plays, and the printing presses, and the care and hope the agencies allied with the UJA were giving to all of these people. Then, as I moved out of Europe, which was hell for the Jewish people, and moved into the sunlight of Palestine, I realized what this massive organization was doing. It was helping to build the State of Israel and helping it absorb mass immigration. And it has persisted with every emergency that has arisen involving Jewish people.

Through the UJA, those of us who care so deeply about the Jewish people have our instrument to work with to get to the deepest recesses of wherever Jews are living and get them whatever they need. My whole life in the UJA has been a life of people. That is why I need a little more reflection before I try to pick out one or two singular events.

M.D.: Mrs. Scagglioni, would you tell us some of your experiences with UJA during this time?

[Mrs. Scagglioni (Jeanne Daman) was born in Belgium. She joined the Resistance and fought the German occupation. She also chose to help rescue Belgian Jewish children. After the war she was a speaker for the UJA in the administrations of Henry Montor, Herbert Friedman, and Irving Bernstein.]

J.D.: I didn't know English. Besides, coming from little Belgium immediately after the war to big New York seemed so overwhelming. I felt totally incapable of accepting any responsibility. I told them, "I can't express myself."

Well, the point of my story is that what they told me, in order to convince me, influenced me for years. They said, "You don't realize that the American Jewish community is very divided, even now after the front-page pictures of the liberation of the camps."

That was something that I naturally didn't realize, not only because I was not Jewish but also because we had concentrated on rescue for so long that we didn't know anything else. They said, "The American Council of Judaism is made up of people who are trying to convince the general American public, and the Jewish public particularly, that the Displaced Persons in the camps—who fall on their knees and kiss Eleanor Roosevelt's skirt while begging for "Palestine, Palestine"—are actually Zionist propagandists. Their members fly all over Europe, trying to talk people into that idea. These people claim that if it were not for those agitators [the survivors], people wouldn't even think about Palestine."

Well, after what I had seen, this naturally fired me no end, because I suddenly realized that there was actually a need for people not only to testify, but to be defenders of the rescue efforts.

On the day of the birth of Israel, of the declaration of the state, I happened to be in Richmond, Virginia. By that time I had become quite a well-oiled campaigner. On that day, I was invited to a cocktail party. I had been warned that I should not be too aggressive, that I should not ruffle the feelings of certain Jews of Richmond. I, in my innocence, thought that this was a cocktail party to celebrate the birth of Israel. So, after two hours passed with everybody having a good time, and with not even a mention of Israel, I said to the UJA representative, "What's going on? I thought this party was to celebrate the birth of Israel." Then he made me understand that I should be diplomatic and silent. Well, when I heard this, I said, "No!" I, a non-Jewish girl, got up and drank the toast to Israel, in which they reluctantly joined me. I think this story is important as an example of how communities have changed under the influence of UJA.

M.D.: Mr. Katzki, would you want to say a word to us about the most important moment for you?

[Herbert Katzki was an executive associate of the JDC who served primarily in Europe during and after the war years (1939 to 1957). After 1957, he returned to the States to serve at the JDC's New York headquarters, as associate executive vice chairman.]

H.K.: Your question, I think, originally was, "What was the most poignant moment?"

Two such moments stand out in my mind. One occurred in Marseilles in 1941, when a children's transport was being prepared to leave for the United States. The children had been gathered in several of the homes of the OSE (Organization for the Rescue of Children). They had either been separated from their parents or their parents had given them up. We went down to the train to see them off.

Among them was one little kid whose only ID was a piece of paper, about two inches by one inch, with his name on it. That was all he had. There was another kid who had written to his father, a French POW, asking for permission to go to the United States. At that time, the permission of the parents had to be secured before you could send them from France to the United States. There were two little brothers—one who had been born in Germany, chased to Belgium and then to southern France. He was being shipped to the United States.

One of the most poignant experiences I ever had was watching these little children of ten and eleven years old go off to the unknown. I knew about their backgrounds, I knew that they didn't know whether they would ever see their parents again, I knew they didn't know what was waiting for them in the United States.

I had another unforgettable experience in Lisbon, when it was still possible for Jews who had visas to come out of Berlin and Vienna. I remember going down to the railroad station to meet a train bringing Jews on their way to the United States. I remember that they crossed paths with non-Jewish Germans from South America who were heading back to Germany. I remember thinking what a crazy world it was. Jewish Germans were fleeing and non-Jewish Germans were repatriating. It just struck me as absurd.

[Lea Horne, as a resident of Denver, Colorado, was active from the 1940s to the 1960s in a number of Jewish organizations: HIAS, JDC, the Israel Education Fund, and the UJA. She chaired the national UJA Women's Division (1954–1955), as well as the New York City Federation Women's Division.]

L.H.: If you will allow me to go back a little further, I would like to tell you about a non-Jewish woman who made me come into this work. A long time ago, Rudolph Sonneborn, from the prominent Zionist family in Baltimore and a Haganah supporter, had a meeting in his home. His honored guest was Mrs. Orde Wingate, widow of the distinguished Christian British intelligence officer who served in *Eretz Yisrael* during the Arab uprising of 1936–1939. She came to tell us about the people that they were trying to get into Palestine. We were told it would cost $500 per person.

On that particular night, some of us became activists on behalf of the Haganah. From that moment on, I worked with the Haganah and for Materials for Israel [a program for getting arms to Israel]. However, I want to emphasize that it was a non-Jew who made me know what it meant to work for Jewish rescue. For me, this was an outstanding thing.

You asked about Dr. Chaim Weizmann. In 1949, I went to Israel because I was fortunate enough to have Dr. Albert Einstein's proxy to the Hebrew University Board of Governors' meeting. In Paris, Chaim Weizmann was at the George V Hotel, which is where I was staying, so I went on the plane with him, his wife, and his grandchild.

It was the first nonstop Air France flight to Israel. There were soldiers on the plane to guard him. When they sang all night long, the hostess went to him and asked, "Are they disturbing you?" His answer was, "When my children sing, it is so beautiful it could never disturb me."

As we were flying, at about four o'clock in the morning, they came to us and said, "Lod is clouded over so we cannot possibly land there." The alternate landing port was Cairo, where we did not dare to set down with Dr. Weizmann on board. They told us we could go to Cyprus. We were traveling in a Constellation, and a Constellation had never landed in Cyprus because the runway was not big enough. But they asked us if we would allow them to land there. "Certainly," we said.

When the plane set down, the people from Cyprus brought a ladder over and came on board with big cans of some kind of disinfectant which they went around spraying on us. Dr. Weizmann and his wife never said a word. I was beside myself. When they came to me, I gave them such a shove and thought to myself, "What are they going to do to me?" Then we climbed down that ladder— if you can imagine Dr. Weizmann and his wife climbing down that ladder. I was heartbroken for them, but they never said a word. When we set foot on the ground, they did not even offer Dr. Weizmann a chair.

There we waited until we got word that we could leave after a couple of hours. They said to us, "We want you to know that a Constellation has never left this runway and we don't know if it can. If any of you want to stay, you can." We all boarded the plane and, as you see from my being here, we made it.

It's a long way from there to the first note that I signed for UJA. As I told you, I signed the $7 million note, but, of course, Mr. Rosenwald of Sears, Roebuck signed way before I did.

[Avis Shulman, a graduate of Northeastern University and Hebrew Union College, spent a year on a kibbutz in *Eretz Yisrael* in the 1930s. Married to Charles Shulman, a Reform rabbi, Avis settled in New York and became active in different Zionist organizations, among them Youth Aliyah, the American Jewish Congress, and the UJA. In 1946 she went to Europe on behalf of the United Nations Relief and Reconstruction Agency (UNRRA) and formed close ties with

survivors of the camps. She later made *aliyah* [the act of Diaspora
Jews settling in Israel].

A.S.: We are going back in time, and I am talking about poignant
moments. The first Haganah office, after the famous meeting at the 21
Club in Manhattan—the site of many critical decisions—was my
apartment on West 72nd Street. It was decided that Henry Montor
would send me to England to conduct part of the UJA campaign,
because that would be a respectable way of getting me into the
Displaced Persons' camps, and subsequently into an UNRRA uniform.

The moment I shall describe occurred in the spring of 1946, just
before Pesach, when we brought the first group of children from
Munich with legal visas for *Eretz Yisrael*. These children were without
parents; they had adopted each other in Munich. Those of us who
worked with them knew how they made their own families, took
care of each other, and were brothers and sisters to each other.

We arrived in Marseilles two days before Pesach, before the *seder*
[the retelling of the Passover story]. The children came and asked
whether they could add a "fifth question" that would embody their
experience from "slavery to freedom." I think one of the most
moving experiences of my entire life was that outdoor seder in the
military camp, with the several hundred children, the official from
UNRRA, and the Jewish Agency, and members of the Jewish Brigade
in Europe who had somehow stayed there. There the children sat,
with the first taste of freedom, one might say, on their tongues, with
a tiny bit of fish, half a glass of wine, and a bit of matzoh. Never did
I witness anything so joyous.

Two or three days later, as we took them down the long hills to get
them to the ship, other children jumped from rooftops and fences
onto the backs of the trucks. By the time we reached the port, we had
not 500 children but over 900. There, the 400 stood and watched as
every one of the children with legal visas was processed.

When they were all on the ship, those on shore gathered around
those of us in uniform. I shall never forget the Dutch boy who said,
"How do you choose who shall stay and who shall go? Have you
the wisdom of a Solomon that you can decide? Have we not lost
our parents and hidden in tree trunks and survived to get here to
go to *Eretz Yisrael*?"

Very quietly, the JDC and UNRRA people and the boy from the

Haganah put them on the trucks and took them back to the camp. There just happened to be another ship leaving the next day. That entire night I stood and shook a table so that the signatures would not be legible on their visas. Uncle Joe [Schwartz] somehow maneuvered all the necessary money and the men of the brigade somehow maneuvered all else that was necessary. The next day, each child went with a new name and a false visa onto that ship, and some of them are leaders in Israel today.

There was a humorous aspect to that day. One little girl really couldn't remember her new name; when the British on board ship asked her, "What is your name?" she said, "*Ani ha-Shomer ha-Tzair*" ["I am *ha-Shomer ha-Tzair*"—"I am a Zionist organization."]

M.D.: It is generally known in UJA history that there was a tremendous leap in giving during the period surrounding the establishment of the State. It represented a real change, a kind of metamorphosis. One of the legendary tales relates to the time Golda Meir came to a meeting at the home of the Mazer brothers' father. That very meeting was a major departure. I'd like to ask the brothers to tell us what happened.

[Joe Mazer is a New York industrialist, an activist in Jewish organizations and a major philanthropist. He is chairman of the Hudson Pulp and Paper Corporation, a leading member of the UJA, and a major contributor to the Hebrew University of Jerusalem.]

J.M.: Well, it was just after the establishment of the State, in May '48. War had broken out and the *Yishuv* was ill prepared for a war. They had no army; they had no money. So Golda Meir came to New York, desperately seeking the maximum amount of cash possible. Well, Henry Montor, who has always been a very clever fellow with lots of imagination, approached my father, who at that time had made, I think, the largest contribution—$60,000. When Henry said he'd come to ask for $250,000, it was quite a shock. But my father, being the idealist he always was, didn't take too long. Nor was he difficult to convince.

Both Golda and Henry were overwhelmed by the size of the gift. It was dramatically announced in the evening at the big meeting held at Madison Square Garden that night. I think it was the first large gift to be made after the establishment of the State, so it had a lot of impact on the Jewish community at the time. Neither Henry nor Golda had expected to get the $250,000 donation. That's what made it more dramatic than normal.

M.D.: As Golda told that story, your father called you in during the course of the conversation and delivered quite a talk about the historical imperative at that moment in history. I think she mentioned that he had a Bible there. "He said, 'This is our belief and our faith and we have to invest in it.'" Then he turned to both you and Bill, and you said, 'We have to go along.' Golda continued: "That's the way with this family. They move together." She remembered this event as one of the singular moments of her visit. Does anyone wish to say anything about the Golda Meir mission?

M.B.: Joe, I recall that a meeting was called at the Astor Hotel, probably after her personal meeting with your family, in which she was asking for support. At that meeting everybody who had made a decision on a very substantial increase changed his or her minds again. As I recall it, Joe, your father announced a gift of $1million that day.

J.M.: It was $500,000.

M.B.: I'm almost sure it was $1 million. Anyway, I do remember that every man, including that dynamo of history, Sam Rothberg, and all the men who had been on the mission and were so active at that time, got up and increased his gift.

I recall so vividly how my husband, who was sitting next to me, said, "You know, the only thing I can think of that we haven't given so far are some paid-up life insurance policies. Do you want to give them now or when I go?" And I said, "Now." So we got up and announced our increase right then.

[Gottlieb Hammer, a New Yorker, was the longtime executive vice chairman of the UJA. He was involved for decades in American Zionist activities.]

G.H.: My recollection of that particular campaign is that a special effort was made to raise $50 million over and above the regular UJA campaign for that year for special needs. In 1946, a unit had been set up in the United States. I was the treasurer of that unit, and as such, I was very much interested in the $50 million that Ben-Gurion had asked for and had sent Golda Meir to the United States to raise.

As the funds came in, the UJA sent them over to my office and I disbursed them according to the instructions I had from Eliezer Kaplan, head of the treasury, whom I represented in the United States. My official job was comptroller of the American office of the Jewish Agency for Palestine. The $50 million came in over a period of time. As quickly as the cash came in, we paid it out.

[Samuel H. Abramson, a Canadian by birth but world citizen by temperament and vocation, served for thirty years in various executive UJA posts. Among other literary achievements, he was co-author with Bernard Postal of *The Traveler's Guide to Jewish Landmarks in Europe*.]

S.A.: I think it's important we clarify that this wasn't a campaign in the regular sense. Golda came early in the year. She wanted $50 million.

How do you get $50 million when your spring campaign is three or four months away? Obviously, it meant that the communities had to borrow, whatever the quota, against their anticipated campaign. Now this was practically a revolution in fund-raising, because never before had communities borrowed in anticipation of a campaign. So the "General," Montor, sent the staff around the country. I went south to Birmingham, Atlanta, Charleston, and places like that—where I had to meet with the boards and say, "Gentlemen, you will have a campaign in April but we'd like you to go to the bank now, in February, and borrow a half million dollars."

I remember sitting with six or eight top leaders in the very beautiful department store office of the leader of the Birmingham community and listening to him tell me, "You Northerners think you can come down here and pull the wool over our eyes?" So I said, "I'm very flattered because, here I am, a young man, sitting with six of the biggest business leaders of the South—and you are suggesting that

I can pull the wool over your eyes. That's a compliment to me."
They laughed, and they borrowed.

At the beginning, in many communities, it meant that fifty, sixty, or even seventy leaders had to put their names on the note, each accepting a piece of the total responsibility. Later, when this procedure was used to raise other money, we worked it out that the president of the local Federation Welfare Fund would sign, without personal responsibility, on behalf of the community.

At that time, however, it was a real breakthrough. For instance, the Stamford community, at first, could not get a comparatively small loan. When I heard that Stamford wouldn't come through, I drove from White Plains, where I lived, to a meeting of the board I knew they were having that night. They said the bank had turned them down. I said, "This is crazy. You have raised $1 million in the course of the past fifteen years; certainly you're good for $100,000. If you ask for alms, hat in hand, from some bank manager, what you're going to get is a *nedovah* [a handout]. Now, Mr. Cohen, you walk in tomorrow, and demand $100,000 on the credit of the Jewish community."

By eleven o'clock the next morning, George Cohen, the chairman, called me in New York and said, "We got the $100,000."

G. H.: I'd like to point out that the UJA, aside from the individual contributions, had a major impact on the American banking system due to the tremendous amount of financing we did. The $50 million that was mentioned was only an incidental part of the whole story, because in 1946 we started borrowing in an organized fashion. In June 1948, after we had already borrowed from Manufacturers Hanover in the name of the Jewish Agency, the JDC was also borrowing for its purposes. We ran into a problem. We needed cash because Eliezer Kaplan, who was in the United States at that time, said he had a cable from Ben-Gurion and needed $10 million right away. So Henry Montor and Henry Morgenthau and I went down and saw the chairman of the bank, Harvey Gibson. The relationship between Gibson and Henry Morgenthau was not a particularly good one. During the war, when Morgenthau had been Secretary of the Treasury and Harvey Gibson president of the American Red Cross, they apparently had had some differences of opinion with respect to their official capacities.

The meeting started off very cool. Morgenthau, who was blunt and direct in his manner of speaking, walked right in and said, "Hello, Harvey." Harvey grunted a very formal "How do you do, Mr. Secretary." I presented the case, and when we were all finished, Gibson said, "Well, I'll have to consult my board," and Morgenthau said, "Harvey, since when do you have to consult your board? Stop kidding!" But Gibson persisted, "I'm going to put it to the board." So Morgenthau asked, "What's your reaction going to be? How are you going to present it?" Finally, Gibson squeezed out; "I'll present it favorably." "That's all I want to know," Morgenthau said. Two days later we had the $10 million.

[Ralph Wechsler, President of the Nopeo Chemical Co., was a leading figure in such organizations as the American Zionist Labor Movement and the Jewish Community of Metropolitan New Jersey.]

R.W.: In the fall of '47, I had the privilege of being asked to become chairman of the '48 UJA campaign. At that time, the UN was already discussing partition and various other things that led to the decision of late November '47.

Instead of waiting for the spring campaign, we decided to start our '48 campaign in 1947. The first thing we did that we had never done before was to call a mass meeting to arouse the wider public. Moshe Shertok agreed to come to that November meeting. [Shertok later changed his name to Sharett.] At the last moment, I was backstage and just prepared to address the group when I was told that Shertok was busy in the UN, that he couldn't possibly come, and that he had sent his assistant, a brilliant young man. This was the first time the community had the privilege of meeting Abba Eban. There were about two thousand people at this meeting. Of course Eban delivered one of his very fine addresses.

Around this time, we felt that we'd never get the community out of the doldrums if we didn't do something dramatic. This led to the second innovation. I went to one of the largest contributors of previous campaigns whose contribution had been in the $10,000 to $15,000 class. I said, "George, we'd like to have a little dinner meeting in your home for about fifteen to twenty men."

"There will be no invitations sent out. I'll make a list, and I will personally call the people and get them to come. Shertok has promised me that he will come as well." I said, "Think of it, George. Here we are, fifty years after 1897, after Herzl, and you have the privilege of sponsoring this kind of meeting."

I said, "We can raise a lot of money at this meeting; it will be an inspiration to the campaign."

He agreed. A small group of people came to that meeting at his home, including Shertok. After dinner, when we went into the living room, I said, "George"—I had prepared him beforehand—"you have got to start this thing off." He responded, "How would $60,000 be?"

Now this was a real jump for George and that group. We walked out of that room with $300,000, which was then a tremendous amount for our community.

In that year, we raised much more money than we had raised before, and much more than our community raised until 1967. You see, I had set a goal in my mind of at least $3 million. When I talked to the president of the campaign, he said, "Ralph, I think you're dreaming, but that's fine if it can be done." Anyway, we reached the $3 million mark before Golda came to the States.

In May 1948, when Golda came, we called another meeting. We also called some of the people together for dinner before the meeting. That event added another half million to the campaign. I must say that the dinner with Golda was one of the greatest moments of my life. I remember getting up and saying, in Hebrew, the *Shema* ["Hear O Israel, the Lord our God, the Lord is One."]

J.M.: We all knew how desperate Israel was for money before the State was established and immediately after. The problem outside of New York City was with the community welfare funds with which the UJA was a partner. It was rather difficult, in many instances, to get the community to borrow. In fact, UJA leaders such as Gottlieb Hammer and Sam Leidesdorf, then treasurer of New York City UJA, rendered yeoman service in getting these communities to borrow monies.

We thought at that time, and now are sure, that they borrowed too little; still, most of them did come through to a greater or lesser extent. Not only did the communities borrow money, but also in '48 and '49, the government had individuals give notes that were discounted by Israeli institutions. Then the funds were turned over to the Israeli government. In fact, only the other day, as I was going through some old papers, I found a letter from Hammer returning a note on borrowed money. The need for cash and dollars was desperate in those days, but somehow or other, we muddled through by borrowing and promising and what not.

M.D.: As we draw our session to a close, I raise a question that goes above and beyond the UJA. It relates to my conviction that while the UJA naturally concentrated on its fund-raising objectives, it simultaneously has built Jewish communities in the process. In terms of your own experience, do you feel that as a result of this twofold approach by the UJA, your community has strengthened and deepened its Jewish roots? Since you are all involved in community leadership, surely you will agree that this is an important issue which we need to evaluate.

[Sidney E. Leiwant was president of Leiwant and Co. Life Agency of New Jersey and Benefit Plans, Inc., West Orange, New Jersey, a former president of the Jewish Community Federation of Metropolitan New Jersey (now Metro-West), and a member of the Board of Directors of the UJA.]

S.L.: I was a relatively young man at the time and had only been active in the "old" Newark community for four or five years prior to 1948. Also, having come from New York City and a small town in Connecticut, my connection with the organized Jewish community was very limited. However, I noticed that even in a city like Newark, where the Jewish population was concentrated, there were basic gaps in organization of the community and a great number of weaknesses.

I was thrilled, of course, by being thrown almost immediately into the company of such community leaders as Ralph Wechsler. As I was right in the middle of it, everything hit me with a great deal of impact.

I did notice, following the 1948 campaign, that the Jewish community tended to become more cohesive. Unfortunately, prior to that time, we had been a community that depended for our largesse primarily on the three families that were connected with the Bamburgers, the department store entrepreneurs.

We had a very difficult lesson to learn when these three families were no longer there, and that was that we had to depend on ourselves. One of the great things that the '48 campaign taught us was that we had the ability to rise to the needs of world Jewry and to do so as a cohesive Jewish community.

Looking back, I probably got both my feet wet in 1946-1947. By 1948, I was in it up to my neck. Since then, it's been over my head. Since I have been active, we have grown into a cohesive Jewish community. As a result of this growth, our agencies have improved. We have gone beyond anybody's dreams of where we can go in matters of education. We have developed new goals and knowledge of how to go about achieving them. We have become a large entity, not only in size, but also in our ability to become a very strong, viable Jewish community.

M.D.: In other words, with about a twenty-year lag, you witnessed the termination of the oligarchic structure that had existed in the early part of the century, wherein the community depended on a very few families. You also witnessed the democratization of giving, which eventually reshaped Jewish community life.

As a beneficiary of what you in this room have accomplished, I cannot resist adding my word of gratitude. All of you, together, have given our people a noble legacy of deed and inspiration.

3

PROJECT RENEWAL:
AN INTERVIEW WITH
YIGAEL YADIN

Preface by
Ya'akov Ariel

Yigael Yadin was born in Jerusalem in 1916, the son of *chalutzim* [pioneering immigrants] from Russia. His father, Eliezer Sukenik, was the founding head of the Institute of Archeology at the Hebrew University; his mother, Hasia, was one of the first kindergarten teachers in *Eretz Yisrael*.

As a teenager, Yadin joined the Haganah, the military organization of the Yishuv during the period of the British mandate. He rose in its ranks to become one of its foremost commanders by 1948. He was later appointed major general and chief of staff of the fledgling Israeli army.

After his release from the army in the early 1950s, he completed his doctoral degree at the Hebrew University and joined the faculty of the Institute of Archeology. He achieved worldwide recognition for his excavations in Hazor and Masada and the publication of a multi-volume work on the Temple Scroll, one of the major Dead Sea Scrolls.

Yadin entered politics in 1977, when he founded a progressive political party—Dash [Democratic Party for Change]—that was the first party to hold primaries for the candidates for political office. Dash won fifteen seats in the elections to the Knesset and joined Menachem Begin's first government coalition in 1977. Yadin served as deputy prime minister and was given overall ministerial responsibility for Project Renewal in spring 1979.

After the dissolution of Dash in 1981, Yadin left political life and returned to the Hebrew University.

He died in July 1984.

Interview by Menahem Kaufman
July 1981

Q: When was your first encounter with the UJA, and in what capacity?

A: I went to the United States for the first time in 1954, two years after I left the army. That was my first direct participation in fund-raising activities in the United States, though I think I had met with most of the leaders even before that. Since then, I have been fund-raising in the United States and in Britain every year or two to date.

There were ups and downs in the development of the UJA, as I see it. The most important change, prior to the introduction of Project Renewal and its merging with the UJA, was the increased emphasis on developing younger leadership during Herbert Friedman's tenure as director.

[Herbert Friedman served as executive vice chairman of the UJA from 1955 to 1971. Prior to joining the UJA staff, he had served as a Reform rabbi and chaplain during World War II, and was active in providing aid to Holocaust survivors after the war.]

Fund-raising activities were the weak spot of the government of Israel and the Jewish people. Public relations with American Jewry, which was mainly channeled—except for Hadassah—through the UJA, meant mainly talking to people who were contributing, excluding the younger generation. This emphasis of directing activities towards the younger generation was a turning point. I participated considerably in a number of those activities.

Q: How did you view the role of the UJA in shaping American attitudes towards Israel?

A: For many years, the UJA, together with Hadassah and later with Israel Bonds, were the main torch bearers of the Zionist message, though the major part was that of the UJA. Both directly and indirectly, it helped create, for better or worse, the Jewish communal leadership in the United States.

The quality of leadership was basically good, but since the criterion was mainly the ability to contribute, it excluded potential leaders who could have been very good. Most of the leaders came from the ranks of UJA contributors or potential contributors, and this included particularly the younger generation. When I talk in my present capacity to UJA missions here, I am thrilled and encouraged to see so many young people. I think that is a very important trend that started at that time.

Jewish leadership in the United States is shaped, firstly, by the synagogues. They are doing a good job in creating a certain kind of leadership—particularly with seminars. They are also doing a good job in the communities where they are educating people about Israel. The second group is that of the voluntary organizations. I think immediately of Hadassah. It is doing an outstanding job. The third group—in quality and also eventually in quantity—is the UJA.

From the Israeli point of view, Bonds and the UJA are taken together as far as creating leadership is concerned. As for the UJA, contributions to Israel have decreased, and this has caused complaints here. Israel and the communities in the United States share the income, although some Israelis feel that the main motivation for contributing is Israel. I think this is a superficial approach on their part, because the local needs of the Jewish communities there are as strong.

One cannot gauge the importance of the UJA in creating leadership, membership, and activities that were directly related to the sums of the money being collected. It is still the largest and the most extensive body that exists in the United States as far as Jewish activities are concerned.

Q: How did Project Renewal answer the social needs of the country as you perceive them?

A: I was bothered for years because half of Israel was not properly integrated socially into the matrix of society—not deliberately, but by mistake. When I was the chief of staff in '50, '51, '52, the years of the big immigration, the army, through my initiative, tried to help the state as much as it could. But when I saw those immigrants seven years ago, when my youngest daughter went as a volunteer to Yeruham [a development town in southern Israel inhabited mainly by immigrants from North Africa and the Middle East], I saw that they didn't have equal opportunities. Their housing was bad, and there were too many children in one room; they couldn't study properly. The fathers had to work; the mothers had to work; there was no one to educate the children. In fact, the gap grew and grew and grew—it had already existed thirty years ago, between the existing *Yishuv* and the new immigrants.

There was a difference between the way I introduced Project Renewal and the way it was announced to the UJA by the Prime Minister. When Prime Minister Menachem Begin first announced this project (a few months before I joined the government), it was mainly to solicit contributions for housing in distressed areas. That was the main aim, and the government took it upon itself to match dollar for dollar. That was the original intention. Yet that was still not the real difference between the original concept of Project Renewal and what it later became—when I entered the government together with my colleague, Dr. Israel Katz, the future minister of welfare.

I changed the nature and concept of Project Renewal. Instead of being a project dealing solely with poverty or with housing, it became a project which actually planned to deal with the approximately 140 to 150 areas in the country with a history of social problems going back thirty years.

Q: Did these new concepts work smoothly in practice?

A: We agreed on the principle very quickly, but the implementation was extremely difficult. I must say that the UJA people abroad made it much easier for me, and for all of us, to deal with them on this issue than it was for us to deal with the Jewish Agency. There was a different problem with the people in the UJA. They wanted to be sure that the money really went to where they wanted it to go and that their people would see results.

Q: Were there any difficulties among professionals?

A: The problem between the fund-raiser and the social worker was of a different order. To "sell" Project Renewal to the Jewish communities in America, UJA had to go about it in a non-abstract way. If they wanted to "sell" the Jerusalem suburb community of Kiryat Menahem, they had to go to the communities prepared with brochures stating problems, solutions, and costs.

We were not prepared for that at the beginning. It was a race. They were already harnessing communities before we knew what the plans were going to be. And I'll tell you why: we had other ideas about how to deal with the communities here. In the beginning, this created a lot of misunderstanding—not so much between the UJA and the government, but between the communities and the contributors. The contributors thought they were going to be given ready-made plans; they were not prepared in the way we thought they would be prepared.

After a time, we overcame the problems and these difficulties diminished. Some problems still exist because of the attitude of the fund-raisers, and I understand them. I'm not criticizing them. They have to go to Baltimore and say, "Look here, we want this and we want that."

We encouraged them to organize missions for the young as well as for the regular participants, and to say to them, "Come and see." They were still accustomed to the older UJA system. When they gave the money, they wanted to see a building or a plaque already in place. It was very difficult to say, "Send them here to see the problem. They don't have to come and see the money at work. Let them see the problem and talk to the people. Let them see how we want to solve the problem."

I have faith in the judgment of the Jews in the United States, provided the situation is properly explained to them. They have seen the failures of slum reclamation in the United States. We have the best advisers here, professors from Princeton and Harvard, who advised the American government on how to reclaim slums. They know why they failed and they advised us how to avoid making the same mistakes. Doing things hurriedly caused the biggest mistakes. We explained all this to them, but we still had misunderstandings from time to time.

At the request of the UJA, I made many appearances. I met missions that came over here, but officially, as far as the machinery with which we work is concerned, my contact with the UJA was through the Jewish Agency, since the UJA money goes through the Jewish Agency and then to the specific locality.

As far as we were concerned, the approach to Project Renewal had to be comprehensive. Therefore, there was need for an administrative interdepartmental committee, which was difficult to create. I am the chairman. It is a committee of the Ministries of Housing, Education, Welfare, Finance, and Health. We have a subcommittee on the professional level, and everything is coordinated. There is also a joint government-Jewish Agency body, of which Mr. Dulzin, treasurer of the Jewish Agency and myself are co-chairmen, that coordinates Jewish Agency and government activity.

We established a principle, which was very important, and I think the people in the UJA understood it quite well—namely, that we didn't want plans to be prepared at the top and then imposed on the people.

On the contrary, we wanted to have the people who were to benefit from the project to participate in shaping the project themselves. So we created steering committees in all these neighborhoods which included its citizens, and we told them, "Look here, you decide what you want."

The principle was accepted enthusiastically by the UJA and by the Jewish Agency. Such a body is working, but it has its problems. Take, for example, the steering committee in Musrara, a neighborhood in Jerusalem that was on the Jordanian border prior to 1967, inhabited by poor families of new immigrants from North Africa. It was a very difficult quarter in Jerusalem. It takes time until they make up their minds what they want, but I am not hurrying them because I think the process—the way they come to a conclusion about what they want—is part of their renewal.

In my opinion, the local steering committees are not only a means to achieving something, they are also part of the target itself, because these people, many hundreds of thousands, came as immigrants from North Africa in 1950-1951. For various reasons, until now they have never been given responsibility to decide what they want. They were always being told what to do, and therefore they were educated only to ask. Now, for the first time, they have been given the responsibility of deciding on priorities. And this is also part of their renewal.

UJA understood the problems. And there are problems. They send a mission, the mission comes and, as I said before, the Americans expect to see everything ready. The UJA and the American community developed a certain mechanism.

Many of these communities have sort of a consul here. Let's say Baltimore has a project in Kiryat Menahem. They hire their own "consul," and trust him to oversee the project and report to them independently, directly, so the people in the Baltimore community have the feeling that they know exactly what is going on. They get reports from the UJA, the Jewish Agency, and the government of Israel, but they also get his report. We tolerate that because that is what we call "participation."

The community there has to adopt a community here. They contribute a certain percentage and earmark it for Project Renewal for this particular place. We encourage them to participate, either by sending a "consul" if they wish, or by meeting the people when they visit. They may even send young people or professional people to work with their chosen community. Take, for example, the Jews of Great Britain. They are doing quite a lot of this in Ashkelon. We formed a joint body with the Jewish Agency and the government, and all the decisions are made jointly.

No new area is designated for Project Renewal unless jointly agreed upon. Any community in America can choose any community in Israel. We don't, and the government doesn't, interfere. We only say that a particular quarter in Ashkelon, for example, is selected for renewal. We don't deal with the missions that come here. We don't deal with training other people. This is the domain of the Jewish Agency and the UJA.

Q: Were there any difficulties among the different agencies dealing with the project?

A: In the execution of plans there are frictions, and they have to be solved. We have agreements. From time to time the top organization, which consists of about seven ministers and myself as chairman, meets with the top department chiefs from the Jewish Agency, headed by Mr. Dulzin, to decide on general policy. The Project Renewal director in my office and the director of Project Renewal at the Jewish Agency carry out the day-to-day business. At the present time, the person at the Jewish Agency is Professor Dan Shimshoni of the Technion, an expert in urban planning.

The frictions I mentioned before are not due to personalities only. Often, there are two sides to an issue. Nevertheless, at this very moment, we are working in seventeen neighborhoods, comprising I think about four hundred thousand persons. Nearly three thousand sub-projects are now in operation. Half of them are under the supervision of the Jewish Agency, half under the government, but all of them are under the supervision of the joint body. And I think we are already seeing the results in many of these quarters.

Q: How would you describe your approach to the project?

A: I've been approaching the problem in a scientific manner, since my upbringing has tended toward a scientific approach, whether it is in archeology or in any other field. That is the way I think. So, obviously, it was not by chance that I put Dan Shimshoni at the head of my team. Because I wanted the project to be based on scientific principles, not just on improvisation, his technical expertise and his ability to deal with public relations made him a logical candidate. I was heavily criticized because politicians don't like professors to involve themselves too much in daily procedures— they insist on spending too much time studying the problem. But because the local people participate in shaping the future and an interdepartmental body exists, it is really impossible for a politician to interfere. These people have now sampled independence. I don't think anybody will be able to take this from them.

Q: Did Project Renewal also deal with improving the educational level of the future local leaders in the Project Renewal areas?

A: We have a project called the Consul's Program of the university. It started with the University of Haifa and it has now spread throughout the country. At this moment, there are about 2,500 people from distressed areas given full stipends by Project Renewal to study in a university. They undertake to work two or three times a week in the place where they come from, and they are committed by contract to go back to those areas for a certain length of time to work as leaders.

We already have seen results. These people are chosen not by parties, but by the steering committees themselves. Of course, they are politically minded people. I hope that in three or four years they will finish their studies. The proper leadership in these areas must also have the proper education—they go together, in my opinion. That doesn't mean that the more a person is educated, the less political he'll be. But I think it is essential that he'll do the work required of him as a leader and will not feel inferior *vis-à-vis* the political parties, the activists, and the government—if he also has a B.A. or an M.A. These 2,500 to 3,000 people will go back every year to their neighborhoods, and they are bound to have an effect on the leadership. I can't give you statistics at the moment because the whole thing started only two years ago.

One has to remember that these new leaders are complex people carrying heavy sectarian or ethnic baggage—even if they get a university education. This is even truer among our teachers at the universities who are already professors: their ethnic affiliations are still very strong. The more enlightened they are, the more educated and the more articulate, the more they manifest their grievances in different and strong ways.

We have to remember that these two to three thousand people being educated by us in the universities—with the specific aim of encouraging them to go back to their areas—may become the torch bearers of anti-governmental or anti-establishment movements— whether to the right or left of Project Renewal's agenda.

Several months ago, I was invited to a Project Renewal activity organized by the people themselves. The older leaders among them arranged a bazaar, with the funds earned being used to help to relieve social problems in their neighborhood. It was the first time that the local leadership in a particular area was not asking anyone to give them something. The young people—boys and girls, local people—were very proud that for the first time they were able to give to others rather than asking others to give to them. So these things are encouraging.

I know that in the last few months, before the elections of 1981, the parties were trying to penetrate all the steering committees in Project Renewal. They suddenly discovered that Project Renewal was a powerful instrument. They had neglected it for years; they had criticized it. However, by then it was too late for many of them. In the future I hope that all parties will participate, in the proper way, within the guidelines and according to the principles.

Q: How do you think Project Renewal will influence the development of Israeli society?

A: Generally speaking, the social problem is the worst the Jewish people have ever tried to overcome in this country. If Project Renewal succeeds, as I believe it will, it will take time because you cannot undo in one year what was done in thirty, forty, or fifty years. I think in five, seven, ten years from now, there will be a change in the whole social structure of the country. When these people see the light at the end of the long tunnel, they will behave differently. They will do whatever they can to educate themselves. If they don't see the light at the end of the tunnel, then an explosion is inevitable. And Project Renewal, I think, has brought the light to many, many of these tunnels.

I can see a difference in the behavior and attitude between the population in those areas being successfully treated by Project Renewal and those neighborhoods where Project Renewal is not successful. My staff is finishing a very quick study to see how certain guidelines were manifested in the last election in the Project Renewal areas compared with the non-Project Renewal areas, that is, in the distressed areas.

We are dealing at the moment with only a fraction of the population. But those who have more time to deal with this directly clearly discern changes in the behavior of children and parents in areas where they had the benefit of better housing, baby homes, kindergartens, old-age clubs, and the other para-social activities— all provided by Project Renewal.

If we leave aside the problems of security, I think the central problem in Israel today is what sort of society we are going to have here. Unless we face that challenge, the whole *raison d'être* of the State of Israel is in doubt. After all, the Zionist dream was not to create another state but to create a state with a society of different standards—Jewish standards and ethics.

Therefore, I think that Project Renewal and the UJA, together with the government, are now facing the greatest challenge of all. It is a long process, more refined than the fund-raising they did before. The machinery must be developed further, and it will take more time, more resources. Yet this is the only hope we have for unifying the Jewish people in Israel.

Project Renewal has helped the UJA. It has brought a new objective to fund-raising. It has injected a new spirit into it. The contributors also saw some new goals for their activities and, what is more important, Project Renewal has brought more young people into the UJA.

I have always regarded the UJA as one of the most powerful instruments keeping the Jewish people together and at one with Israel. Many of those hundreds of dentists who came and worked for some two or three weeks in Ashkelon had not been to Israel before. Now they are tied to Israel—not only to Ashkelon, not only to Project Renewal, not only to the dental project of Ashkelon. They are now tied through commitment to Israel.

The UJA should encourage more such groups to organize themselves on a trade basis so that they participate not just with money but also personally, in the areas with which they are connected. I think this is of the utmost importance. I've seen quite a number of successful cases like Ashkelon. I saw Ramat Gan and what happened in Yeruham with a Canadian group.

Young people are coming. They have an address. When a Jew who participates in Project Renewal visits Israel now—not only in organized groups—he comes to see Israel generally. But he should also be encouraged to see the area with which his community is connected. He can get in touch with it through the Jewish Agency, the UJA, and Keren Hayesod. He can be shown the highlights and the dark spots of the problem, and he can go back and report to his community on what he has seen of "their" project. Then maybe more people will come. Yes, I think these personal, physical contacts are just as important as the contribution of money.

Project Renewal is one vital common ground of activities between the Jewish leaders in United States Jewry and Israel in which they have a legitimate right to participate and to have a say. This is one of the great assets of Project Renewal within the UJA.

4

PROJECT RENEWAL: RETROSPECTIVE

P roject Renewal was born in controversy, raised in confusion, and choked by doubts and antagonisms in Israel and America. It was kept alive by the dedication and zeal of individual members in the government of Israel, the Jewish Agency, the World Zionist Organization, the UJA, Keren Hayesod, the fund-raising communities, and participating Israeli neighborhoods. They all believed in its value for both Diaspora Jewry and the people of Israel.

Even at Project Renewal's inception, a prominent government minister used a Yiddish colloquialism to pronounce the program illegitimate. Most American Jews saw it as a gimmick. Many in Israel regarded it as lacking credibility, thinking it was proposed solely for political purposes. The wonder of it all is that today all take pride in its record of achievement and its becoming a role model for Diaspora-Israeli interactions.

By bringing hope to neighborhoods, Project Renewal proved the doubters wrong and added depth to Diaspora-Israeli relations. It succeeded because a minority of its supporters in both countries were practitioners in the field, not politicians or theorists. They were sent to Israel by their communities, unfettered by their establishments, unburdened by the painful labor of Project Renewal's birth, to develop the *modus operandi* for a totally new UJA enterprise. They were to stimulate citizens of deprived neighborhoods to improve the quality of their own lives, to improve their living conditions, and social and educational structures through involvement in the decision-making process.

Those who came from overseas had to achieve these ambitious goals. At the very same time, the main thrust of the agencies that sponsored them was the effort to raise the enormous funds required for the Jewish Agency's annual budget for *aliyah*, absorption, Youth Aliyah, and rural settlements.

In the neighborhoods of Israel, participants found partners like themselves—storekeepers, laborers, housewives, and social workers—who were also not involved in national priorities. Together, Diaspora representatives and community citizens initiated the first hands-on involvement with the people of Israel since the founding of Keren Hayesod in 1920 and of the UJA in 1939.

In many instances those involved in Project Renewal were not in their community's first level of leadership. But in the process of creating and building programs and relations with each other, Jews from the Diaspora and their Israeli counterparts gained confidence, knowledge, and ability. They accepted commitment and rose to higher ranks in leadership.

Among the many in Israel who became nationally recognized for their creative efforts and public growth through Project Renewal were Moshe Katzav and Meir Shitrit. Katzav was mayor of Kiryat Malachi; Shitrit, mayor of Yavneh. They reflected the new generation of immigrant Sephardic Jews who grew to regional and national stature because of their Project Renewal experience. Both Katzav and Shitrit were elected to the Knesset. Katzav became deputy minister of housing, then minister of transportation; Shitrit became treasurer of the Jewish Agency.

An example of the enormous impact of Project Renewal on Diaspora leaders is contained in an excerpt from a letter to UJA from Edward Goldenberg of Philadelphia [November 8, 1992]:

> In the 1970s, my attitude was still very much that of an assimilated American who was Jewish, with very little knowledge of his religion. In 1979, I was asked to attend the Jewish Agency Assembly. Philadelphia had accepted Project Renewal in principle in 1978, twinning with Ramat Gan, but deferred any active participation or fund-raising for a year, due to a capital campaign going on to pay off our new Jewish Community Center in Northeast Philadelphia. I was asked to investigate and report back to the Federation.
>
> At this Assembly, Israel Peled, mayor of Ramat Gan and a member of the Board of Governors of the Jewish Agency, announced that Philadelphia had not lived up to its agreement. I introduced myself to him after the session. What followed was a visit to his office and my first visit to Ramat Gan.
>
> As you know, the early years of Project Renewal was a "hands-on" experience for those who made the effort. I returned to Israel

in the fall of 1979 to begin work with the professionals in the neighborhood. If I was going to be an effective fund-raiser for Project Renewal in Philadelphia, I needed to know all aspects of the program. We endeavored to involve the residents in the decision making process, with some success.

I began going to Israel three times a year, working within all facets of the program. I became the advocate and go between for the neighborhood activists with the municipality and my new friend Israel Peled. I became very close with those working in Project Renewal from the Jewish Agency for Israel. I established a working relationship and sometimes a personal one with those in the government who had responsibility for Project Renewal. I couldn't get enough of it. I have not been the same person since.

Although many in the Diaspora and in Israel rightfully share credit for this mutually productive program, the truth of the matter is that it would never have come into existence had it not been for Menachem Begin.

It all began in October of 1977, just two hours before the closing dinner of the UJA Prime Minister's Mission in the Knesset, the most important mission each year. Members' pledges made at the Knesset determine the success or failure of each annual campaign. The mission had spent the week in Israel prior to the Knesset gathering studying and reviewing the proposed Jewish Agency's annual budget. They were prepared to make their commitments on that basis.

As we were dressing for dinner, an urgent call came in from Yehuda Avner, then Menachem Begin's aide, advising us that the prime minister planned, during his address to us, to propose a special emergency campaign to raise $1 billion for housing Israel's poor.

Fearing that such an unexpected proposal would destroy the initiative that had been the basis for the mission and confuse our contributors, I insisted that we have an immediate meeting with the Begin, which Avner quickly arranged. I alerted our key leadership and we rushed to the prime minister's residence.

I went with Max Fisher of Detroit. Max had been chairman and president of national UJA and was the founding chairman of the board of governors of the Jewish Agency. He was influential in Republican circles and was involved in negotiations between Israel and Washington.

Others who came with us were Frank R. Lautenberg of Montclair, New Jersey [now senior U.S. Senator (D-NJ)], then UJA's national chairman; Leonard Strelitz of Norfolk, Virginia, and Gordon Zacks of Columbus, Ohio. They were the incoming national chairmen; Alex Grass, a UJA national vice chairman from Harrisburg, Pennsylvania, joined us.

We were dressed for dinner. The Prime Minister had only just returned home from his office. He met us in his robe. He was obviously annoyed at our intrusion and perplexed and disturbed by our resistance to his proposed program. He turned to us, and in a stern voice very different from his usual courteous manner, asked, "Mr. Bernstein, are you and your colleagues trying to tell me that I, the prime minister of a sovereign nation, cannot say whatever I would like to say in the Parliament of this sovereign nation?"

"Of course not, Mr. Prime Minister," I replied. "You can say anything you wish to us at any place, anytime."

We explained to him that announcing a billion-dollar housing campaign without any prior notice or discussion, and without giving the group time to study what was involved, especially after we had spent so many days reviewing other budgetary proposals, would confound the audience and negate the mission's purpose. At the same time, he would be creating insurmountable difficulties for his projected new effort.

After considerable discussion, the prime minister relented and agreed not to launch the new program. Instead, he announced it as a critical item for the future Jewish agenda. We advised Begin that a committee headed by Max Fisher would be appointed to plan a viable framework for the prime minister's proposal—one that would heighten the possibility of success and would be accepted by UJA and community federations. Members of the committee were drawn from the UJA, the Council of Jewish Federations (CJF), UIA, and JDC.

As preconditions for our involvement, we concluded that a comprehensive social component had to be added. Our primary concern was to avoid repeating the failures of such well-intentioned programs as "wars on poverty" that dealt only with housing. Our committee deliberated with Federation representatives and with those in government and social agencies who had experience in similar efforts, and we realized that it was essential that a special or ministerial authority be appointed.

Our committee's report was delayed because we sensed opposition in Israeli ministries, Jewish Agency departments, and American Jewish community federations to funding a program above and beyond their regular budgets. After all, the funds raised would not be available for allocation by the respective ministries, Agency departments, municipalities, or community federations for their ongoing budgetary needs. The funds were to be earmarked solely for this special project.

In view of his promise to Menachem Begin, Max Fisher felt morally obligated to respond and forced a timetable to report the program out of committee. He understood that a perfect order might never be realized.

As a result, the UJA national committee picked up speed, raising the priority of its discussions with community leaders and professional executives. After a decisive meeting with the "large city" executives at their annual retreat in Hyannis, Massachusetts, we came up with the name Project Renewal—just in time to present it to the April 1978 CJF quarterly meeting in Washington, D.C.

Morton Mandel of Cleveland was then president of the council. Leonard Strelitz, UJA's national chairman, and I represented UJA and Project Renewal. The debate was stormy. Difficult questions were raised regarding the structure and process for the programs both in the United States and in Israel.

The hostility of several executives from America's major communities was apparent. They looked upon it as similar to war emergency funds for Israel—that drew contributions out of their communities in which they did not share. It was clear to us that if we presented the program for a vote, it might not pass.

To avoid a negative decision—a failure for UJA on behalf of Israel and an embarrassment for the prime minister, his government, and the people of Israel—I urged that we try to reach a consensus on the basis of community option rather than a compulsory agreement.

We then arrived at a reluctant consensus among those attending the quarterly meeting: that local communities would have the option of accepting or rejecting the effort for Project Renewal. That decision added pressure on UJA to spend a great deal of its time persuading reluctant communities to endorse the project.

Thereafter, we learned by trial and error, since both countries were not properly prepared to carry out the program. Because of inadequate research and planning in America and Israel, American and Keren Hayesod communities were at times twinned to incompatible neighborhoods in Israel.

We limited Project Renewal to a five-year timetable in order to overcome community resistance to any extended fund-raising in which the community would not share. However, almost 25 percent of those communities that eventually participated continued working on Project Renewal, on a limited financial basis, long after the five-year limit because of the friendships they had developed over the years with their twinned communities.

To many communities, the program has become an object lesson on Israeli-American relations for new leaders and contributors. Communities that remained involved on a financial basis, directed their efforts to university scholarships for neighborhood children, creative social programs, and economic development.

There was also unequal community response to contend with. Local options of American communities ranged from enthusiastic community acceptance to hesitant participation limiting involvement, to choosing select groups for involvement, or to outright rejection. But as the program succeeded, many of the communities that had previously rejected the program or limited their participation ultimately joined it. Some of them even expanded their relationships to neighborhoods beyond the one with which they had originally been twinned.

Inappropriate budgets and authority inadequate to the task in Israel—in the government and the Jewish Agency—combined with the reluctance of communities in the United States, were the most significant obstacles that prevented Project Renewal from achieving far more.

Despite Prime Minister Begin's wholehearted support and the endorsement of both chairman of the board of governors Max Fisher and chairman of the Jewish Agency executive committee Leon Dulzin, neither the Agency's functional departments nor the government's ministries reflected or reacted with the same enthusiasm, support, and cooperation. To a degree, their response was understandable: none of them had enough funding to carry out their normal functional responsibilities. It was obvious that Project Renewal would add to their burdens, as Americans, British, Swiss, and scores of others from the Diaspora joined in partnership with neighborhood residents to bring added pressure for items not included in their current budgets.

It became clear to us that for Project Renewal to succeed it had to be on a twinning, hands-on basis and not just by the allocation of funds to the Jewish Agency—which would then distribute the funds through ordinary allocations for regular Agency activities. Since much of the resistance was also parochial and institutional, it was critically important to the UJA and to Keren Hayesod that Menachem Begin appoint a special minister with responsibility for Project Renewal.

That was how Yigael Yadin came into the program.

Frankly, we would have preferred the establishment of a separate ministry that, in our experience, would have endowed Project Renewal with greater influence and priority in governmental decisions and financial allocations. Under the circumstances, Yadin was a more than welcome and respected partner—because of his personality, integrity, intelligence, and his belief in the program.

Yadin was familiar with the Diaspora, particularly North America and Britain, but, like many Israelis, he could not fathom its multiple organizations and the process of community development. He believed, for example, that the synagogue movement was the source of community leadership, a fact no longer true by the early 1950s. In the same vein, Yadin's reference to decreasing campaigns reflects his and his colleagues' lack of grasp of the fund-raising realities in the United States and Keren Hayesod campaigns. Despite dips along the way, the UJA and Keren Hayesod campaigns had been steadily increasing.

The 1973 Yom Kippur War campaign reached record-breaking levels that were not broken until the campaign to fund the exodus of Russian Jews in 1992-1994.

It is true that throughout UJA history, campaign levels reached during Israel's wars and immigration emergencies could not be sustained immediately after the crisis was over. However, to our surprise, succeeding campaigns continued on a higher plane than existed prior to each emergency effort.

Yadin was an effective promoter of the Project Renewal program and was able to explain its growing parameters in oral and written communications. He was always available for meetings with individuals and groups in Israel, the United States, or other countries. He believed as much as we in the United States did, that social programs were critical factors in raising the quality of life in neighborhoods. The question of whether he or we introduced it is moot. The UJA would not have become involved without this critical social element. Yadin believed in it from the day of his appointment. We were all on the same track.

Just as not all of UJA's conduct toward Project Renewal was perfect, and despite Yadin's total support, neither was Israel's. Yadin was both a gentleman and a gentle man, but he lacked the political elbows essential for persuading ministerial colleagues to make Project Renewal a priority.

He was sometimes frustrated with the zealousness of twinned overseas communities regarding their partnership with their neighborhoods. In my opinion, that was because of the complaints and resistance he encountered in the Israeli ministries involved with the program. However, Yadin clearly understood that once such twinning began and interaction took place in neighborhoods, it would be virtually impossible to limit or restrain the new partners. It was pointless to think that those living and working together in deprived areas would not act on their shared dreams and visions. His fellow ministers did not understand this basic truth. His own difficulties with the program are evident in his requests that "there not be interference with the function of government." And he often contradicted himself.

On action-partnership, he said, "They [UJA] do not decide where nurseries and baby homes go or what the educational agenda is. On the other hand, Yadin also said explicitly to Diaspora communities: "Let's be partners." "Be active." "Participate in shaping the project." "You have a legitimate right to have a say."

On participation, he said, "It is the *raison d'être* for Project Renewal's success." Although the overseas partners, lobbying with their neighborhood partners, may have gone to extremes at times, in all my years with Yadin, he accepted the process as long as it did not breach the line of reason and civility.

Yadin differed with the Jewish Agency for similar reasons, but more often than not he reacted in the same manner as other government ministers did to the Jewish Agency. Since Ben-Gurion's days, many officials have found it difficult to accept the Agency as an equal partner with government. The Agency is, after all, a quasi-public body and not a government instrumentality.

Furthermore, since many in government did not have experience and knowledge of the Jewish Agency, they often failed to understand the fact that Agency funds are restricted and limited by the tax requirements of the respective countries in which the money is raised. That is especially true of American money and contributors. Therefore, it is the Jewish Agency, not the government or any other instrument, that is UJA's agent in Israel. This is also true for Keren Hayesod communities—although several of their countries have less rigid tax requirements.

The Jewish Agency by itself does not meet American standards of accountability for tax purposes; therefore, UIA, an American affiliate of the UJA, also has an office in Jerusalem. That office has ultimate responsibility for the accountability of UJA funds spent in Israel in accordance with U.S. regulations. For many in Israel, at times including Yadin, the overlapping agencies were perceived to be unnecessarily duplicating and interfering with their normal procedures. To the UJA, UIA, and our community federations, this was a matter of the highest priority on which there could not be any compromise—as donations from our contributors depended on the inviolate sanctity of their tax integrity.

Yigael Yadin had still another problem. Although he had the key responsibility in the government for the program, Menachem Begin had mandated that he share it equally with Jewish Agency chairman Leon Dulzin, especially in their meetings on policy and program in an inter-ministerial Jewish Agency committee. Although the two men worked very well together, differences necessarily occurred because each represented different constituents and interests.

UJA's problem with the Jewish Agency was on another dimension. At the very beginning, UJA felt that a separate department for Project Renewal should be created in the Jewish Agency with authority equal to that of other Jewish Agency departments. This was not achieved in the beginning because people weren't convinced that

Project Renewal was viable. Instead of a department, an office was established in the Jewish Agency under Leon Dulzin that, in perception if not in fact, was equal to other Agency functions. UJA therefore established its own unit for Project Renewal in its Jerusalem office so that our constituents would not be totally dependent on those over whom we had no control. By having our own office, we would be able to liaise directly not only with the UJA in New York, but with all our constituents who arrived in Israel on behalf of Project Renewal.

Yadin raised a valid and serious critique regarding the "hurry" in our planning and our rush to implement programs in neighborhoods. Theoretically and academically, he was right. Practically, in regard to the reality of communal life in America, he was wrong. During the 1967 and 1973 wars, every Jew, every Jewish organization, every federation, immediately reacted to the need for a separate campaign for Israel's needs. This was not the same in 1978, as Project Renewal never exuded that same sense of urgency or immediacy, particularly since it was being projected over a five-year period.

Since our federated communities functioned on the basis of local option, it was vital that UJA achieve immediate positive and productive results. If we were ever to overcome the reluctance of American communities and persuade them to join the program, it was critical to the success of twinning that those who had accepted it and came to Israel to work in their twinned communities would return home with stories of achievement.

It was impossible for us to delay and wait until Yadin's office completed its research and planning. We had an absolute need to participate with Yadin's director general, Dan Shimshoni, and his personnel, as well as with neighborhood residents. Although this "hurry" created undue conflict and differences of opinion, in the final analysis it enabled us to launch the campaign successfully in the United States and even convince resistant Israelis of its viability.

Yadin's comment describing the newly opened Federation offices in Israel as community "consulates," was not, in my view, meant in any pejorative sense, but stemmed simply from his familiarity with British colonial symbols. In the beginning, even UJA did not support the establishment of these offices, which were initiated by Rabbi

Brian L. Lurie, then executive head of the San Francisco Federation and later UJA executive vice chairman.

UJA was also concerned about duplication and a possible separation of communities from UJA. In fact, it worked out to both UJA's and Israel's benefit. Lurie's intent was constructive, for the opening of community federation offices in Israel brought their communities closer to Israel and UJA—and thus proved to be another fringe benefit of Project Renewal.

As Project Renewal grew in importance and funding, in 1980 the Jewish Agency recognized its value and established the program as a separate department equal in status to all others. Max Fisher played an important role in heightening the image of the program by appointing Jerrold "Chuck" Hoffberger of Baltimore to head Project Renewal in the Jewish Agency. The appointment was significant, because Hoffberger was slated to succeed Max Fisher as chairman of the board of governors of the Jewish Agency. In the government, however, Project Renewal never again reached the level of prominence it had under Yigael Yadin. Today, it is dealt with in separate ministries insofar as the program's activities relate to their respective areas of responsibility.

Both Yadin and UJA envisioned the Project Renewal twinning process as the wave of the future. Although this did not entirely come to pass, there has been a new trend in that direction. UJA has again, under Brian Lurie's initiative in 1994, begun fostering partnership and twinning for economic development. The program is again directed at Israel's underdeveloped neighborhoods. This time the Jewish Agency responded quickly, and the Project Renewal Department has itself now been restructured as the Department of Renewal and Development.

It is interesting to note that UJA's role—both in the genesis of Project Renewal in Israel, in terms of its substance and its title, and in persuading the federations to participate in the program—has rarely been recognized in Israel. Historians and journalists tend to describe Project Renewal as fully born with Prime Minister Menachem Begin's initial announcement, not realizing that it was then limited to housing rather than social renewal.

Project Renewal's record deserves the acclamation it has received. It is a success story about Jewish communities of the Diaspora responding to Israel's needs and improving Israel's neighborhoods. Since its inception, 230 American Jewish communities, through their federations, and 20 Keren Hayesod communities and countries have been twinned either singly or in combination with 95 Israeli neighborhoods.

Although the program never realized its original intention of covering 160 neighborhoods in Israel, it is still a unique accomplishment—particularly since it was achieved while the annual campaigns were raising record amounts for ongoing programs. [That includes the special Peace for the Galilee campaign in 1982.]

As of January 1, 1993, the Project Renewal campaign throughout the United States and Keren Hayesod had raised over $368 million— an investment that dramatically changed the people and landscape of Israel's neighborhoods. There are dental and medical clinics, day-care centers, services for the elderly, recreational programs, parks, nurseries, community centers, cleaner towns, and—most importantly—more involved citizenry.

No less significant is the fact that Project Renewal stimulated more than equal participation from the government in improving housing conditions to a far greater degree than would otherwise have been accomplished.

Does the process uplift people in Israel? Does it strengthen Diaspora relationships with the people, land, and State of Israel?

Yigael Yadin believed that Project Renewal is "the only hope for unifying the Jewish people and Israel." If he is right—as we at UJA believe he was and still is—isn't it time for communities outside of Israel to begin to be less selective in their participation and involvement? Isn't it time for the government and the Agency to deal with renewal at an appropriate level in every ministry and every department, with budgets commensurate to the challenge and the opportunity?

With Western *aliyah* hardly extant, with fund-raising campaigns at times barely meeting inflation, with Zionist entities finding it difficult to recruit support, should not the lessons learned in Project Renewal be transmitted to other areas of potential interpersonal-Diaspora-Israel involvement: education, settlement, immigration, absorption, and industry?

If, in the secular, pluralistic societies of the Diaspora, fund-raising for Israel is "adult Jewish education," then working together with Israelis in Project Renewal is "postgraduate Jewish education" because it shapes and enriches Jewish identity in the fullest sense of belonging and kinship.

The secret has always been in the process—the personal involvement of people working together in partnership—that today can be expanded with energy and capital for the absorption of Soviet as well as Ethiopian immigrants. It is a process essential for a younger generation in the Diaspora to understand, as they tend to take Israel for granted and need such personal involvement just as much as do the recent immigrants. One can only imagine what could have happened if Project Renewal had been funded on a scale appropriate to its challenge and potential. One could only dream of what could have been accomplished had Project Renewal been fully accepted by the government of Israel and the Jewish Agency, open to all generations, no matter what their level of giving or role in their communities.

In 1979, Max Fisher led the way to Project Renewal's acceptance. In 1994, his daughter, Jane Sherman, became the chair of the Jewish Agency's Department of Rural and Urban Development, including Project Renewal—from generation to generation in so short a time.

More than two decades have passed since Menachem Begin stood in the Knesset and proposed a partnership to resolve a crisis not based on war. He reacted viscerally to the tangible problem of inadequate housing. Others in Israel and in the Diaspora added social substance. Project Renewal can still make a difference. In the decades ahead, it is possible that the creation of Project Renewal may become a pattern of life for Israelis and Jews throughout the world.

5

THE YOM KIPPUR WAR: FRANK LAUTENBERG WITH IRVING BERNSTEIN

B orn in Paterson, New Jersey, Senator Frank R. Lautenberg (D-NJ) grew up in a series of working-class neighborhoods throughout New Jersey. Lautenberg enlisted in the U.S. Army and served his country during World War II in the European theater. After returning from the war, he attended Columbia University on the G.I. Bill.

After college, Lautenberg joined with two other young men, Henry and Joe Taub, both future UJA leaders, to help found the nation's first payroll company, Automatic Data Processing (ADP). Lautenberg and his partners developed ADP into the largest computing services company in the world, now providing jobs for thirty thousand people. Throughout his business career, Lautenberg ensured that ADP never forgot its obligations to its employees and to the community.

Senator Lautenberg also has a long record of involvement in the Jewish community. He was general chairman of the national UJA campaign from 1975 to 1977. During his tenure, the campaign raised more than $1 billion—about $450 million in 1975–1976 and $454 million in 1976–1977. Lautenberg is a past president of the American Friends of the Hebrew University. He was appointed by President Jimmy Carter to the U.S. Holocaust Memorial Council, which eventually designed and established the U.S. Holocaust Memorial Museum in Washington, D.C. He also endowed the Center for General and Tumor Immunology at the Hadassah Hebrew University Medical School in Jerusalem, and has visited Israel more than seventy times.

To help American families that have been victims of terrorism, he authored a law that gives American citizens the opportunity to sue individuals in the U.S. courts who commit terrorist acts on behalf of foreign governments. He also authored a law to ensure that state sponsors of terrorism are barred from receiving preferential trade benefits, and he secured additional funding to bolster the FBI's efforts to prevent illegal fund-raising by terrorists.

Lautenberg fought the Arab boycott and authored another law to end the Arab practice of refusing entry to American citizens who have Israeli stamps in their passports. He also wrote a law banning all foreign aid to countries that sponsor terrorism, forcing executive directors of international financial institutions to vote against all loans to terrorist countries, and denying foreign tax credits to U.S. companies that operate in countries that actively support terrorism. He believes that Jerusalem is the unified capital of Israel and voted in favor of moving the U.S. embassy in Israel from Tel Aviv to Jerusalem.

As a member of the Helsinki Commission, he has fought for the freedom of Soviet Jewry. He has worked against tobacco companies and for the environment, and helped write the Clean Air and Safe Drinking Water Act. Supporting the Brady Bill, he has fought the National Rifle Association in an effort to reduce gun violence and has also sponsored a bill to prevent men convicted of wife- battering from buying guns.

He supports reforms in the areas of campaign finance and lobbying. He believes in expanding education, especially computer education, in the nation's schools; is in favor of greater public funding for AIDS programs; voted for the Family and Medical Leave Act; and supports a host of other domestic laws that reiterate his humanity and commitment to community.

Interview by Moshe Davis and Menahem Kaufman
June 19, 1975

Q: The news came across last week that you reported a phenomenal growth during the past few months for the UJA. From a historical and a fund-raising point of view, it seemed totally inexplicable. We are in a period of recession, when everybody is complaining and frightened. You have indicated that the pledges this year are less than last year. And then suddenly comes a report that you have more cash. How was this accomplished? Something basic has occurred here.

F.L.: I see a couple of reasons. Number one, and most important, is the ideological basis for the surge. I think that the Jews view the threat to Israel as almost as serious, if one can say that, as the war. There has been a sense of isolation between the United States and Israel, a perceptible weakening of the traditional relationship. The agendas of Israel and of the United States in the postwar negotiations on the cease-fire lines have not always been identical.

Countering this, remarkably, was the surge in cash flow in the wake of the '73 War. The emotional response raised the levels of giving the following year to unprecedented heights. In 1974 we saw a greater cash flow than in December '73, and that again was because of the war, so the UJA had the greatest concentration of pledges of any period.

Q: But something had to have happened during that period to account for this seeming contradiction.

F.L.: I think the campaign is broader based in '75. In answer to the question as to the reasons for the cash flow, it was a combination of the deep concern in the community and the dramatic response of the UJA that galvanized community action. There was the failure of the Jackson Amendment. Then came the Kissinger shuttle. There was confusion in the community as to the nature of the American government's response.

What the UJA did this time was to relate to the concern for Israel and for Jewish life and develop a mobilization program which would not have been credible if it hadn't been for the community's concerns.

I.B.: There was also a question of leadership. There always is when problems are not resolved and there is no clear direction. But the fact that Frank and the veteran group of leaders around him were calling for mobilization made the difference. At that moment, UJA was one of the very few entities acting nationally. We were asking American Jewry to rally together, to listen, to learn, to act, and while in the process, to finish their campaigns and pay their pledges. We couldn't wait because in campaigning, like everything else, timing is everything.

We stated honestly: If we have *mazel* [luck], out of the Rabin-Ford relationship could come a warmer period, a period of an improved mood, the course of action would have to change.

Q: I ask again: There must have been other factors in addition to exhortation.

F.L.: The main factors were the sense of isolation in the Jewish community because of Kissinger's Middle East shuttle diplomacy; the beginning of the opportunity to rescue Soviet Jewry; and the emergency nature of UJA's crisscrossing the country with authoritative Israeli and American leadership. They rallied communities in support of the immediate cash collection programs.

I.B.: In analyzing the negative climate between Washington and Jerusalem that affected our community, UJA had a critical role to play. Either to continue to do what we're doing and try to do it better, or assess the situation and take major corrective action.

Q: Can you give us some examples of what you encountered as you moved around the country to illustrate this process of "corrective action"?

F.L.: Irving is right. I think we can give you general examples. It was his concept to step into the breach and provide the leadership and rallying point for the community to come together. Among the major cities we covered were Miami, Dallas, Los Angeles, Chicago, and New York.

Q: Why did you choose those cities?

I.B.: They are centrally located major Jewish centers. A meeting in California brings together leadership from the other western states.

Q: Did any Israelis come in and help you on this?

I.B.: Yigal Allon, foreign minister and deputy prime minister, traveled with us, as a result of arrangements made during Frank's and my quick overnight trip to Israel to meet with Prime Minister Yitzhak Rabin. We told the Prime Minister: "We need one of the people who participated in the cease-fire negotiations. If you give us the right person, we will give you the leadership of every Jewish community in America."

F.L.: Rabin at first said nobody could go. But we kept pressing, as we believed it was in the best interests of American Jewry and Israel, and we forced Allon's visit. The press in the United States carried a story that even though no meeting had been scheduled in Washington, Allon would meet with Kissinger. While no meeting was scheduled in Washington, the fact of his public presence decided the issue. He received an official invitation to visit Washington, and he did meet with Kissinger.

Irving and I had met with Allon in Jerusalem in order to get his agreement, but he said he wasn't sure and he had doubts. After his tour of the UJA was over—we met with him the night before he left—he told us that without a doubt it had been worthwhile. He had no regrets.

I wondered whether we had pressured Israel too far. I was concerned. Allon said, "No, don't worry about it, I have no doubts. It was exceptionally worthwhile on all counts, especially in Washington with the strength of that tour behind me."

He also said that Kissinger noted directly to him the effectiveness of drawing the Jewish community together. When he went to the State Department, Kissinger told him, "I see that you've been meeting with the American Jewish community." That had significant meaning. It publicly showed that Jews care, are not daunted by pressures, and that Washington does take note.

And isn't it remarkable to wonder if thirty years ago, if that kind of grassroots pressure had been applied, what might have happened? This was grassroots pressure of the Jewish citizens expressing themselves and letting others feel the pulse of the Jewish community around the country. We weren't trying to get involved in any governmental process. Our purpose was to fulfill leadership responsibility and our mandate: the success of the UJA campaign.

I.B.: It was a non-political action that to others may have seemed political. We could not have done this thirty years earlier, because UJA then could not have drawn out the leadership of the communities who responded as they did in 1975. Thirty years ago, we were not that well organized, anti-Zionism was very strong, and our constituency was not united. At that point in history, communities regarded the UJA with antagonism. Today there is unity within American Jewry. Today, UJA leadership has greater credibility, as they have risen from the ranks of community federations.

Q: Did you have a meeting in Washington when Rabin was there? Isn't it unusual to have had a campaign meeting in Washington at a time when the Prime Minister comes to see the President?

F.L.: Washington is like any other city. Our meeting was with its Jewish community. We did not initiate Rabin's presence in the community. We did, however, gain one advantage from his official visit to Washington. We initiated the Allon meetings and the mobilization campaign. UJA put that program together. Allon was there for our purpose, to show Israel's face to the American Jewish people. We alerted the communities. We saw it as doing our job, getting the cash in, bringing leadership up to date, raising gifts, and uniting communities. The end result was that communities came with declarations as to how much their cash goals would be in the days ahead.

Our goal was to collect $100 million in cash. We assigned each community a quota for the $100 million, which was accepted, sometimes with resistance. But our task was made easier by the fact that the community representatives had to make public declarations in front of their peers. We also asked them to finish the campaign and to resolicit inadequate gifts. The meetings were directly related to the campaign, but at the same time they were showing support for Israel. At the end of each meeting, in spontaneous reaction, we would sing "Hatikvah" [Israel's national anthem].

Q: Was that new?

F.L.: Yes, because these were informal meetings. When we hold a formal meeting, we always begin with "The Star Spangled Banner" and conclude with "Hatikvah." At these meetings...it just happened naturally, feeling the tone of the room.

Allon would stand between the two of us. You could feel the excitement and emotion in the room. And due in part to Allon's friendly, outgoing personality, it just happened as if we had planned it. As we went from meeting to meeting, Allon would sing a little louder.

When we got to New York, this little man stood six feet tall, and sang like a baritone at the opera. He led that audience in "Hatikvah." This was before he went to Washington. He had grown in strength as he went through this trip, experiencing and feeling the response of Jews in cities as far apart and disparate as New York City; Helena, Montana; Seattle, Washington; Barstow, California; and Texarkana, Texas.

Q: Thirty years ago, if he were on his way to Washington, it would have been a meeting organized by the Zionist organizations.

I.B.: Thirty years ago, before the state, there was no Israel Bonds drive. The UJA was still in its infancy. Whatever was done for Zionism or Israel was done for Israel by the Zionist organizations and their leadership. Their constituency was then limited. They could reach neither the organized nor the non-organized Jews in their major federation communities.

Since the 1967 war, there is greater unity in the American Jewish community. Today, all major Jewish organizations unite in meetings of their presidents in the Presidents' Conference. Today, UJA, Israel Bonds, and other Israel-oriented entities set up meetings with prominent Israelis.

A key difference, however, is that it is only the UJA or the CJF that can bring the leadership of federations and independent communities together. The meeting that was held in Washington was possible because it was the only time and place Rabin had for us. We planned for two to three hundred people, but six hundred attended. It was an unbelievable response.

F.L.: This connects directly to the fund-raising. Whatever meetings we have arranged lately have drawn greater numbers of people than we have seen before.

Q: So, it's really not only due to good organization? And it's really not all technical?

F.L.: No. There is a groundswell of support as we view it, and it's being manifested in many ways, not the least of which is this phenomenal turn-out that we just described, especially when there seem to be threats to the American Jewish community or to Israel.

The Rabin meeting was an operational uplift. It was designed to bring together the Jewish community to hear from the Prime Minister. Rabin's official talks were not concluded, and he couldn't make a statement that could be carried in the media. It was therefore a show of strength and support. Rabin moved his audience with statements such as, "I didn't come here in June to give away what we wouldn't give away in March." This drew thunderous applause.

Q: Was it new for this audience?

F.L.: It is one thing to read about it, but it's totally different to hear it directly and bear witness.

Q: It's pretty clear now that you have much more credibility with the Jewish Agency power structure.

F.L.: The main funding instruments of Israel today are Bonds and UJA. If we are now raising twice what Bonds do, it doesn't mean that Bonds are ineffective, it just means that the UJA is the agency that has the capacity for greater outreach. UJA still raises two-thirds of world Jewish funds, with Keren Hayesod raising one-third. UJA at this moment in time has been very fortunate.

I.B.: Leaders are only human and not cut from any mold, there are times when there has been conflict between lay and professional leaders. The problems exist because of the permanence of the professionals and the transitory nature of volunteer leadership. These situations have to be worked on all the time because captains of industry have their agendas and professional leaders have theirs. I have not been exempted from that.

This period has been a blessing for the UJA and me. Whenever there is conflict, the campaign suffers. Frank and I have had a symbiotic relationship. We can differ with each other without ego problems. We have confidence in each other's judgments.

The public tends to see UJA through the image of its leadership. Their sense of that person, even more than their position, often determines their perception of UJA. Therefore, as Frank meets with leaders from around the world, they relate to the UJA through his person, as well as his position, and it has been an unbeatable combination. Every UJA chair therefore exerts as much influence by their person as they do by their efforts.

F.L.: There is a demand by the American Jewish community today, and perhaps, by Jews around the world, for deeper Jewish content in the UJA and in programs that relate to Israel. It is no longer sufficient for wealth to be the only factor in the leadership. There is a second and third generation that desperately needs that content.

Q: In the quality of ideas?

F.L.: Absolutely. And there are other factors that have begun to percolate in the world. Money and physical assets as a commodity do not alone provide security in our own country. The man who lives on Park Avenue on the thirty-sixth floor, when the doorman doesn't show up, is liable to get mugged and killed on the way up to his apartment. The things that used to represent security no longer do so. The whole world is seeking deeper values, and particularly the Jewish community, which always recognizes that first. They are looking for answers. We've provided a channel for them, and we have a response. In that way Israel becomes aware of the more serious side of a developing, thoughtful Jewish community.

Q: And the representative personalities?

F.L.: We think that we bring credibility to the leadership—our people in the national leadership are serious men and women.

Q: What you are saying is that what you do in campaigning really builds national Jewish leadership?

F.L.: I believe campaigning will become a regular part of one's communal life. That obligation is now accepted as a fact of life. Judaism is important, and if Judaism is important, Israel is important. If Israel is important, we must convince Jews in the Diaspora to support it.
There's been a great change in the magnitude of the budget. The budget of Israel is roughly $3.5 billion dollars. From the Keren Hayesod and UJA campaigns, we'll bring in over 15 percent of Israel's budget! This is from a non-voting constituency. It's a unique phenomenon. Jewish energy, a resource that's there, has just evolved and is developing. You can't understand it in strict rational terms.

Q: Are you saying that the leadership of the UJA has more and more become the leadership of the American community?

F.L.: We'd like to believe that, but we are not the only leadership on the American scene. Based on our perspective and experience, we have gained credibility and we have made an impact in Israel, as well as back home, that has gone beyond our mandate to raise funds.

6

FRANK LAUTENBERG: RETROSPECTIVE

It was early summer in 1974. UJA faced a crisis in leadership continuity for only the second time in its fifty-five-year history. Despite careful planning, Albert Adelman of Milwaukee, an experienced and veteran UJA leader, a former All-American football player from Northwestern University, had to withdraw for personal reasons after he had been chosen to serve as chairman for 1975 to 1977.

The first time it happened was in 1961, when Philip Klutznick of Chicago, after serving three months as chairman, bowed to pressure from President John F. Kennedy and resigned his post to serve as U.S. Ambassador to the United Nations.

At that time, my predecessor, Rabbi Herbert A. Friedman, after consulting with leadership, persuaded Joseph J. Meyerhoff to step into the breach. To Meyerhoff's credit, he proved to be a unifying force during the difficult years prior to the 1967 war—when anti-Zionism was still a potent force.

[Meyerhoff was the director and president of the PEC-Israel Economic Corporation from 1957 to 1963. He was also president of the Baltimore Symphony Orchestra; president of Baltimore's Jewish Welfare Fund from 1951 to 1953; and a member of the boards of directors of the Technion-Israel Institute of Technology, the Hebrew University of Jerusalem, Tel Aviv University, Ben-Gurion University of the Negev, the Weizmann Institute of Science, and the Tel Aviv Museum. He was general chairman of the UJA from 1961 to1964.]

When Adelman left, the 1975 campaign was still in the shadow of the extraordinary 1973 war campaign—an effort that raised the highest totals in all of UJA history (surpassed only by the Operation Exodus campaign of 1991).

A period of lower giving became the pattern after every surge in funding—in the war years of 1948, 1956, 1967, 1973, and 1982 and the historic, dramatic rescue operations: Magic Carpet (1948–50) [Jews from Yemen] ; Project Ezra (1950–51) [Jews from Iraq];

Operation Moses (1984–85) [14,600 Ethiopian Jews in 36 hours from Addis Ababa]; Operation Solomon (1991) [Ethiopian Jews from Sudan]; and Operation Exodus (1990–94) [Jews from the former Soviet Union].

The large amounts raised during these unifying moments in Jewish history were predictably followed by decreases when the crises ebbed. Still, levels rose above those of previous non-war years.

To make sure donations increase in non-crisis situations, special leadership effort is required, as are innovative, inspirational, and emotional programs involving major contributors.

After record gains in 1973, made under the dynamic leadership of Paul Zuckerman of Detroit, it was evident we needed a respected, influential, and well-recognized leader around whom the community could rally.

Among the UJA officers and board members were an impressive group of younger leaders whom we had been grooming, and newer members whom we had added to the board. Among them were Henry Taub and Frank Lautenberg of New Jersey, partners in ADP— one of the largest automated computer service companies in the world. The company was founded by Taub with Lautenberg as its president. Taub had been president of the American Society for Technion-Israel Institute of Technology and later rose to become chairman of Technion's international board of governors. Taub became the only American Jewish leader ever to be honored by holding the chairmanship of both UIA and JDC.

Lautenberg was president of the American Friends of the Hebrew University when the UJA leadership decided that he was the prime candidate to assume its chairmanship. He had the potential to meet UJA's internal and external challenges with our federations in the United States, the government of Israel and the Jewish Agency.

I was assigned the task of sounding him out for the position because we had both been appointed by President Carter to the U.S. Holocaust Commission [which later became the U.S. Holocaust Memorial Council] and had worked together closely. I had also spoken at UJA meetings in Lautenberg's home. [Together with our wives, we had accompanied Elie Wiesel, the chairman of the U.S. Holocaust Commission and then the Council, on a diplomatic mission to Poland, Russia, Denmark, and Israel to generate research materials for a museum.]

After dinner with Lautenberg and his family, we met in his study for more than two hours. Although he was honored and excited about the opportunity and challenge UJA offered, he felt that he was not ready for it. He also preferred his involvement at the university, as it demanded less of his time and resulted in less conflict with his duties at ADP.

It was an exhausting two hours, since I realized that a further meeting with UJA leadership might be just as fruitless. Then I remembered I had an appointment the very next day in New York City at the UIA with Pinhas Sapir, the legendary finance minister of the State of Israel.

I asked Lautenberg to join me. At first he was reluctant and hesitant. But he finally agreed because Sapir was a unique character, respected and beloved by all UJA leaders and professionals.

Sapir was a huskily built man with a gleaming bald head, piercing eyes, and a guttural voice that rarely completed a sentence. Yet he ably communicated with and persuaded Rothschilds and Rockefellers to see things his way.

As we walked into the small office Sapir had taken over for the day, before we could sit down, Sapir pointed his finger at Frank, looked him directly in the eye, and in his distinctive accent, emphasizing each word, said, "Lautenberg, you must be the UJA chairman."

To my consternation and Sapir's joy [since he had been briefed about my meeting the previous day] Lautenberg said, "Yes."

The rest of the hour went by in a blur. I was happy but bewildered by the turn of events. I could not understand what had happened to change the situation since the night before. When Lautenberg and I walked out, I asked him, "How could your first thirty seconds with Sapir so suddenly change your decision after our two hours yesterday?"

His unforgettable reply was, "How could I say no to a man who wears high-button shoes?" It was then I learned that Lautenberg's father had worn high-button shoes.

Lautenberg was born and raised in Paterson, New Jersey, then the center of the silk industry. Although his father owned a bar, the majority of Paterson's large immigrant community worked in the silk mills. As a young man, Lautenberg ventured into driving racing cars. He met Henry Taub at Columbia University, where both were majoring in business administration. After graduation, Lautenberg sold insurance. Taub opened a storefront operation that computed payroll checks for small companies. As his business grew, he asked Lautenberg to be his outside man. The two of them built ADP into an international corporation.

It was abundantly clear to Lautenberg and me, as well as to the leadership, that it would be difficult to achieve the same numbers in volunteers and funds that we had done in the aftermath of the Yom Kippur War. We knew we had to inspire our fellow Jews, raise their spirits, reawaken their interest and energy, and unite them with their fellow Jews in Israel and all over the world on the principle that we were one people.

"We Are One" was the statement of faith we adopted after Yom Kippur 1973, and we maintained it throughout my tenure at UJA.

Our key aim was to reach out and involve as many Jews as possible of all generations, the unattached as well as those already involved, so that the priority of Israel and Jewish need would mean as much to them in peace as it did in war.

In conducting a campaign, any campaign of any year, it is essential that those who lead it be aware of the conditions in Israel and Eastern Europe, of world events and issues that affect Diaspora Jews and Israelis. The challenge is to assess the impact of these events and issues on the giving public, and to plan in a manner that gives direction and support to 164 federation campaigns and 283 smaller, non-federated communities.

Lautenberg's reference to the Jackson-Vanik Amendment and Kissinger's shuttle diplomacy relates to these events that unsettled American Jews, leaving them with mixed emotions—concern, anger, despair—as they waited for signals and direction from responsible national Jewish bodies.

The Jackson-Vanik Amendment, if passed by Congress, would have forced the President to withdraw "most favored nation" trading status from the Soviet Union, making it more costly for them to trade with the United States. It was proposed in order to exert pressure on Soviet rulers, to force them to withdraw the head tax imposed on each Soviet Jew who wanted to immigrate to Israel. The net effect of the tax was to stop the flow of Jews to Israel.

When the amendment was first proposed in 1972, President Nixon opposed it. President Ford maintained that opposition during his administration. Henry Kissinger, who served both of them as Secretary of State, also opposed it. Both administrations tried to convince Jackson, Vanik, and the Jewish leadership that the amendment would be counterproductive and that they could achieve the same goals with personal diplomacy.

It was this resistance to the amendment and the continued shutdown of Soviet emigration that disturbed American Jews and the Israeli leadership. Because of the continued obstinacy of the Russian leadership, the Nixon-Ford-Kissinger "personal diplomacy" tactic failed. When Congress passed the amendment in 1972, President Ford had no alternative but to withdraw "most favored nation" status from the Soviet Union.

In 1985, Gorbachev removed the tax penalties on emigration and opened the exit gates wide for Soviet Jews. The Jackson-Vanik Amendment had served its purpose. Natan Sharansky said that one of his interrogators in Russia told him the amendment had cost the Soviet Union $1 billion. Beyond that, the Russians had clearly learned a bitter lesson by losing the goodwill of the American Jewish community and its friends in Washington.

An interesting footnote is that both Senator Henry Jackson of Washington state and Congressman Charles Vanik of Ohio had Jewish administrators who went on to higher positions: Richard Perle worked with Jackson, and Mark Talisman worked with Vanik.

Perle later served as assistant secretary of defense under President Reagan and was instrumental in the SALT II [Strategic Arms Limitation Talks] negotiations with the Soviet Union. During the summit in Reagan's second term, Perle forced through the breakthrough "zero tolerance" nuclear arms agreement that led to the dismantling of all nuclear warheads in Europe.

Talisman became the Washington director of the CJF and was also responsible for bringing the Precious Legacy Exhibit from Prague to North America. My wife Judy, Sandra Weiner of Houston, and I accompanied him on one of his organizing trips to Prague. The exhibition consisted of Judaica and artifacts from Jewish community life that had been stolen by the Nazis. The show, which toured the major cities, was very effective and had a deep emotional impact on those who viewed it.

Kissinger's shuttle diplomacy between Israel and Egypt caused even deeper concern than the two Presidents' resistance to the Jackson-Vanik Amendment. The Jewish perception was that Washington was leaning harder on Israel than on Egypt. They worried that this pressure might irretrievably weaken Israel.

To ease those concerns, the UJA decided to bring one of the three Israelis who had negotiated with Kissinger and the Egyptians to the United States for a lightning tour. We believed that this was the most effective way to bring the facts directly to the Jewish leadership and their constituents, clarify the issues, and give them a sense of direction.

Lautenberg and I flew to Israel for thirty-four hours, intending to return with any one of the three: Prime Minister Yitzhak Rabin, Foreign Minister Yigal Allon, or Minister of Defense Shimon Peres. We needed a well-known personality and an authoritative voice.

Although Prime Minister Rabin offered us other ministers, we held out for one of these three. In the end, Rabin agreed to send Allon. Allon was reluctant to come, but we finally convinced him that it was vital for him to brief American Jewish leadership in the United States.

After a very positive meeting with East Coast leaders in New York City, we flew to Chicago for our second meeting. Aboard the plane were national vice chairmen representing all the UJA divisions, including the Women's Division and Young Leadership. We had staff support, press, and members of Israel's embassy in Washington with us.

The Allon visit and his subsequent tour of major cities was not the only UJA mission of its kind. It was an approach UJA had used whenever a crisis threatened Israel, whenever there was a need to call for Jewish unity, for American Jews to stand with one another and with Israel.

This was UJA at its best. For UJA to be productive, it must be able to respond to emergencies in the same manner as police officers or firefighters, without falling prey to the bureaucratic process.

Lautenberg correctly states that UJA does not enter into political arenas. However, we know from long experience that our people do not respond by giving or becoming involved when they feel disheartened, despondent, or isolated because of current events.

What we did with Yigal Allon in 1975 was a repetition of what we had done during the Yom Kippur War, when we brought Finance Minister Pinhas Sapir, Jewish Agency Treasurer Leon Dulzin, and General Chaim Laskov to America to address meetings in New York City, Chicago, Los Angeles, Dallas, Atlanta, and Miami.

We did it again with Defense Minister Moshe Dayan when Jimmy Carter became President, and relations between Washington and Jerusalem looked as if they were deteriorating. At each of these meetings, Jewish leaders from the regions surrounding each host city were invited. The purpose was to keep our fellow Jews apprised of current Israeli positions and the positions of the Jewish communities around the world—to let them know that we stood together, that the immediate task was to complete the campaign at appropriate levels. We did not in any sense ask for, or discuss, political action.

In Washington, at times these tours were seen as being politically oriented. If so, it was an unplanned benefit. Our programs were about unity, financial needs, and Jewish fulfillment. Our goal was to stimulate Jewish hearts.

Although the sums UJA raises are not for political purposes, it is a fact that in many capitals of the world, leaders are aware of the extraordinary sums raised by UJA through the will, strength, and determination of the Jewish community. And they read that as a political statement.

[A brief humorous incident occurred on Yigal Allon's visit to Palm Springs, California. Secret Service agents are always assigned to foreign dignitaries for their protection, and four were assigned to Allon. Allon, an expert horseman, decided to go riding. The agents, who were not experts, joined him reluctantly. As they galloped through the canyons of Palm Springs, it was a sight to behold Israel's foreign minister far ahead of the pack, while his four protectors strenuously straggled far behind in a futile effort to close the gap.]

It is axiomatic that the success of annual campaigns also depends on the ability of the UJA leadership to design campaigns that continually capture the attention and participation of major contributors.

In 1975, in consultation with the CJF, and for the first time in their then forty-eight-year history, with CJF's full support and cooperation, UJA held a national Big Gifts fund-raising meeting on the eve of the annual CJF General Assembly in Chicago. This clearly was an indication to the entire country that there was unity of purpose in the Jewish community and in the goals of our campaign.

On November 10, 1975, the United Nations, to its eternal shame, passed the infamous resolution equating Zionism with racism. Like all Jewish organizations in the United States, UJA held meetings and rallies to protest. We involved Ambassador Chaim Herzog [later President of Israel], Elie Wiesel, and other public figures and distributed their statements to all communities. In addition, UJA produced and distributed large buttons with the imprint, "We Are All Zionists"—just as we had done, and continued to do, with our "We Are One" buttons.

During Moshe Dayan's visit to the United States on our behalf in December 1975, I accompanied him to a reception hosted by the well-known television personality Barbara Walters. I usually pinned the button on automatically when I dressed in the morning. As we came into the reception, a well-known television star, also Jewish, accosted us and screamed at me, "How dare you wear that slogan?! We are not all Zionists." Startled, and somewhat embarrassed by the silence and stares in the room, Dayan stood still by my side. The moment seemed like an eternity, until Dayan replied for all to hear, "You don't know what you are missing," leaving her standing alone as we joined the others.

Frank Lautenberg aptly refers to the ideological backbone of the campaign. Such under-girding becomes visible when Israeli leaders visit the United States during periods of crisis.

It is also apparent in the popularity of teachers and writers like Elie Wiesel and Moshe Davis. It is the basis of the personal encounters with contributors on behalf of UJA. UJA fund-raising is rarely, if ever, just a matter of dollars. From its very beginning in 1939, it has been clear that for UJA to succeed, it had to serve as a Jewish educational instrument.

The degree of its educational outreach, however, always depends on the symbiotic relationship between UJA's professional and volunteer leadership. Increased levels of educational outreach were particularly heightened during my predecessor Rabbi Herbert A. Friedman's tenure, my own term of office, and later Rabbi Brian

Lurie's term. Our principal texts were based on *Klal Yisrael* [the people of Israel], *kehillah* [community], and physical and spiritual ties to Jerusalem.

The texts applied directly to the fund-raising process. In the United States, the bedrock of fund-raising is the solicitation of one person by another. In the Keren Hayesod world outside the United States, our colleagues describe it as canvassing. But the fact of the matter is that both soliciting and canvassing are one and the same—it is a uniquely Jewish experience, not just a financial negotiation.

A UJA solicitation means that one Jew shares with another the meaning of physical and spiritual Jerusalem, the Jewish future of their children and grandchildren, the relationship of both to their respective communities. It is only in this way that the act of giving has any meaning and value to the one who is asking and to the one who is giving. When the encounter fails, it means that one or both have forgotten who they are and the purpose of their meeting.

It must be borne in mind that at UJA, during my tenure as well as that of my predecessor, everything we planned was based on the understanding that if UJA wanted to raise more money, it had to be rooted as an organization in the history of the Jewish people and in the significance and meaning of the State of Israel. Elie Wiesel summed it up this way:

> Just as a man needs other men to be human, so does a Jew need other Jews to be Jewish. He chooses to define himself not in relation to the hate he elicits from strangers, but rather to the faith he inspires in people. Community is the key word. It indicates what path to follow, it opens hidden gates and bestows ancient strength on every day formulae. A vital, vibrant word, a primary that cuts through all other words, challenging them, enriching them: community.

Since Lautenberg and I shared the same vision of the Jewish role in the UJA, we were able to project, create, and plan programs that were entirely new or incredibly large. Among them was the film production of Elie Wiesel's play, *Zalman, or the Madness of God*, at Carnegie Hall in New York City. It starred, among others, Joseph Wiseman, Theodore Bikel, and Herschel Bernardi, who performed to packed houses. It was produced and directed by Issachar Miron of UJA's staff.

Miron, the educational director for the fledgling Israel Defense Forces in 1948, wrote the popular song "Tzena, Tzena," which became the only song from the Middle East to climb to number one on America's hit parade. Composer, artist, producer, director, and educator, Miron continued, with UJA's blessing and support, to produce spiritual performances based on UJA's theme, "We Are One." His work resonated with thousands of people in practically all the major communities in the United States.

In 1977, UJA for the first time published a major supplement in *The New York Times* and arranged for it to be distributed to the American Jewish community, where it immediately became a keepsake. In it, President Jimmy Carter summed up the essence of UJA:

> In your humanitarian work, UJA reflects a heritage that is both uniquely American and traditionally Jewish—alleviating human need and suffering both at home and across the globe. In your campaign, you collectively express a spiritual bond that transcends national boundaries. In crisis and in hope, UJA symbolizes for Jews a determination to live by ideals—in keeping with American principles.

Frank Lautenberg wrote:

> The challenge is to know that we are links in the chain of generations; that we transcend geography in expressing our unity with the people of Israel—and that we have the ability to make impossible dreams come true . . . if we act together in strength, and truly believe that Jewish destiny is in Jewish hands.

Academics became involved with UJA, spreading its message and programs. Elie Wiesel, Moshe Davis, and Yehuda Bauer of the Institute of Contemporary Jewry at the Hebrew University in Jerusalem [now at Yad Vashem] delivered the first three Louis A. Pincus memorial lectures at successive annual December conferences. Wiesel, who delivered his famous address "Against Despair" at the first Louis A. Pincus memorial lecture at the 1973 conference, became a significant voice for the UJA in both his spoken and written words.

"Against Despair" was distributed throughout the United States, reprinted time and time again for contributors—no matter what their level of giving—and was disseminated to campaigns in Australia, Canada, the United Kingdom, South Africa, and other countries conducting similar campaigns. Wiesel included the entire address in his 1978 book *A Jew Today* published by Random House.

During those terrible moments of the Yom Kippur War when it appeared that Israel might be destroyed by the combined Arab attack, Wiesel wrote:

> We owe it to our past not to lose hope. Say what you may, despair is not the solution. Not for us. Quite the contrary: we must show our children that in spite of everything, we keep our faith—in ourselves and even in mankind, though mankind is not worthy of such faith. We must show our children and theirs that three thousand years of history cannot end with an act of despair on our part. Other peoples have more reasons to give up in despair. To despair now would be a blasphemy—a profanation.

Each of the 1975 and 1976 Young Leadership missions, *Koach* [strength] and *Dor le-Dor* [from generation to generation], brought more than one thousand young leaders to Israel. They were the largest missions since Young Leadership programs were introduced in 1963.

In 1976, we organized the "This Year in Jerusalem Mission" to bring three thousand people to Israel. My initial projection was for a mission of ten thousand. But in meetings with the management of El Al, it was clear that in order to cope with a mission of that dimension, El Al would have to assign every plane in its fleet to the task and cancel its entire regular schedule—with negative commercial consequences in Europe and elsewhere.

Even though we then planned to use TWA as well, we realized that our goal of ten thousand was not feasible. The largest number we could agree on was three thousand, and even then we had to combine El Al with TWA. [I still wonder what might have happened in Israel and in the United States if we had succeeded in bringing ten thousand American Jews to Israel at one time!]

To this very day, it remains the largest Jewish mission ever to have visited Israel. It was an enormous undertaking to gather three thousand plus visitors representing 124 communities from all fifty states—including Anchorage, Alaska and Honolulu, Hawaii.

En route, participants visited concentration camps and remnant Jewish communities of Eastern Europe and North Africa—and then they came to Israel. They came from eighteen nations and four continents, in more than 350 flights. In Israel they filled eighteen hotels, traveled in one hundred tour buses, and visited two thousand Israeli homes.

Effective and motivated communal leaders led the mission. By the end of the week, these inspired communities had raised $40 million, an increase of more than 20 percent over the previous year's giving.

Why did it work?

Because thousands of individual experiences were taking place throughout the land: in the home of the president; in the apartments of ordinary citizens; in universities, rural settlements, urban centers, stadiums, convention halls, and the streets of Jerusalem; and in strength and prayer at the Western Wall.

An Arab shopkeeper watching a plane skywriting the words "Welcome, UJA—We Are One" was asked by another Arab what he thought of it. He answered, "Yes, they are one."

At the closing session, general chairman Frank R. Lautenberg expressed the emotion that was driving the mission:

> That soaring of the Jewish spirit—that sense of renewed strength—was symbolized in the Negev by the Kfir [Israeli fighter jet] soaring skyward like the spirit of the independence of the Jewish people. As the *Kfir*—soaring like eagles' wings—thrust upward, it spoke of strength, excellence, courage, and life. Perhaps some day this, too, can be turned into a pruning hook. But until then, the guardian of the people of Israel neither sleeps nor slumbers.

The editor of *Al Hamishmar* was moved to write describing the spirit of the event:

> The old Western Wall has many faces. I visited it in those distant days when we stood like poor people at the door. I saw it on the day after it was liberated, when the late President Zalman Shazar prayed there with a trembling voice. I stood in the shadow of the Wall in hours of mourning and in moments of protest, and I enjoyed it on holidays and during celebrations. I also passed by the Western Wall on an ordinary day, which is never ordinary at

the Western Wall. But now, the Western Wall had a new surprising face: the Western Wall of the UJA.

The words UJA Campaign have a rather prosaic sound. But in the same way as the poor beggars of the Western Wall described in the novel of Ari Ibn Zahav were not just beggars, because the divine presence of the Holy Place gave them an extra soul—and in the same ways as the hundreds of Jews all year round become on the holidays a holy community wrapped in their *tallitot* [prayer shawls]—in the same way, as this unique event turned the businessman from Boston, the society lady from Los Angeles, the successful physician from Chicago, together with the Israelis who accompanied them, into "We Are One"—a blue sea of three thousand blue jackets on the gray background of the Old Wall—*tachlis* [purpose] became destiny.

In the days and weeks following this mission, a flood of calls and letters with poems and stories expressed the impact of the experience on individuals, families, and communities. It was the first time in UJA history that a mission had generated such a post-mission emotional response.

7

GOLDA MEIR

Golda Meir, longtime labor leader and Israel's Prime Minister from 1969 to 1974, was born in 1898 in Kiev, Russia. Because of extreme poverty, the family immigrated to the United States in 1906 and settled in Milwaukee, where Golda was graduated from high school and enrolled in a teacher's college. Because of her childhood memories of Russian pogroms and anti-Jewish massacres, she embraced Zionism.

In 1921 she and her husband, Morris Myerson, settled in Israel and joined a kibbutz. Golda soon became involved in political and social activities.

She was sent as an emissary to the Pioneer Women's Organization in the United States from 1932 to 1934. When she returned to Palestine, she was invited to join the executive committee of the *Histadrut* [the Jewish labor movement, founded in 1920]. There, she rapidly rose in the hierarchy and was appointed head of the Political Department, which proved to be valuable training for her eventual role as leading statesman of Israel. Golda was also a gifted orator in Yiddish and English.

Among her many achievements was the ability to raise desperately needed money for the new emerging State of Israel. In January 1948, she visited the United States and was extremely successful in presenting the seriousness of the situation to the American Jewish leadership. Her goal on that first trip was to raise $100 million.

Golda will also be remembered for her bravery, among her many attributes. On May 10, 1948, just four days before the proclamation of the state, she made a very dangerous and dramatic journey across the Jordan to meet secretly with King Abdullah—hoping to persuade him not to join the attack on the newborn Jewish State.

After the establishment of Israel, she was appointed minister to Moscow, a post she held until April 1949. Her presence elicited an extraordinary appearance of Jewish masses at the Moscow Great Synagogue on the High Holy Days.

Later, as minister of labor, she initiated large-scale housing and road-building programs and supported the policy of unrestricted immigration, despite the great economic difficulties faced by the newly established state.

In 1969, after the death of Levi Eshkol, Golda became the fourth Prime Minister of Israel. She paid an official visit to President Nixon in Washington and led her party to victory in the next general elections. Golda was one of the few women in the world to hold the office of prime minister, becoming a famous figure on the international scene. She displayed an extraordinary capacity to convey, in public and private talks with foreign statesmen and representatives, the moral aspect of Israel's vital interests.

Her concept of Israel as a focal center of a united Jewish people was conspicuous and dramatically evident in her activities as prime minister.

She died of leukemia in December 1978.

**Interview by Jeff Hodes, Shulamit Nardi
and Menahem Kaufman
June 8, 1975**

Q: Mrs. Meir, the UJA has always been close to your heart, and whenever you could free yourself from vital responsibilities in Israel, even for a few brief days, you accepted our pleas to come and address our people. In this interview, we would like to get your impressions of the UJA, given what you experienced in the States during your visits there. We are particularly interested in your personal impressions, especially during the early State period, of the people that you met.

A: My relationship with the UJA, as such, started in 1948. Until 1948, my visits to the United States were on behalf of the *Histadrut* or the *Mo'etzet ha-Poalot* [Working Women's Council, the women's branch of the *Histadrut*].

That is why until then I didn't meet any of the people that were active and responsible for UJA, and who have since become very close friends of mine. I had not even met Henry Montor. Of course, I knew that he was a great power and did great things, but I didn't know him.

My first contact with the UJA was rather dramatic. Eliezer Kaplan [Israel's first minister of finance, previously a member of the *Histadrut* executive], obtained the first foreign loans for the State of Israel in 1949. He later served as deputy prime minister. The Kaplan School of Political and Social Science at the Hebrew University of Jerusalem was named in his honor. He was then treasurer of the Jewish Agency and had just returned from a visit to the United States and Canada and reported before the Jewish Agency meeting in January 1948 that he had succeeded in getting a loan of, I think, $7 million. This was to carry us through until the new fiscal year of April 1948.

However, here we were practically already in the war, which began openly the moment the United Nations decided on the partitioning of Palestine. I remember sitting there at this meeting of the executive committee of the Agency and watching my good friend Ben-Gurion boil while Kaplan was reporting. I thought, my God, this building is going to explode in another minute.

Finally, I proposed that Kaplan and I should go immediately to the United States to get the necessary monies. Jerusalem needed a lot of money then, and we had to prepare for a real war. I also said that Ben-Gurion must remain in Israel, since what he was doing, nobody else could do. He was really preparing the Haganah, and making plans for the war that we knew would break out.

I said, "I think that I can do what you want to do in the United States." He said no, he must go. I said, "Okay, but first we'll take it to a vote." This was the one time I voted against Ben-Gurion, because everybody in the Agency realized that it was impossible for Ben-Gurion to leave the country at that time.

I can't say that I was very courageous; I was terribly afraid of going to these people who didn't know me from Adam. Before I went, I asked Kaplan to write Montor that my visit is the decision of the Agency and that he should be helpful.

I came to New York on a Friday night toward the end of January, during one of the worst blizzards New York ever knew. New York was cut off—there were no planes, no trains, nothing! Both of my sisters—Clara who lives there, and Shayne, who was there for surgery—met me at the airport. The sister that lives in the States was at that time the head of the Bridgeport Federation Council in Connecticut. When I told her what I came for, she said, "Look, there's a Federation meeting now going on in Chicago which I think you should go to."

Up to that point, I had no itinerary.

As I requested, Kaplan had notified Montor that I was coming. However, Montor was in Chicago, so his second-in-command met me at the airport. He said no to my sister's suggestion. He said that since there are no Zionists at the Federation, it was not the place for me to go.

I stayed overnight at my niece's house in Brooklyn, and when I got up in the morning, I decided that maybe the Chicago meeting was a good idea. So we tried again. Montor said, "Look, I'm not directing this thing; they have an agenda, but I'll talk to them."

When he called back, he said, "Okay, they're prepared to let you speak, but, how do you propose to get to Chicago?"

There were no trains, nothing. All this occurred on Saturday. Montor told me they were prepared to have me speak at lunch Saturday or on Saturday night.

"I can't get there," I told him. Then he told me they were prepared to let me speak on Sunday noon. Luckily, there was a breakthrough and a plane did leave for Chicago. I think it was the only one that left that day.

There in Chicago, for the first time, I met Montor and Harold Goldenberg, Bill Rosenwald, and Eddie Warburg. I admit I was shaking. This was an audience I didn't know. All I knew were the men's names. I had no idea what was going to happen.

[Goldenberg was vice president of the Council of Jewish Federations and Welfare Funds (later CJF) in 1948; chairman of the national UJA cabinet from 1945 to 1949, and national vice chairman of UJA from 1949 to 1950. Bill Rosenwald was director of Sears, Roebuck, had been active in philanthropic activity since the 1930s, and was both president of New York City's Jewish Federation and chairman of the national UJA campaign. Eddie Warburg was president of the JDC and the New York City Jewish Federation and was also national chairman of UJA. He took office in 1951.]

When I spoke, I told them that I wanted $25 million in cash within two or three weeks. I didn't tell them that the only way that I knew that we could get the cash was if leaders in the various communities would take loans from the bank, to be paid off afterwards with the income from the campaign. Interestingly enough, the Dallas delegation immediately held a caucus among themselves and announced that they were going to take loans.

Now, when I returned to New York, a very serious question arose. The JDC people said to me, "Look, if these men go to the bank and get loans, that will have to be paid off from the collections of the UJA. Then, with all this money going to Israel, where is the share of the JDC?" JDC needed money also because of the work they were doing in the Diaspora.

At that time, someone from New York who was very important in the JDC, and who later went to work in the government, came to tell me that no war was ever won on donations. I answered that we were a special case. He wanted to know what was going to happen to the JDC.

I told him the following story: There was, in a small Russian town, a Jew who made a living by going to another town and speaking in shul on Saturday. There he would get a few rubles, which his family would live on for a week. The next Saturday, he would go to another town.

Once, when he came to a town, he stayed overnight in a little inn where he had his Friday night meal. On Saturday, he went to shul, but there he met a Jew who didn't give him anything. So, on Sunday morning, as he took his bundle and was preparing to go, the innkeeper asked him what he was doing leaving without paying. The Jew said, "You are right, of course, but I didn't get a *kopeck* here."

Then he said, "I have a suggestion. I'll go from house to house now, and everything that they give me, I'll give to you. But," he continued, "maybe you don't trust me, so let's go together from house to house asking for something. Or maybe you think it's not becoming for you to go with me. So you go, and whatever you collect among the Jews in the city will be yours."

After telling this story, I said to this man, "I don't want to upset anything. I want to do this within the framework of the UJA, so either we do it together, or you do it alone and give me $25 million, as that's what I need. Or I'll go out and cry to the Jewish community that we need this money."

The compromise that evolved was that instead of asking for $25 million, we decided on my suggestion: $50 million. The JDC people thought that was "nuts" anyhow, that I wouldn't even get $25 million, but I felt, what's the difference. We might as well ask for $50 million. And as a matter of fact, we got it.

Q: What was the division to be?

A: Fifty-fifty. At the time, the UJA worked on this basis: 50 percent was to go to the Jewish Agency, and 50 percent was for the JDCs outside of Israel, primarily in Eastern Europe.

Q: When you left the States, were you aware of any divisiveness and of some of the conflicts that existed between JDC and the United Palestine Appeal (UPA)?

A: No, there really weren't any conflicts; there was an agreement between JDC and the UJA, and they worked harmoniously. In fact, the fifty-fifty basis is the reason I suggested we ask for $50 million. I saw it simply as a way to get $25 [million] for us and $25 [million] for them. Nobody believed a word of it, of course, but we did it.

Q: Who led the effort?

A: The men were fantastic. Sam Rothberg, Bill Rosenwald, and Eddie Warburg worked day and night. Samuel Rothberg was national Big Gifts chairman of the UJA. In 1954 he became active in Israel Bonds and served as general chairman of the organization.

Q: After the Chicago meeting, which was the breakthrough, how did Montor proceed? Were there personal meetings?

A: Yes, we went from city to city. The procedure was that we would meet with the leadership, who had to decide that they were prepared to go to the bank for loans. Each time, Montor worked out a list with the Council of Federations of how much we could ask for. Then, we would have dinners for the UJA where people would give their gifts.

Q: Did Montor think the $50 million goal was possible?

A: Not really, but he worked hard. He thought maybe that they would give $10 or $12 million.

Now the only difficulty was that as I went from city to city, coast to coast, and was every day in a different city, these men had to change off. They couldn't take the schedule. But I must say that as I traveled from coast to coast, I got to see how wonderful the Jews were.

Q: Did you have any private, personal solicitations?

A: No, that I never did. Miami is a good example of what we did. For instance, in Miami we first had a breakfast meeting, then a luncheon in a nightclub, and in the evening we flew from Miami to Palm Beach for another meeting in the big hotel there.

Henry Morgenthau, Jr., was with us that time. Bill Rosenwald, Eddie Warburg, and the fellow who afterward went to work in the government in Washington also traveled with me, on an alternating basis. There were others, among them Moe Leavitt, chief executive of the UJA, and people in New York like Sonneborn and, of course, Paul Baerwald, who was fantastic. Both Sonneborn and Baerwald were non-Zionist leaders in New York.

Q: Did you feel that they were already Zionists emotionally, or was it just your personal Jewish appeal?

A: Not all of them were Zionists, but they all realized what was at stake. When we went to Miami, Morgenthau said that this was his first trip to Miami. The breakfast meeting was for the local Miami community, while the luncheon was attended by Jews that were spending their vacations in Miami. At both, we did very, very well.

Then in the evening, as I mentioned, we flew to a hotel owned by a Jew where fund-raising was forbidden. I remember coming down to the patio, which was so beautiful, and seeing the people there dressed with all that beauty, and thinking that this I couldn't take.

Morgenthau was conducting the meeting; Montor, Rothberg, and Goldenberg were there. As I looked at the audience, I was sure that when I'd begin to speak, they would walk out of the room; I was sure they couldn't care less. As I sat there, I didn't eat anything. I drank black coffee and smoked my cigarettes, tears coming to my eyes.

I thought, "How can I, in this beautiful atmosphere, tell what's happening at home." So I told Montor how I felt. Morgenthau said to me, "Look, I understand perfectly how you feel. What I'm going to do is to get up, never mind what the manager of the hotel said about not having any fund-raising here, and say, "Friends, you're here on a vacation which you deserve. Nobody has the right to trouble you, and since I don't want to keep you here under false pretenses, I have to tell you that we intend to do business tonight. Anybody who wants to walk out, we'll do nothing against you; you can just get up and walk out!"

Of course, nobody walked out after this, and believe me, that evening we raised $150,000 in cash. In fact, I think we ended that day in Miami with about $4 to $5 million.

Q: How did you handle the problem of the Haganah and the UJA in raising arms? Did you talk about military funds?

A: What I said was that we have to fight and that we have to prepare. I said that American Jews can't decide whether we should fight or not, since that's our decision. But I also said that you *can* decide whether we should win or lose. If you'll be with us, then we'll win. If not, we may lose.

I told them that we're going to fight anyhow, that we're not going to give up. Of course, I didn't go into details. I knew that we could get planes and tanks in Europe. I didn't go into that in public, although the leadership knew about it.

Q: Do you mean that even the non-Zionists in your mission, such as Bill Rosenwald, knew about it?

A: Yes, because there had been many warnings. Really, to understand the situation, we have to go back a little in time. In 1945, when Ben-Gurion was in the United States, he said to Montor that there was going to be a war with the Arabs. Then he said, "Call a group of Jews who will be prepared to do whatever we need so that we will be ready to defend ourselves when war breaks out."

Montor made up a list of men who met at Sonneborn's home or office. Every single Jew who was asked to come appeared, even though they didn't know what for. Evidently Montor phrased it in such a way that it was understood to be of great importance. Among them were Dewey Stone [later UJA chairman and UJA national vice chairman], Harry Levine, and Haim Slavin.

[Levine was the treasurer and member of the board of governors of the Weizmann Institute of Science and a member of the national

UJA cabinet. He sponsored the Negev Water Experiment with Harvard University. Slavin was the engineer responsible for coordinating Haganah arms production.]

They really saved us, not only with money but also by their conduct. They were fantastic in what they did, and they did all this separate from the UJA. They did it for *Rekhesh*. [*Rekhesh* is the Hebrew for "acquisition," referring to Materials for Palestine.]

For instance, at a very nice dinner in St. Louis, I said that if the American Jews would help us financially, then I was sure that by the end of the year we would have a State. They were very nice and generous.

Immediately after the State was declared, I received a cable from Montor that I should come back so that we could raise another $50 million. That's why on the 17th of May, I flew again to the United States, revisiting all the cities, including St. Louis, where Melvin Dubinsky, one of UJA's best leaders, was with us from the beginning.

There, in the same St. Louis hotel, the same chairman said that now it could be told that the day after Golda had spoken, a few of the men had commented that although she had made a very nice speech, she had talked a lot of nonsense. "How can a group of people so outnumbered have a State in a gulf of hatred?" they asked. "But now," he said, "I can see that you were right." Of course, I was then returning as an Israeli citizen. The Jews were fantastic then and have been ever since.

I must say that Montor has a critical share in all this. In '46 he dared, during the first UJA conference, to ask for, I think, a $100 million and beyond this. He was "mad." I've never seen anybody that worked like he did.

Also, it was incredible the way he knew what every Jew had, what his problems were, and how much he should give. Believe me, at that time, Montor, Rothberg, Venezky, and others used to "terrorize" the Jewish community; they would tear the house down if they weren't getting what they thought the Jews ought to be giving.

Q: Was there much interaction between the Zionists—the ZOA [Zionist Organization of America]—and UJA in those years? What was the level of the Zionists' participation in terms of big giving?

A: Essentially, the Jews gave as Jews. I was once at an afternoon meeting in the garment center in New York. My late sister, who was there for medical care, went with me. I said at that meeting, you have the choice either to meet in Madison Square Garden to rejoice in the establishment of a Jewish state or to meet in Madison Square Garden at another memorial meeting for the Jews in Palestine who will be gone.

My sister wanted to choke me; she could not understand how I could talk like that. But the Jews were wonderful to me, and they responded fantastically.

Q: Is it possible to measure the significance of the UJA after the war, in the formative years of the State, when you were head of the Labor Ministry?

A: Look, what the UJA was giving us was our source of income. In March 1949, we got a bank loan from the United States, but that was for machinery and other things that we needed to buy in the United States. The only cash we had before income tax was introduced was what the UJA gave us; and remember, when income tax was introduced, what did we have?

UJA money was the lifeline for the big immigration coming in. Of course, little by little, JDC money was also spent in Israel; as the Jews came from the camps, the JDC and their money went with them; that is how the proportion of UJA funds to Israel became larger and larger all the time.

Q: Was that how the JDC came to be introduced to Israel? Was that, along with the creation of Malben, part of anyone's deliberate policy? [Malben is the acronym for the Hebrew words *Machon le-Tipul be-Ochlosiot Nechshalot* (Institute for Care of the Underprivileged), a unit of the JDC functioning in Israel at the invitation of the Israeli government to cope with the social services required for aged new immigrants to Israel.]

A: Well, in the first place, as the Jews were coming in large numbers, the agreement as to proportions changed. Beyond that, such JDC activities like Malben became extremely important.

Q: In the formative years of the 1950s, once the State was established, how was the momentum of UJA giving sustained? Did anyone ever sit down and think about the question of whether this could continue indefinitely?

A: Well, I did. When I came back from Russia in 1949, I remember bringing this problem before the cabinet.

I said I didn't think that giving would remain on that level, that it was bound to come down. However, I also said that we needed money. I suggested that we look for some way to take a loan, that perhaps the Jews should give us a loan for a number of years, or that they should guarantee a loan. All I wanted was that the government should allow me to investigate this possibility. This was the first step toward Israel Bonds, although both the Jewish Agency and the UJA people were terribly against it. They thought it would be at the expense of the UJA.

At the start of my investigation, I went to see a Wall Street banker who was a great friend of Ben-Gurion. He told me how the Dutch government, based on its gold deposited in the United States, had just floated an $18 million loan, which proved to be a failure.

I said that I could understand that, because they didn't have five million Jews in the United States behind them. It was a big battle for Israel Bonds. There was tremendous fear that this would destroy the UJA until Ben-Gurion, toward the end of 1950, called a big conference where four methods of helping Israel were decided. The "four-point program" consisted of UJA, American government aid, private investments, and Bonds. When I went to the conference that was called in Washington, first I was to go in the name of Bonds; then I think it was decided to be in the name of UJA. Of course, there were ups and downs.

Q: Did you negotiate at all, initially, in the conflicts that arose between Bonds and UJA?

A: Sure, I think I was proven right. Bonds did not hurt UJA. Of course, there was a big discussion about whether Israel could really take it upon herself to pay back the loan, with interest. I don't know what we would have done without Bonds. We developed it, and everyone got his or her money back.

Q: Both Bonds and UJA are two totally unique institutions. Have you ever thought to yourself what basically motivates people to give to UJA, or why it has been the more successful?

A: I think the people are interested in Jewish life; they're interested in Israel, and whether they have worked it out logically or whether they feel it instinctively, they realize that without a Jewish State, the continuation of the Jewish nation is not guaranteed.

For me, the thing that is so gratifying is to see the personal connection of Jews that were never Zionists and who have become so devoted and so thoroughly identified with Israel. Many of them have their children here. I meet Jews over and over again in the United States who have a daughter or a son who lives here. This is unique. It certainly is unique to see men who have their own business spending so much life energy on Israel, and not for a year or two. This has been true ever since '48.

Q: You say that people, not Zionists, are very interested in the existence of the Jewish people as a nation. What do you mean "as a nation"?

A: Although they are not Zionists, they want us to exist as a free, organized nation, as a State. Take Bill Rosenwald as an example. He was never a member of a Zionist organization, but he's been supporting us for years. He has a fantastic way of working. When he goes to see somebody to get a gift, he sits and waits in the room. He doesn't take no for an answer. If he has to, he comes back again. Really, I don't know what would have happened to us during the War of Liberation and the years after that without men like Bill.

And now I see younger people in every delegation that comes from the UJA. I see many of these men coming with their sons. It is wonderful to see the Young Leadership; these young men in their early forties or in their late thirties, who are in business for themselves. It's wonderful to see them. It's not only the money that is important, but it's the interest these people are showing.

Q: Were those groups in 1948 an older age group, as you look back?

A: Well, look, those that were there are thirty years older. They weren't old people then. Sam Rothberg, who is now sixty-five, was a young man, as were Harold Goldenberg and Bill Rosenwald. If you're asking me whether youth used to come to these dinners, I would have to say no, not then. But now, yes!

Q: Did you have any experiences in fund-raising outside the United States?

A: I did not have many, but I did go to Latin America and France.

Q: Did you enjoy it?

A: Well, in Paris, I had a language problem. I don't speak French. I hope they'll forgive me, but they never gave me a translator. They should have. In Britain I fared much better. I remember opening the appeal, which until very recently was called the United Palestine Appeal, when the target was 2.5 million pounds sterling. They never reached that target until the Six-Day War. They're good Jews.

Q: Is there any difference between the reactions in the United States and England?

A: Now, I wouldn't say that there's a difference, and I was just in London a few months ago, on my way back from the United States, after Arafat was hailed in the UN and accepted into the "family of nations."

You know, I remember being in England on the tenth anniversary of the State, and there was a big fight within the Zionist group about whether they should take the Albert Hall or not. People were afraid that the Albert Hall would not be filled. But, finally, it was decided that they should take the Albert Hall, and it was packed.

Now this time when I came to the Albert Hall, there was no such debate. There were eight thousand people at that meeting, and it took two hours to get into the hall, since security was so tight and everybody had to be checked.

The meeting was fantastic. Lord Samuel was there, along with lots of young people. [Lord Herbert Louis Samuel was the first high commissioner of Palestine during the British mandate. He led the Liberal Party in the House of Lords in 1944–1945 and was instrumental in influencing Great Britain to follow the United States and the Soviet Union in recognizing Israel.]

What is truly gratifying now is that wherever you go, in Europe and in the United States, there are young people.

Q: Over the years, each of the different governments has approached the UJA leadership with a different perspective and different expectations. Given your approach, can you describe what they expected from the leaders of the UJA as a collective entity?

A: Well, there's never enough, but I don't think that anybody is justified in expressing disappointment over the reaction of Jews, especially in the United States. Also, as I said, in the latter years England and France have picked up. In 1967, things occurred that we never believed could happen in Switzerland and every country in the world. In England, during Israel's so-called normal years, Jews have continued to come through.

The one thing that Jews don't do as they should is make *aliyah*, but in that the UJA can't help much. Though perhaps it has that potential.

Q: Other than with respect to *aliyah*, have you, over the years, looked to the UJA leadership collectively or individually for political support in the States, even though the UJA itself is not political?

A: Many of the people who are active in UJA are also active in every aspect of Israel and the United States. You might remember the old man, Judge Joseph Proskauer, he was a fantastic person. [Proskauer was a jurist and president of the American Jewish Committee in 1949; he was also a consultant to the UN Conference in San Francisco in 1945.]

Q: But he was an anti-Zionist, wasn't he?

A: He was, but that was a long time ago. I remember during one of my trips to the United States, at a meeting with the executive group of, I think, the American Jewish Committee, somebody got up and asked, "Mrs. Meir, do you have an atomic bomb?"

Old man Proskauer was sitting next to me and said, "You don't say anything." Then he got up and said, "I don't know whether they have it or not, but if there's one country in the world that is entitled to have an atomic bomb, it is Israel."

To go back to your question about political support, the American Jewish leadership was faced with tremendous problems. First, they were faced with the Holocaust, and then they were faced with what was happening here.

Since then, every time there's a crisis, like the Six-Day War, the Sinai Campaign before that, and the Yom Kippur War, Washington calls upon them. They see the Jews who are active in UJA as the leadership of the Jewish people, although they've never been elected as such. When the State Department wants to influence the Jewish community with respect to an issue that is being discussed between the United States and Israel, they call in those Jews and try to influence them. I remember the time Proskauer was called in. And I must say, we were never disappointed in their stand; they were always with us.

Q: Over the years, I'm sure you've had some extraordinary personal involvement and incidents with people like Warburg, Max Fisher, Eddie Ginsberg, and Paul Zuckerman. Can you tell us any interesting anecdotes that stand out in your mind?

A: I remember a UJA dinner at the Shamrock Hotel in Houston. The hotel had just opened and was really beautiful. Sam Rothberg and Julian Venezky were there.

Before the dinner, I was told that there had been a big discussion during which one of the community leaders said that they could not display an Israeli flag because I was a foreign agent. Imagine, I was minister of foreign affairs, and he was saying I'm a foreign agent. So the others said, "Okay, then there's no American flag either."

After I spoke, they began calling cards. Let me give you the picture first. As I came up to the table, a man came over to me, and when he saw that his card was next to mine, he excused himself, saying that there were other people who deserve it more. We found out later that he was the one who didn't want the Israeli flag. He also didn't want to be photographed with a foreign agent, which explains why he gave up his place.

The response was miserable. At the end, $4,000 was needed to make a round figure. The chairman, who wasn't getting anywhere, finally got up and said, "I usually don't take advice from my wife, but this time I think she's right. There are four hundred people in the hall and we need $4,000. We'll pass the hat and each one will put in ten dollars." I said to him, "Don't you dare do it! If you do it, I'll leave the room."

Poor fellow, he didn't know whether he should listen to his wife or to me. So the hat began passing around. I got up, and so did Julian, and we marched out of the room. I wasn't going to watch a charity collection for Israel. Still, they're wonderful. For me, if they would all come here, it would be fine.

Really, I feel so privileged to have worked throughout these years with these people and those who came in later. Eddie Ginsberg was not among the first at that time, nor were Max Fisher and Paul Zuckerman. However, all those that have come in, and the old-timers who still go on, have been just excellent.

Q: What about the new generation of newcomers?

A: The young generation is wonderful. I have met them on the missions that come here. About three or four years ago, there was a dinner at the Knesset for a group of young people. I asked, "How many of you are here the first time?" Quite a few raised their hands.

Then I said, "Tell me your impressions." The youngsters got up, one after the other, and said what this meant to them. Then, in a corner, one of five young modern American boys asked for the floor. He said, "I am here with four of my friends and I want to tell you about our experience. We have been to Poland. First we went to Warsaw, to the place of the ghetto, and then to Auschwitz. After that, we came back to the place of the ghetto, where we found ourselves, instinctively, walking with our arms linked. Then, we came here. This morning, we were in Yad Vashem. The circle is complete now."

Q: You may be happy to know of our plan to have a thousand young leaders come over here in the fall. We will describe the group with one word: *koach* [strength].

A: A lot of the young men who are now moving up in UJA have come through Young Leadership. By the way, Moses Leavitt [Secretary of the Palestine Economic Corporation, 1933; Executive Vice President of JDC in 1940] was a wonderful person. He had his share of experiences after the war when he went to the camps in Europe.

Q: Another wonderful fellow, the very active Charles Jordan [European Director, JDC; National Executive Vice Chairman, JDC] ended up in the river in Prague on August 16, 1967, the victim of terrorists. He was the head of JDC, a large man, deaf in one ear and terribly active. He was with President Shazar, speaking at a meeting of the Study Circle on World Jewry, the night before he left.

A: I knew him, as a matter of fact. Charles Jordan was here just before he went to Prague. He was the professional head of the JDC. He said, "I'll come back; we'll continue our conversation."

[Someone comes in and offers coffee.]

G.M.: You want some coffee? Anybody want tea instead of coffee? Talk, people!

8

GOLDA MEIR: RETROSPECTIVE

Golda was Golda to everyone, whether typist or chief execu-tive. She was Golda to a UJA professional meeting her in some distant community as well as to its largest contributor. She was possessed with a movie star quality and drew people of all faiths to her. They attempted to shake her hand, touch her, and ask for her autograph. She was always approachable, greeting people with a smile and a touch of humor, then excusing herself with grace. When Golda would visit the Oak Room at the Plaza Hotel in New York or go to a theater on Broadway, diners and theatergoers would give her a standing ovation. Even when, for security reasons, the Secret Service would bring Golda into the theater just as the lights were dimming, the audience would somehow sense her entrance and begin to applaud. The curtain would be delayed until she was seated and only the curtain's rising would silence the enthusiastic crowd.

Golda, unlike many Americans and Israelis, did not keep a stiff upper lip at moments of discomfort or disagreement but let herself go emotionally. When it came to making difficult decisions, she did not procrastinate or take the easy way out. She would be decisive and direct and, when she felt it necessary, tough.

Golda's brilliance on the American scene, besides her unique personality and image, was in her language. She spoke *mama loshen* [Yiddish] and never used a multi-syllable word if she could avoid it. There was never any confusion as to where she stood on an issue or about her expectations from her audience. Golda was Israel's most requested public speaker in America, since everyone felt she was speaking personally to him or her.

As a woman, Golda was perceived by the Americans to be an equal in Israel's hierarchy—long before equality and feminism became the accepted norm in the United States. Her reference to herself at the 1948 Israeli cabinet meeting, when she persuaded them to let her come, instead of Ben-Gurion, to the American Jewish community to raise the $25 million, is pertinent to this perception. "I was terribly afraid of going to see these people who didn't know me from Adam," she said.

One might have expected her to compare herself to Miriam or Ruth, and yet the general perception here is that she believed that she was the equal of any man, whether Adam or David. Because Golda was a woman with a rare combination of strength and compassion, which she could express both personally and publicly, she was beloved and admired [and sometimes feared] by Americans no matter what their faith or position in life. I witnessed many examples of her effect on people; among them are some of the following unforgettable moments.

In 1978, Irwin Field of Los Angeles was elected as the youngest national chairman in UJA history. His had been a remarkable rise in growth and stature from his days as a student leader to his prominence in the Young Leadership Division. He soon became campaign chairman for Los Angeles and then national vice chairman of UJA—that led to his unanimous election as national UJA chairman.

Field was reluctant to accept the position because his wife, Joanna, was seriously ill with cancer. But she, the daughter of an old-line Zionist family, insisted that he take it, despite the difficulties it would mean for her. Because of his new role, Field would frequently be absent from home.

In the spring of that year, on her last visit to the United States, Golda came to a UJA executive committee retreat in Southbury, Connecticut. Frank Lautenberg, the former UJA national chair, presided over the meeting and Irwin Field was chosen to make a special presentation to Golda. Joanna, because of her deep admiration for Golda, came east with him to hear her. By then, Joanna was using a walker.

She sat in the back of a long, rather narrow room. Golda arrived late, delayed by traffic. I didn't get a chance to talk to Golda until she was being introduced, when I whispered to her that Joanna's cancer was incurable and that her time was limited. I explained that because of her deep respect and love for Golda, she had come all the way from Los Angeles to see her. Since Golda had to leave immediately after the meeting for another commitment in New York, I asked her to stop and greet Joanna on her way out.

Golda did not even nod. I had no idea whether or not she had heard me. She spoke in her usual manner—moving, direct, demanding—and closed on an inspirational note of unity. She was given a standing ovation and rose to leave.

As she wended her way out of the room, she stopped to greet Joanna and asked her how she was doing. Joanna answered that she was as well as could be expected, that coming to hear Golda was worth all the travail. Golda then invited her to come to Israel, to call her so that they could have tea and a heart-to-heart talk in Golda's kitchen. Joanna told her that she would love to do it but didn't know whether she could.

The next time Irwin led a UJA mission to Israel, Joanna found the strength to come along. She called Golda, and Golda remembered and invited her to tea. Irwin accompanied his wife, but when they arrived Golda asked Irwin to wait so that Golda and Joanna could drink their tea and talk—in the living room, not the kitchen. They were together for more than an hour. Joanna returned home exhilarated by her visit with Golda, and was energized and happy to the last with the memories of that day.

For those of us in UJA who shared common causes with Golda, her compassion and ability to give of herself to Joanna was not the exception, but the rule. But the other side of Golda—the strength, direction, and dominance—was just as evident.

It was 1972. Paul Zuckerman of Detroit, UJA's only Sephardic leader, was our national chairman. A man of boundless energy, he was the right man in the right place to lead the record-breaking campaigns during the Yom Kippur War. Golda was then Prime Minister and had been invited by Paul to address the annual December conference. At the close of the meeting, even as the four thousand people on the floor and dais were still applauding Golda, I led her party out through the curtain behind the dais. She had to catch an El Al flight plane back to Israel, and the flight was already delayed because we had run into overtime.

The members of Golda's party were Foreign Affairs Minister Abba Eban, Ambassador to the United States Yitzhak Rabin, Ambassador to the UN Yosef Tekoah, and Director General of the Prime Minister's

Office Simcha Dinitz. As we neared the ballroom elevators being held by the Secret Service and Israeli security officers, New York City police, and hotel security, Shlomo Argov, then deputy to Rabin in Washington, came running toward us. Argov grabbed Rabin and took him aside to give him a message from the White House. Rabin then spoke to Golda and then Golda told me that a private room with a telephone was needed immediately.

To the consternation of the security people who were holding the empty elevators, I told them we had to go to my room on the forty-first floor. That meant pushing buttons for passenger elevators. When they first arrived, it was full of elderly couples who were startled by the sight of the police and security, but complied when they were asked to leave the elevator. In the confusion to get into the elevator, which is far smaller than those for the ballroom, I was one of those left out. Golda noticed and asked a member of the security staff to leave so that I might enter.

When we arrived at my room, the security officers remained outside; only Golda's party and I entered. Golda sat on a chair in the middle of the room in her black dress with her feet planted on the floor, surrounded by powerful men—among them a future Prime Minister—leaders of the government and her party. It was clear that she was in control. Argov asked whether I should stay, since the matter was so sensitive. No one said anything, but Golda answered that I should remain as I might be needed.

Golda then told Rabin, who was seated by the telephone, to call Kissinger, who was waiting. Rabin did so, spoke to Kissinger, and then addressed Golda and the others in Hebrew. She explained the urgency of the situation in English so that I might understand. Henry Kissinger, on behalf of President Richard Nixon, had called the embassy to alert Israel to the fact that Syria was threatening Jordan's northern border and that Syrian tanks were already on the move. The President was asking Israel to mobilize its reserves as a signal and to put a brake on Syria's threat. Golda asked Rabin to tell Kissinger he would call him back, but first to reach Moshe Dayan [then minister of defense] in Israel—where it was 5 A.M.

Rabin realized that he didn't have Dayan's number with him and asked the others if they had it. They all shook their heads. At that moment I raised my hand. Golda, for the only time during the hour and a half we spent in my room, chuckled and said, "See! I told you we might need him."

Rabin called Dayan, who agreed to mobilize but urged Golda first to get President Nixon's assurance that he would back Israel if the Soviet Union entered the fray on behalf of Syria. Golda then asked Rabin to call Deputy Prime Minister Yigal Allon to brief him. Again, the same search for the phone number and again, I raised my hand and gave it to Rabin. Rabin called Allon, who agreed to the process. Golda then told Rabin to call Kissinger and to ask for the assurance from President Nixon.

We then waited ten mostly silent minutes until Kissinger called back with Nixon's approval and the additional assurance that elements of the Sixth Fleet would be directed to Haifa. Golda then told Rabin to call Dayan and give the order to mobilize, which Rabin did. The strategy was successful. The Syrians blinked. They withdrew their troops and tanks and the crisis was over.

It was after midnight when we were led down the long hotel hallway to the elevator. But even at that hour, every door was open, and hotel guests—some in their robes or pajamas and some still dressed—cheered, applauded and threw kisses as Golda swept by.

Golda was revered for her loyalty to those she met and worked with when she first came to the United States on behalf of Ben-Gurion in 1948. Among them were Henry Montor, Sam Rothberg, Harold Goldenberg, and Julian Venezky, who remained her close friends even when they were no longer affiliated with UJA or Israel Bonds. Her friends, however, were not limited to those mentioned but extended also to many others beyond UJA and Israel Bonds.

[Venezky was a member of the UJA national campaign cabinet; was national chairman for regions [1947-1948]; the first chairman of the national UJA campaign cabinet [1948-1950]; and a founder of Israel Bonds.]

My first meeting alone with Golda took place in 1950, on my first visit to Israel. UJA sent two staff people to Israel every year in recognition of their work. Although my supervisor had recommended me, I was not chosen and decided to go on my own. I then asked for a meeting with Henry Montor, insisting on it when his office was reluctant to grant it. Montor apparently thought I intended to question his judgment in not choosing me.

When I did get to see him, he was somewhat hostile until I told him that I was paying my own way and that all I wanted from him was the same treatment in Israel that he was getting for the two he had chosen. He agreed, and I left.

The cheapest way I could get there [my salary was $3,000] was on a chartered DC-4 from Montreal to Rome—which was flying Catholic families to meet the Pope during Holy Week. When I landed in Israel on a connecting El Al flight from Rome, I was met by a delegation led by a member of Golda's staff and informed that I was to have lunch with Golda the next day at the Eden Hotel in Jerusalem. I thought the lunch would be for all three of us from UJA, but I learned that it was only for me. I was bewildered, since they held higher positions in UJA than I did.

I was in awe of Golda, but she immediately put me at ease with her warm and open manner. She discussed the key issues concerning Israel and UJA. Then she surprised me by asking me what I thought of the viability of the sale of Israel Bonds in the United States. I told her exactly what I thought: "It will never work."

Although my reply was foolish and based on inexperience, Golda recognized even more than I that the reasons I gave to justify my reply were not only valid but would be critical to the success of the Bond effort. It was launched in 1952 and headed by Golda's friends: Montor, Rothberg, Goldenberg and Venezky. Although there were conflicts, especially of timing, there was also cooperation, and as a result, many pitfalls were avoided. When I returned to New York, Montor invited me to join him at Bonds. After considerable thought, I decided to remain at UJA. I felt I would have a better opportunity to teach and reach a larger share of the Jewish community there than I would through Bonds.

Although I traveled throughout Israel with my two UJA colleagues, I was continually singled out for individual meetings with other members of Israel's hierarchy. I couldn't understand the reasons for this special treatment and tried to find out about it when I returned home. But no one knew or would tell me, until a member of Montor's inner circle showed me a copy of a wire Montor typed the moment I left his room. As a former PR man, Montor kept a typewriter behind his desk and used it as thoughts crossed his mind. The wire read as follows: "Billig, Panzer outstanding members of staff. Bernstein future leader of UJA. Treat each accordingly." This was 1950. In 1971, I became Executive Vice Chairman of UJA.

Golda makes several references to JDC and UIA that require clarification. She speaks of the lack of antagonism between the two agencies, the equal allocations they received from UJA, and JDC's beginning in Israel as Malben. The fact was that JDC and UIA reflected two totally different views—that had hindered and delayed their coming together until 1939. The marriage was conflicted until the early 1950s, when the State of Israel was a fact and the Displaced Persons (DPs) in Europe were flowing into Israel.

UIA represented the Zionist community at a period when the Zionist movement was the American arena of support for the *Yishuv* and the early state. JDC was an old-line German Jewish entity founded and led for the purpose of rescue, rehabilitation, and reconstruction of threatened Jewish communities throughout the world. JDC's first contribution to the *Yishuv* years was in 1914 when the then U.S. Ambassador to Turkey, Henry Morgenthau, wired JDC to send $50,000 to the starving Jews in Palestine.

A remarkable footnote is that Morgenthau's son, Henry Morgenthau, Jr., became UJA's national chairman after serving as Secretary of the Treasury in Franklin Delano Roosevelt's cabinet. Like his father, he had been a non-Zionist until he encountered, and was appalled by, the negativism and hostility of his government (particularly the activities of Breckenridge Long of the Department of Immigration and Naturalization) to rescuing the beleaguered Jews of Europe.

When the two agencies came together in the UJA, the larger share of UJA funds went to the JDC, since they were dealing with the huge postwar problems of 250,000 Jewish DPs in Europe. With the birth of the State and the massive emigration from North Africa and Europe, the equation of division of UJA funds changed, with the larger share going to UIA for Israel. After 1948, differences between the two lessened, and the division of funds was negotiated between the two in a cooperative and businesslike manner. Still, in 1962, by its hesitation, JDC vetoed the appointment of Dewey Stone, the most active Zionist in UJA's fold [National Vice Chairman, UJA;

Chairman, UIA; and Chairman of the Board of Governors of the Weizmann Institute of Science], as UJA's national chairman.

Ideological differences between the two agencies haven't existed since the 1970s. Henry Taub, in fact, served as chairman of both UIA and JDC while he was a member of the executive committee of the Jewish Agency and the UJA. In fact, in 1949, JDC was invited by Israel to help with the enormous number of aged people coming to Israel, especially from Romania. Despite its agreement with Israel to send Jews of all ages, Romania relieved itself of all its aged Jews before freeing the middle-aged and young. JDC thus set itself up in Israel at that time as Malben.

In 1972, again at the request of the Jewish Agency and the government's Ministry of Social Welfare, JDC opened its own offices and maintained staff in Jerusalem so that it could share its expertise and become involved in Israel's wide range of social services. To help Israel develop its own skilled personnel, JDC established the Paul Baerwald School for Social Service Work at the Hebrew University. [Baerwald, was the first chairman of JDC, and became a member of President Roosevelt's Advisory Committee on Political Refugees in 1938.]

Golda refers to Montor's role in bringing leadership together to help provide war materiel for Israel. At Ben-Gurion's request, Montor presented a list of leaders who might possibly be helpful. But he did not play an active role in the group of the so-called "Fourteen." They were so named because they met at 14 E. 60th Street in Manhattan, the location of Hotel Fourteen, which housed the famous Copacabana nightclub in its basement.

That was where the Fourteen, also known as the Sonneborn Group, held their regular meetings. The club's landlords were Fanny Barnett and her husband, Ruby. During World War II, Fanny was Chaim Weizmann's secretary at the Jewish Agency. In 1945, Ben-Gurion was a guest at Hotel Fourteen, marking it as the meeting place of many future leaders of the State of Israel. The group's efforts, led by Rudolph Sonneborn [the president of the American Financial Development Corporation for Israel and president of the Israel America Petroleum Corporation], have been well documented in *The Pledge*, a book by Irving Slater published in 1970.

Golda understood American organizational life better than most Israelis did, even those who had also lived in the United States. In this regard Golda's sister Clara was exceedingly helpful. She was the executive director of the Bridgeport federation. Their relationship and Clara's experience helped Golda gain knowledge of, and insights into, Federation structure and needs, as well as the UJA and the attitudes of Americans to Israel.

Golda speaks about her devotion to the UJA personalities. Indeed, the relationship between UJA and Golda was a close one, beginning with her first encounter with the organization in 1948. In 1974, in the aftermath of the Yom Kippur War, UJA still played a unique role in Golda's life in Israel.

It was during the UJA Prime Minister's Mission to Israel in October of 1973, held just days after the outbreak of the Yom Kippur War, that UJA, under the leadership of its national chairman Paul Zuckerman, produced a special performance of hope and unity at the Mann Auditorium.

It was for Israelis as well as Americans—UJA's tribute to the people and army of Israel. Its theme was "The Night Shall Shine as Day." The performers and artists were all Israelis. Among those invited were Ben-Gurion and Golda, who had not, or had only rarely, spoken to each other since their political rift in 1965. [At that time, Ben-Gurion had attempted to return to active political life and abandoned Mapai to form a new party, Rafi *(Reshimat Po'alei Yisrael*-the Israel Workers List*)].*

Both came to this testimonial to Israel's unity. We brought them together in a separate room with Zuckerman, Louis Pincus (then chairman of the Jewish Agency), Teddy Kollek, and myself. After some awkward moments, the two came together like the old friends they once were. Then we arranged for them to enter the packed hall together and to be seated next to each other, all to thunderous applause.

I remember we were in the Chagall Hall of the Knesset, at the final dinner of the 1972 Prime Minister's Mission led by Zuckerman. Golda sat between us. Zuckerman introduced her. Then, as Golda finished speaking and returned to her seat, he leaned over and kissed her. The mission members, who were still standing, with tears of joy and pride in their eyes, responded with even greater applause. The Israeli and foreign press captured the moment with television and still cameras.

Golda was a world-class personality. President Nixon, in documents at the Nixon Library in San Clemente, labeled her as one of the ten greatest leaders he had ever met. So it was no surprise that this was a kiss that echoed around the world. The photograph of "the kiss" appeared in newspapers in Jerusalem, Lisbon, London, Paris, New York, Detroit, Los Angeles, Melbourne, and scores of other cities.

In December 1978, with Golda's death, a beloved relationship ended. It was never replaced. During many historic moments, when joy is mixed with sorrow, I am always reminded of the message Golda Meir gave us in 1973, in the midst of the Yom Kippur War—when the world seemed to stop and life almost came to an end.

On Yom Kippur, she sat in the War Room, deep under the *Kirya* [Defense Ministry] in Tel Aviv, a woman among men, a leader of generals and ministers, head of her nation, but alone and tense and frightened by the reports from the Golan and Suez, as Israel's young defenders fell before the Egyptian and Syrian onslaught.

Then, at this lowest point in her life as mother, woman, and leader, she heard her commanders in the north and south, the east and west, all calling to their men, *"Lo la'atzor! Lo la'atzor!"* ["Don't stop! Don't stop!"].

She regained her confidence, strength, and courage, and went on to lead the nation to victory.

Lo la'atzor—Don't stop!

In that spirit of Israel's valor and sacrifice, in Golda's spirit of devotion and dedication to Jewish unity and solidarity, we, too, did not stop.

9

MAX M. FISHER

Max M. Fisher was born in Pittsburgh, Pennsylvania, but spent his early years in Salem, Ohio. He graduated from Ohio State University in 1930 and moved to Detroit, where he joined his father's oil business.

In 1933, he and two partners formed the Aurora Gasoline Company, where he eventually became chairman of the board of directors. Aurora became a wholly owned subsidiary of the Marathon Oil Company in 1950, and Fisher continued to serve in his board chair until Aurora's dissolution in 1962. He then joined Marathon's board of directors.

A giant in Jewish philanthropy, Fisher has served as chairman of the board of governors of the reconstituted Jewish Agency in Jerusalem, general chairman of the UJA, chairman of the UIA board, and past president of the Council of Jewish Federations and Welfare Funds (later CJF).

Max Fisher has also been a supporter of the Republican National Committee for more than forty years. In addition to being a charter member of the Republican Eagles and a founding member of Team 100, he chaired the 1991 Inaugural Anniversary Gala which raised $7 million for the Republican Party. He has been an adviser and supporter of the last four Republican Presidents: Nixon, Ford, Reagan, and Bush.

Fisher's civic activities have included many positions in varied organizations, including founding chairman of Detroit Renaissance and founding member and former chairman of New Detroit. He is a member of the boards of Sinai Hospital, the Detroit Institute of Arts; the Greater Detroit Chamber of Commerce, and is President and Chairman of the United Foundation of Detroit. Fisher served on President Reagan's Task Force on Private Sector Initiatives and President Nixon's National Center for Voluntary Action.

Fisher has continued his business interests and is currently on the board of Comerica and Sotheby's. He has also served on the boards of numerous companies, including Owens-Illinois, Inc.; the Irvine Company; United Brands; Michigan Consolidated Gas Company; Michigan Bell Telephone; and the Fruehauf Corporation.

His credentials include fourteen honorary degrees from higher learning institutions, among them Ohio State University [his alma mater]; Michigan State University; Eastern Michigan University; the Hebrew University of Jerusalem; Yeshiva University; and Brandeis University.

His over forty-seven awards include the Presidential Citizen's Award, presented by Ronald Reagan; the Alexis de Tocqueville Society Award of the United Way of America; the William Booth Award by the Salvation Army; the Distinguished Citizen Award from Wayne State University; and the Ben-Gurion Centennial Medal from State of Israel Bonds.

Fisher now lives in Detroit and Palm Beach with his wife, Marjorie.

Interview by Irving Bernstein
August 30, 1995.

Q: You have the unique distinction in American Jewish life of being the only person to have served as chairman of the CJF, national UJA, UIA, and the Jewish Agency for Israel. Some of these entities have conflicting interests. For example, CJF's major agenda is the American Jewish community, while UJA, UIA, and the Jewish Agency view Israel as their first priority. How do you explain your acceptance in agencies with such different points of view and interests?

A: Chuck Hoffberger mentioned that I was the only man he knew who could bridge the cultural differences between the agencies. In truth, I never really had much of a problem—I thought they all had similar purposes, to provide for Jewish needs, but different ways of achieving them. I used to say UJA and the Council of Federations are two sides of the same coin. They all had an objective of saving Jews and providing for the needs of the Jewish community. There are local needs and overseas needs, and both are very important.

[Jerrold Chuck Hoffberger was president of the Baltimore Orioles from 1956 to 1979; a trustee, of UJA; president of the Council of Jewish Federations and Welfare Funds, 1975–1978; National Vice Chairman of UJA 1978–1983; and Chairman of the Board of Governors of the Jewish Agency, 1983–1987.]

When I was with UJA, I urged UJA people to get involved with their local federations, because real leadership comes out of the local communities.

Remember our good friend Mel Dubinsky from St. Louis? He was very anti-Federation and later became president of his federation and one of the most active Jewish leaders in America. [Dubinsky was president of the St. Louis Federation, UJA national chairman, UIA chairman and treasurer of the Jewish Agency.]

When I became general chairman of UJA, the UJA and the CJF would never get together—there was a great schism. One of the first things I wanted to do was create unity, so I asked Herb Friedman to invite council staff to be part of the effort as we prepared for one of our big UJA conferences. I said each member of the council staff could be a salesman for the cause. You ought to make them feel welcome, let them know that they should be a part of the whole effort. That made a difference.

Q: You are as easily at home in the non-Jewish community as you are in the Jewish community. Did your early years and experience in the small community of Salem, Ohio, which barely had a *minyan* [prayer quorum], influence this aspect of your personality?

A: Yes, I think it did have an effect. After all, I didn't have any Jewish friends, and I was able to relate to non-Jewish friends. Later on, in the business world, in politics, and in community work, I took the position that a good Jew is naturally a good citizen, and so I made it a point to be involved in many non-Jewish causes. I think you have a responsibility to the community in which you live.

When I was president of the Federation, I met with and addressed the United Way. They didn't understand why the Jewish community was not involved with them. I told them we wanted to be involved, and I explained to them that as of centuries ago, *tzedakah* [charity] was a core deed in Judaism. The result was that the next year, out of the blue, they invited me to head the United Way, which I accepted. And my Jewish involvements continued to increase year by year.

Q: Were you the first Jew in the country to be the head of the United Way?

A: I was chairman and then I became president and chairman of the board of the United Way for almost seven years. They all knew I was Jewish, and I induced many of the non-Jewish industrialists to become involved in Jewish causes. For example, Chrysler

Corporation, General Motors, Ford, and many others became contributors. We still get contributions I initiated from banks and the automobile companies. All this is a result of my philosophy that a good Jew is a good citizen.

Q: Though that's an essential point, there must have been times when you had to balance various interests carefully. You were at one time a major stockholder in Marathon Oil, which was heavily involved in Libya. Were you in any way able to influence Libyan policy toward Israel? And when you left Marathon, did you leave of your own free will or due to pressure because you were Jewish and so heavily involved in the UJA for Israel?

A: No, there was no pressure put on me. But this is what happened. I couldn't change the policy. Qaddafi was a real radical, far to the left, and they started exploiting the fact that "Max Fisher the Zionist" [they called me that in Libya] was robbing the wealth of Libya to support their enemy, Israel. I felt I had to make a choice that would benefit the shareholders of the company. I either had to keep quiet about my activities in the Jewish world, or I could no longer continue with Marathon. As a Jew, I had to be a supporter of Israel and our own Jewish causes, so I resigned.

I remember the board of directors' meeting. There were tears in some of the fellows' eyes when I explained why I had to resign. They had no idea I was going to leave. But it was more important to me to espouse the cause of Jewish life than to become richer through Marathon Oil Company.

Q: During this period, when the greater majority of American Jews were affiliated with the Democratic Party, you chose to be a Republican and became active in the Republican Party. Why? And did your identity with UJA and Israel in any way inhibit your influence and advancement in the Republican Party?

A: Well, first of all, I believe that the Jewish community should be represented in both political parties. I became a Republican when Roosevelt indicated he would run for a third term. I thought it was a mistake to prolong a dynasty, even though I voted for him the first two times.

I remember a meeting I had with then-former President Eisenhower in Gettysburg. He told me, "One day I was sitting on my porch, and in reviewing my decisions as President, I felt that I had made a mistake back in 1956." I asked, "Why do you say that?" He said, "At that time I felt that the United Nations was an idealistic agency. Later in life I found that they voted in blocs—not on the basis of ideals but on their own parochial interests and prejudices."

Eisenhower was referring to his decision to force Israel, Britain, and France to withdraw from the Suez Canal. He then added that he didn't have any Jewish friends or Jewish advisers. He did mention the names of a couple of people who were Jewish, but not involved in the Jewish community and with Israel. Before we met, I thought about becoming involved in the Republican Party at a level where I would have influence and access to the Republican Party. What Eisenhower said pretty much decided it for me.

I worked pretty hard at it. I had many friends in all the Jewish organizations, and they were very supportive. I don't know how many voted Republican, but as far as finances were concerned, they created and gave me a base of support that allowed me to make inroads in the Republican Party. I knew Nixon in the sixties, also Nelson Rockefeller [governor of New York and vice president of the United States under Gerald Ford] and Bill Scranton [governor of Pennsylvania]. I could go on and on with all the names . . . George Romney [president of American Motors, governor of Michigan, 1963-1969, and a presidential candidate, 1968] and Jerry Ford [vice president under Richard Nixon and President of the United States after Nixon's resignation].

These were all great friends, and I helped them all. By helping them, I think I bettered the Israel-American relationship during the years the Republicans were in power. This is something that most people don't know. Until Nixon came into office, the Democrats were never interested in giving Israel any military supplies. In the days of the Kennedy and Johnson administrations, Israel didn't receive any arms or any large financial support; Israel bought arms from France and Germany. I had to intercede with John Mitchell to work on Nixon to get him to deliver the fifty Phantom aircraft that Lyndon Johnson had promised to Israel.

The airlift in 1973 was the beginning of real aid to Israel. I think that when you look back at the last twenty-eight years of Republican administrations, the relationship between Israel and America has improved. It was a very interesting and satisfying period in my personal life, because I had the opportunity to deal privately with the prime ministers and the presidents on those issues.

Q: You became a confidant of every Republican president beginning with Eisenhower, and you always disclosed your Jewish commitments and ardent support of the UJA and Israel. How did this affect your relationships with the presidents, secretaries of state, or cabinet members who often differed with the American Jewish community in terms of their American policy toward Israel?

A: Well, I don't think it hurt. Please remember: I never sought or accepted a position with any administration. In politics there is a quid pro quo. When one works for a President he can often get a position—an ambassadorship or cabinet post. I turned down a cabinet post with the Department of Energy and an ambassadorship, among other positions, because I knew it would limit my freedom by accepting such a position. What was most important to me was to have access. Since the early days of the Nixon administration, I carried a pass to the White House. I wanted to be able to see the President without any restrictions.

Also, the minute you accept a position, you have to follow the line of the President. By being an outsider with both the President and the Secretary of State, whoever they were, I could tell them what I believed. They might not have accepted it, but the fact is they listened and did not get angry with me.

I was being honest and forthright with them. I used to tell them, "Look, I have no monopoly on wisdom, but I must tell you this is the way I feel about this matter." I earned their respect. And I never gave a press conference. I had more visits than some cabinet officers did in the Oval Office, and I never once gave a press conference or stated what purpose I had in mind.

I also dealt with issues other than Jewish issues. I dealt with economics. I was adviser, at that time, to Arthur Burns and to Paul McCracken in the energy field. [Arthur Edward Burns was a member of the French Legion of Honor, U.S. Ambassador to the Federal Republic of Germany; chairman of the president's Advisory Board on Economic Growth and Stability, 1953–1956; President, Council of Economic Advisers, 1953–1956; Chairman, National Bureau of Economic Research, 1967–1968; and Chairman, Board of Governors, Federal Reserve System, 1970–1978. McCracken was the Director of the Federal Reserve Bank of Minneapolis, 1943–1948; Chairman, Council of Economic Advisers, 1969–1971; and member, President's Advisory Board on Economic Policy.]

Q: Was this in a voluntary capacity?

A: They asked my if I wanted to be the energy czar. I said no. I spent six months in the White House volunteering my services, helping to stabilize the energy crisis that we had in 1973. John Ehrlichman [Nixon White House presidential adviser] wrote that he learned more about energy in the few days he spent with me than he ever thought possible. But I never had a hidden agenda. I didn't want anything for myself personally. I just wanted the ability to be able to accomplish what I set out to do.

Q: As you look back now at your relationships with Presidents Eisenhower, Nixon, Ford, Reagan, and Bush, to what extent were you able to influence their policy in their relationship with the American Jewish community and Israel?

A: Politics is a very fine thing. You know that you press buttons, but you never know exactly what happens. The fact that I was able to express my opinions must have had some influence. I don't mean I always got what I wanted, but expressing my thoughts, my honest opinions and assessments, had some impact. There were times when at least I had the ability to sit across the table and they would listen to me. The ability to talk to a person means a great deal. There are times when it is a valuable thing.

Q: Was helping the Ethiopians one of those situations?

A: Yes. I went to President Bush and talked to him about trying to help the Ethiopians in the Sudan. He was going to North Africa at the time, and he was the one who was responsible for the rescue of those North Africans. He told me later that the man he worked with, the minister of the interior of the Sudan, ended up in jail. He felt sorry for him.

Then there were the Ethiopian Jews in Addis Ababa. I had a meeting in my home with Uri Lubriani [secretary to Moshe Sharett; Director, Mideast Division of Arab Affairs, 1955–1961; ambassador to Uganda, 1963–1965; ambassador to Ethiopia, 1968–1971; and coordinator of Israeli activities in Lebanon since 1982], Sylvia Hassenfeld [chairman of the UJA Women's Division, 1975–1977] and Michael Schneider of JDC.

During the meeting, I picked up the phone in my library, called the White House, and talked with President Bush. We started a process right then and there. The president asked me if Rudy Boschwitz [U.S. senator from Minnesota, 1978-1990] would be a good person to work with.

Operation Ezra started right from that telephone call in my house, during the meeting with Lubriani.

Q: During the '73 War, when Nixon was President, there was a delay in sending arms to Israel. Did you play any role in getting them to expedite the supplies?

A: I delivered a message from the Conference of Presidents of Major American Jewish Organizations, which every member signed. It asked Nixon to help Israel as quickly as possible. I gave it to Nixon. I did talk to him. Whether I was the one to push the button at the right time, I really don't know. I visited with Henry Kissinger, and we talked about it. And I also spoke to then Attorney General John Mitchell, who was also helpful.

Q: You and Henry Ford and your families were close to one another. Probably due to your influence, Ford became a large annual contributor to the UJA, and in 1973 visited Israel, where he helped Israel produce and assemble cars and trucks. Was his interest in Israel due to his guilt over his father's antisemitism, or was it because of his relationship with you?

A: The answer is neither. Let me tell you a little about Henry Ford. I knew Henry since the early fifties. We first became acquainted when my wife, Margie, and Ann Ford were co-chairmen of the Metropolitan Opera when it came to Detroit. Henry didn't like the opera, I remember—he used to sneak off during intermission. I worked with Henry on many community causes. He was one of the founders of the United Way and I found him to be easy to work with in our common interests. He was interested in the plight of African-Americans, as I was.

When I talked to Henry in later years, he told me that from speaking to his grandfather he knew very little about the man's view of Jews. [Henry Ford, Sr., published the antisemitic *Protocols of the Elders of Zion* in his newspaper, the *Detroit Free Press*, as well as a series of antisemitic screeds.] His grandfather lived on the west side of town, and Henry lived on the east side. He would see him occasionally, but conversations about Jews were not major topics of discussion. But I used to tell him, Henry, the reason that Ford Motors was not popular among Jews was because of what did take place.

I'll never forget 1967. I was on a boat trip in the Mediterranean with Henry Ford, and I was called to Israel, because that was the beginning of the 1967 war. I arrived in time to attend that dramatic cabinet meeting. Then I returned to the boat and told Henry what was taking place, and that I had to leave to start the '67 campaign. I was chairman that year. When I returned home, there was a letter for me written in Henry's handwriting: "I'm sending you this check, not because you're my friend but because I believe in the cause." I still have that handwritten note. I received a check for $100,000 every year until his untimely death.

Henry used to speak for UJA, and he came to Israel twice [once with UJA and once with the American Manufacturers Association]. Pinhas Sapir encouraged investments in labor-intensive industries in development towns to employ mass immigration. He came over and we had a big meeting. In 1973 Sapir was desperate, so I called Henry Ford and said, "Henry, we may need your help." He answered: "All I can tell you is that if we have any facilities available to help, we will." You were there with us.

[Sapir held the post of director general of the Ministry of Defense in 1953; was minister of trade and industry, 1955; took on the additional portfolio of minister of finance in 1963; and was again minister of finance in 1969 during Golda Meir's tenure as prime minister.]

Several years later, some of the Ford executives I talked to told me he raised hell and told them that they were going to help in whatever way they could.

And then there was the "incident": Ford of England refused to ship Ford engines to Israel in 1973. Others tried to put pressure on them. And I went to see Henry. He said, referring to the British subsidiary, "No one is going to tell me what to do." I brought in Abe Harman, and he told Abe the same thing. The result was that British Ford shipped the engines.

[Harman was Assistant Director General, Ministry of Foreign Affairs, 1955–1956; Counselor to the Israeli delegation to the United Nations; Consul General to the Israeli delegation to the United Nations; Consul General, Montreal, 1949; Consul General, New York, 1953–1954; ambassador to the United States, 1959–1968; President, Hebrew University of Jerusalem, 1968–1983; and Chancellor, Hebrew University of Jerusalem, 1983–1988.]

Q: Max, let me shift a little bit. During the Nixon administration, there were whispers by some members of the Conference of Presidents of Major Jewish Organizations that you were the "court Jew," in spite of your leadership in the UJA and the Jewish Agency. Why was that issue raised, and how was it resolved?

A: Most of the presidents of the council were Democrats, and they thought I was there to control them. But they discovered the truth by experience. If you read the history of the Presidents' Conference, you will note that I took them to Washington, to the White House, to the State Department. I did everything in the world to make them feel comfortable and to present their points of view.

That's how the issue resolved itself. They found out for themselves that my interest was Israel and not myself. If you read the notes of the then director of the Presidents' Conference, Yehuda Hellman, they state that the Democrats would never have been able to do that on their own. I brought them to the White House.

[Hellman headed the Jewish Telegraphic Agency in Paris and was

Executive Vice Chairman, Conference of Presidents of Jewish Organizations; he was also a member of the International Steering Committee, World Conference of Jewish Communities on Soviet Jewry, 1971.]

Q: In 1971, as President of the Council of Federations, you and Louis Pincus, the Chairman of the Jewish Agency, forged the reconstitution of the Jewish Agency. In view of the fact that all previous efforts failed, why did you take on the task?

[Pincus was Chairman of the South African Zionist Socialist Party, founder of Habonim in Israel in 1958; legal adviser and Director General, Ministry of Transport; Managing Director, El Al Israel Airlines 1949–1956; Treasurer, Jewish Agency 1966; Chairman, Board of Governors, Tel Aviv University, 1967–1970; and afterwars remained as honorary chairman.]

A: Well, years before, I had started talking with Louis Pincus about my main purpose—to work for the unity of the Jewish people, and to get everyone to work together. Working that way has always been in my background—from the days when I was president of the Federation in Detroit. So we worked at it. I spent hours, days, weeks and months, to try to achieve that. It just took personal time bringing people together and breaking down the distrust.

By the way, when I first announced the agreement to the Federation, I got some criticism. There were members of the Federation who were not very happy. But I remember suggesting that they get involved. And they did. It was a matter of just letting things work, of breaking down the distrust on both sides.

Zionists distrusted the fund-raisers, their emphasis on control of budgeting; and of course the fund-raisers didn't appreciate the political affiliations of the Zionists. But in the end, it worked for two reasons: patience and perseverance. In fact, I brought Louis Pincus to speak to the CJF.

Q: And throughout all this, you were able to maintain unity and gain the respect of the World Zionist Organization [WZO] members. This was quite a feat, considering, as Eddie Warburg once pointed out to me, that the Zionist versus non-Zionist conflict defeated his father's and Chaim Weizmann's efforts to unite the two sides. How were you able to do it?

A: First you have to develop trust. When I became a chairman of the Board of Governors of the Jewish Agency, I never looked at myself as a representative of the American Jewish community. I represented the whole Jewish community. I was chairman of all of them. I looked out at whatever audience was there and I insisted that the seating at the tables be mixed. I insisted people mingle. When they first came in, the Zionists sat here and the fund-raisers there.

You gain trust and respect by your actions, the deeds that you do. It took time. You mentioned Eddie Warburg [President of the JDC and of the New York City Jewish Federation; National Chairman, UJA]. When I reorganized the United Palestine Appeal into the United Israel Appeal, I remember that we had two-thirds representation. I couldn't get the others to join. I believe it was Eddie Warburg and Bill Rosenwald who refused, because they didn't want to sit with Zionists. But Zionists are Jews, and non-Zionists are Jews. They all have some mutuality of purpose. Over a period of time they found out they were wrong, and I said so. You had to be sort of a mediator between them.

I wanted to promote Jewish education. You recall, I wanted to put $5 million into the budget; and Frank Lautenberg, Michael Sacher, and you opposed me on this. When I first went into the Jewish Agency, I spent time in all the departments, including education. I tried to get to know them and their programs. There were many rough periods, but a trust developed, if only because I always tried to bring together different points of view.

Q: What led you, who grew up without a Jewish education or any Jewish involvement, to become such a passionate and zealous advocate and Agency spokesman for Jewish education and the establishment of the education authority? At the time, there was enormous pressure on the Jewish Agency and the world Jewish community to fund the flood of immigrants pouring into Israel.

A: Maybe it's because I didn't have any Jewish education. I did not even have a bar mitzvah. I figured that if we did not have a good Jewish educational system, we were going to lose our Jewish people. I felt that very keenly.

As early as the Jewish Welfare Federation Assembly in Kansas City, I espoused the cause of Jewish day schools, and even that early, there was criticism from some of the members of the federations. Time and history have proven me correct, though we've got a long way to go. My feeling was: now is the time. I feel this is a very important cause, so much so, that the one official involvement I've held onto is the Louis Pincus Fund that we established twenty-five years ago. I'm proud of the results.

Q: Today's Jewish organizations mimic corporate culture by hastily dismissing professionals, regardless of cost. Then they go out to hire the best staff, again, regardless of cost. How did you, with your history of organizational leadership, develop constructive and long-lasting relationships with the professionals you worked with, even after they retired? And why do they speak of you with such affection and respect?

A: I believe that when working with a professional, you should not work around them. Occasionally, somebody comes in and wants to take over. I believed in working with all the professionals, and as a result, I developed lasting relationships and friendships and then when I moved on to the next job, I still kept in touch. We developed camaraderie. I treated them as peers, I didn't have to have a staff— my staff was the corps of professionals I worked with. If I wanted to get information or do something about UIA, I'd call whoever was there or at the CJF.

Q: Why did you, just as you were growing to prominence in the economic world and influence in the public sphere, suddenly become involved in the UJA?

A: It goes beyond just UJA. I always felt I was Jewish, even in Salem, Ohio, and especially when I went to Ohio State. I was involved with a Jewish fraternity, Hillel, and many organizations—

including political ones—and football. I always had a feeling for Jewish unity and fellowship.

I always liked community life, and I always felt that it was part of my life. When I came to Detroit during the Depression, one of my father's attorneys had a friend, Fred Butzel, who was very well known. I think I was earning $15 a week. I gave him $5 for UJA/ Federation. That was in 1932 or 1933, when $5 was a lot of money. I got involved in the Jewish Community Center; I worked for the aged; I worked in many causes.

Then came my first trip to Israel in 1954. I was on a UJA mission composed of fourteen people, traveling on non-air-conditioned buses. Joe Schwartz was there with Eddie Warburg and they elected me as chairman.

[Schwartz was a Semitic scholar who taught at the American University in Cairo and who, with the approval of the U.S. War Refugee Board, negotiated the rescue of thousands of Jews from Germany and occupied countries during World War II. He was the chairman of the JDC in Europe, 1940–1949. After the war, he supervised the transfer of over a half million Jews to Israel from Europe, North Africa, and the Middle East. He helped one hundred thousand Jewish refugees immigrate to Canada, the United States, and Latin America and was Director General, JDC, 1950–1951; Vice Chairman of UJA, 1951–1955; and Vice President of the State of Israel Bonds, 1955–1970. He established new records in large-scale fund-raising for Jewish causes.]

I remember my first speech was terrible. As I got involved, I became intrigued with what was happening as Israel was building itself up, and it thrilled me. I decided that I had a responsibility to try to unify the Jewish people in whatever way I could. There were so many groups. When I first started, the rabbi at Temple Beth El in Detroit didn't believe in the State of Israel. The American Council for Judaism was publicly opposed to Israel.

Q: In eight years of leadership in UJA, four as national chairman and four as president, do you believe you brought to the UJA something that didn't exist before?

A: I think I brought a spirit of togetherness. For example, I saw to it that the leadership came from the communities. I brought

Council of Federation leadership into UJA and UJA leaders into the council. I think I brought the federations closer to the UJA, and that enabled me to move on to the Jewish Agency to bring people together from all over the world, regardless of whether they were non-Zionists or Zionists.

Q: You were UJA chairman in the 1967 war, and you were chairman of the Board of Governors of the Jewish Agency in the 1973 war. Do you recall any dramatic incidents either in the States or in Israel that you experienced at that time?

A: Of course, 1967 immediately comes to mind. I was called off the boat to a meeting of the Israeli cabinet. And there was the time when Ambassador Eban [Abba Eban, Israeli ambassador and UN representative] called from the States and said that although Eisenhower had promised in 1956 to keep the Straits of Tiran open, President Johnson was not ready to do that. I remember we sat around the table trying to decide the fate of the Jewish people and how much money could be raised, how much support Israel would get. At that time, I sat next to a man in a uniform. I turned around to him and introduced myself. His name was Yitzhak Rabin.

Q: That was your first meeting with Yitzhak Rabin?

A: That's right. I asked him, "What do you think of all this?" I'll never forget his response. He said, "I hope they don't rob me of the element of surprise."

That was one of the amazing things that happened. To be involved in a period of crisis, to be able to play some part, gives you a great deal of satisfaction. There is comfort and pleasure in doing the right thing.

Q: You have often said, publicly and privately, that the results of the UJA annual campaigns are closely watched in Washington and have an impact on American-Israel relations. Can you recall any specific incidents that indicate this type of UJA campaign impact in Washington?

A: Of course. When the Soviet-Jewish problem came up, we were working together on Jewish emigration to Israel. I recall talking with President Bush. At that time we were raising $800 million. I told them that we're not asking for money, we're asking for help to get the Jews out of the Soviet Union, and it did have an impact.

I also recall talking with President Nixon right after he took office. He said, "You know why I feel very comfortable in a relationship with Israel? They don't ask, like many countries do, for us to come over there and build roads for them. They say that they don't want our soldiers. They say, give us help, and we'll do our own job."

Q: Did anyone in Washington ever refer to the amounts the UJA raised?

A: Oh yes! We used to hear that all the time. They were amazed at the ability of the Jewish community to raise so much. I think that was very helpful.

Q: You were associated with every Prime Minister since David Ben-Gurion. Do you recall any memorable incidents, agreements, or differences?

A: I remember our cooperation with Golda Meir. I told her about Nixon when he was elected. She said, "Either we will get help by his doing the right thing, or we will get punished."

Golda and Nixon kept up their relationship after the war. They liked each other and continued to communicate.

Nor can I forget a moving conversation with Levi Eshkol [the third Prime Minister of Israel] about the meaning of immigration to the State of Israel. It was back in the fifties, when we didn't have enough money. I was picked to suggest a cutback on immigration. He said to me, "Young man, let me tell you something. As long as there is a State of Israel, the borders will always be open. We may go down, but we'll go down with the borders open, and we'll fight and starve to keep those borders open, whether you give us one dime or not."

Q: Did Menachem Begin accept you in the same way?

A: Oh yes. He and I differed quite a bit and had some very interesting visits. I carried some messages back and forth. He was a man of courage and I really liked him.

Q: You have been intimately involved with Shimon Peres in his many ministerial roles. Would you comment on that relationship and the areas you worked on together?

A: Our discussions dealt primarily with arms and materiel when Peres was minister of defense from 1974 to 1976. In 1984, when he became prime inister, they were concerned with the status of the West Bank and peace. It was during this time that Peres described me as one who occupied a position, not a post, and said that I was politically adept.

In 1984 Prime Minister Shimon Peres asked me to take the chairmanship of Operation Independence to stimulate investment in Israel. He felt that I probably could get more support from other leaders. I took the job feeling we had to start something which would eliminate the negative balance of trade that Israel had while developing the business sector so the country would not have to depend on foreign aid.

There were many issues with Operation Independence that I had to review and resolve with Shimon Peres. First of all, it was necessary to convince Israel to privatize industry, to change the culture from a socialist state to one that was capitalistic.

This was no easy task. It meant that the government would have to give up ownership and control of much—up to 35-40 percent— of Israel's industry. It was also necessary to convince Israeli manufacturers to follow the model of the West in packaging, promotion, and publicity. In my opinion it was the only way Operation Independence could attract American investors to Israeli industry, to help the country achieve economic independence, and to close the growing gap between Israel's exports and imports.

In the beginning, Operation Independence was a success. It flourished with the help of George Shultz, the Secretary of State. I asked Schultz to invite American industrialists and entrepreneurs to a meeting at the State Department to encourage them to invest in Israel. Shultz explained to them how vital it was for Israel to move along the path to economic independence, since the United States might not be able to continue its present levels of foreign aid in view of American obligations all over the world.

My relationship with Peres was excellent during his term as prime minister. I spent many hours with him. He was, and is, a visionary leader. Our relationship was widely known in Washington, and Shultz authorized me to tell Peres that when it came to arms sales, Israel would have priority and its security would in no way be hampered.

Q: You're now eighty-seven. You are still active and attend every important meeting. How do you explain your continuity and involvement to this very day?

A: I stayed with it because I deeply believe in it. Things are not the same when you step down as they are when you're a chairman or president or executive. Some people don't want to be in a position of second-guessing the next president or chairman. But I never had that problem. I was able to relate to my successors. People come up and ask, how can you sit up there on the dais for hours without saying anything? I talk when I feel it is important to talk, but I do feel that my presence alone also means something.

Q: What do you consider your greatest achievement? Do you have any regrets about things you couldn't do?

A: Well, I don't think I can really answer that. I look at the total achievement. Any one accomplishment, like the $350 million I raised, or the '67 war, that really doesn't mean anything. Did I contribute to organizations? Did I contribute to Jewish unity? Did I contribute to better relationships between Israel and America? All those are things I played a part in. It is left to history to answer exactly what that part was. I can't answer that.

Q: What do you feel you personally gained from all those years of involvement and leadership in UJA?

A: It's not a matter of getting a title or a plaque or anything. There was a feeling inside me that was my personal reward. Not everybody is elected to serve. The fact that I was chosen for leadership, and had an opportunity to serve, means a great deal to me.

Q: When did you first get the idea to become a bar mitzvah? Why did you decide to do it at age seventy-five at the Western Wall, after a board of governors meeting on June 25, 1984?

A: I have always regretted my lack of Jewish education, and felt that the lack of a bar mitzvah, which we couldn't do in Salem, diminished me as a Jewish leader and spokesman.

In the spring of 1984, I attended a meeting of the Jewish Agency Jewish Education Commission at the Waldorf Hotel in New York City. The meeting was chaired by Morton Mandel of Cleveland, who I had appointed to the chairmanship of that committee. He and I both spoke on the priority of Jewish education.

After that meeting, although I knew my aims and goals were on target, I deeply felt my own inadequate Jewish education. Going back to the hotel, I shared my thoughts with Rabbi Zelig Chinitz and broached the idea of having a bar mitzvah at the *Kotel* [the Western Wall]. Chinitz agreed to arrange a low-key service in June of '84 with the minister of religion, Yosef Burg, father of Jewish Agency executive chairman Avrum Burg [both of them Orthodox]. It would be a private service to the left of the Wall.

It was a bright, sunny morning. There were thirty-five members of my family; Chuck Hoffberger, chairman of the board of governors of the Jewish Agency; Leon Dulzin, chairman of the Agency's executive; members of the executive; and many friends, including you.

Rabbi Mordechai Kirshblum made a brief speech about the occasion, but I was too tense to remember his words. I was then summoned to the Torah to recite the transliterated prayers wearing a *tallit* and *tefillin* [phylacteries]. It was an Orthodox service .

I then went to the Wall and ran my hands over the stones. With tears in my eyes I remembered my *Yiddishe mama* in Salem, and the great difficulty she had in keeping the house kosher; the trips

I made from Salem to Youngstown to the *shochet* [butcher]; and I realized that I had come full circle from Salem to Jerusalem.

Q: Do you believe that your involvement in UJA and the Jewish Agency heightened your sense of Jewish identity and consciousness, and were they factors in your decision to be bar mitzvahed?

A: Certainly I've always felt an important link missing for my lack of having a Bar Mitzvah, and the fact that I was able to do it at the Wall in Jerusalem, at that age, was of special significance to me.

10

SHIMON PERES

F ormer Prime Minister Shimon Peres was born in Poland in 1923 and made his way to Israel at the age of fourteen. By 1948 he was head of Israel's naval services, and at the end of the war he was appointed to head a Defense Ministry delegation to the United States. While there, he completed his education at New York University and at Harvard.

Politically active from the age of twenty, after a number of years in Kibbutz Geva and Kibbutz Almanot, Peres was elected secretary of the Labor youth movement in 1943. In 1947, after being conscripted to the Haganah by David Ben-Gurion and Levi Eshkol, he was assigned responsibility for manpower and arms purchases, continuing this post during the early part of Israel's War of Independence. A year later, in 1948, Peres was appointed head of Israel's navy, and at the war's end he assumed the position of director of the Defense Ministry's procurement delegation in the United States.

In 1953, at the age of twenty-nine, Peres was appointed by Prime Minister David Ben-Gurion to the post of director general of the Ministry of Defense, a position he held until 1959. During that period he developed the special relationship between Israel and France, established Israel's electronic aircraft industry, and was responsible for Israel's nuclear program.

In 1959, Peres was elected to Israel's parliament, the Knesset, and has remained a member ever since. From that year, until 1965, he served as deputy minister of defense. In 1965, together with David Ben-Gurion, he left the Mapai [Labor] Party and became Secretary General of Rafi. In 1968, he initiated bringing Rafi back to Mapai to form the Israel Labor Party.

The following year he was appointed minister of immigrant absorption, and from 1970 to 1974 served as minister of information. Peres was then appointed minister of defense, a position he held until 1977. It was during this term of office that he masterminded the rescue of the Entebbe hostages in 1976.

After the election in 1977, which placed the Labor Party in opposition to the Likud government, Peres was elected chairman of the Labor Party, a post he held until 1992. During that period he was elected vice president of the Socialist International.

Upon the establishment of a national unity government in September 1984, Peres served first as prime minister and between 1986 and 1988 as deputy prime minister and minister of foreign affairs. From November 1988 until the dissolution of the national unity government in 1992, he served as deputy prime minister and minister of finance.

In July 1992, after the election of the new Labor government, he was appointed minister of foreign affairs. He was awarded the 1994 Nobel Peace Prize for his effort in advancing peace in the Middle East.

On November 5, 1995, following the assassination of Prime Minister Yitzhak Rabin, Peres was appointed Acting Prime Minister; and on November 22, 1995, after Knesset approval, he was sworn in as prime minister. After his defeat in the May 1996 elections, he continued to serve as head of the Labor Party until June 1997.

Shimon Peres has authored ten books, including *The Next Step* [1965]; *David's Sling* [1970]; *Entebbe Diary* [1991]; *The New Middle East* [1993]; and *Battling for Peace* [1995].

He is currently a member of the Labor Party, and he and his wife, Sonya, have three children.

**Interview by Irving Bernstein
in the Labor Party office in Tel Aviv
June 25, 1996**

Q: You will recall the national conferences UJA held every December in New York City at the Hilton Hotel—with the five-tiered dais and four thousand campaign and community leaders, from the smallest to the largest Jewish communities in the United States. At the 1975 conference you were the principal speaker and you said that since 1940, "we had been focused on building a state," and that for the next thirty-five years, we would need to build a model society for a model state.

Although it is less than thirty-five years since you told us what our goals should be, do you feel we have been successful in building at least the beginning of such a society and state? Or have we failed?

A: In many ways it is more than I hoped for, and in some ways it is less. In 1948, it was hard to imagine that Hebrew would become the language of four and-a-half million people. That is more than Danes who speak Danish. It was, at the beginning, hard to imagine that Israel would reach such heights in education, in research and development, in technology. It was hard for me to imagine that we would overcome wars and begin a real peace movement with a real introduction to peace. But it is clear that to build a civilized society it is essential to have civilized relations with your neighbors.

In those days it was also difficult to predict that we were going to have close to eight hundred thousand immigrants from the former Soviet Union. It was hard to see that in the historic struggle between communism and Zionism, Zionism would win and communism would fail, and that large emigrations from Romania, North Africa, and the Soviet Union would add to our strengths.

Israel is not yet a great nation, but she can thrive on our greatness in human terms. Because of all the different kinds of immigrants we have brought in, the fabric of our nation is very sturdy, much better than it used to be. And today, Israel can live on its brains. The country is being developed in a very attractive and appealing way. We are recognized by most nations, including China and India—who between them represent one-third of the world's population. At the same time, we have diplomatic relations with seven Arab countries, and together with Jordan, we are trying to solve the problems of the Palestinians. All these events have exceeded our dreams and expectations.

On the other hand, there are still problems and setbacks. There is fragmentation of society between non-religious factions as well as ethnic groups. Still, every development has its dialectical side—you go up and down and usually up again. Right now, we are at an impasse. I don't know when things will move on and up, but I know opportunities exist.

Until now Israel's greatest struggle has been with the outside world. I really believe that today we do not have to win a military war, but we do have to win over the world's good opinion. Until recently, Israel was seen as a compensation for the Holocaust and our people's historic suffering. Today, Israel must become an invitation for the un-Jewish generation. We have to build on new ideas, new attractions, and new agendas.

We will have to redefine who is a Jew. The religious definition of a Jew was that a Jew is a person whose parents are Jewish, or that at least the mother is Jewish. Today, the answer to who is a Jew should be that a Jew is a person whose children remain Jewish. You cannot change your parents, but you have to keep your children.

Q: In speaking of the younger generation, I noticed as I came into your office that everyone here, male and female, is young. Is this deliberate?

A: Yes. It is a statement about the future. In this last general election, the real gain was in our younger generation. This young generation mobilized itself in an unexpected manner—with devotion and sincerity. I still receive thousands of letters from young people who tell me that what we are doing gives them hope and promise. We must learn from the content of these letters.

Q: You also said that Judaism is not a sum of statistics but a divorce of it, not a sum of reality but an attempt to enrich it, to change it. Would you elaborate on that? The concept has puzzled many of us and stimulated a series of debates without resolution.

A: Jewish history is a contradiction. What happened to us didn't happen to anyone else, and what happened to everyone else didn't happen to us. Namely, from our earliest days, there was a contradiction between the size of the spirit and the size of the body that we have possessed. It is a very small body. If you count the number of Jews all over the world, we are a tiny minority, one of the smallest among the nations, as the Bible itself describes.

Yet spiritually and religiously, we are the equal of the Christians and the equal of the Moslems even though there are 1.3 billion Muslims and approximately 16–17 million Jews in the world. We have had a great deal of character and tenacity not to divorce ourselves from the spirit that created so much resentment and challenge throughout our history. We have kept that spirit alive, and the spirit has also kept us alive. We had nothing else to nurture us—nothing in real estate, no state and no army.

Never in history has a nation that was exiled from its land for thousands of years and scattered all over the world rebuilt itself on the land it was exiled from and renewed its ancient language. We are the only nation in the Middle East that speaks its original language. The Egyptians do not speak Egyptian, in Rome they do not speak Latin, in Athens and Damascus they do not speak their ancient languages.

And even though we were out of business for such a long time, we renewed the land in an agricultural miracle, built industry, an army, and a democracy in less than fifty years.

Q: Do you recall where you first became involved with UJA? It seems to me that you were there at UJA's inception, then the youngest among the Israelis who helped launch the UJA, just as I was one of the youngest in UJA in '47.

A: I recall Henry Montor, one of your predecessors, coming here from time to time and almost giving us orders. However, I had respect for him as a great organizer and leader. I remember traveling with one of your first chairmen, William Rosenwald, who would not fly—we always traveled by train and car. I will never forget one night on a train traveling across America and seeing this unique person of German-Jewish background, a multimillionaire, taking care of every detail of our journey and meetings while taking care of his own business. I also remember Sam Bronfman of Canada, the father of today's Bronfman brothers, Edgar and Charles, who followed their father into the liquor industry and in his devotion to Israel.

Q: Do any meetings come to mind?

A: Yes. An inspiring meeting in the home of Max Fisher in Detroit. The meeting that began my relationship with Max is one I will always treasure. We became friends and partners during the historic struggle for Jewish statehood, Jewish survival, and Jewish unity. As fellow Jews came together in his home to serve and build Jewish lives, the room became so crowded that many had to stand. But no one complained. They were absolutely inspiring. All they wanted to know was whether Israel would survive and what could they do to help. Their gift to UJA, and their emotional words, sent me out of Detroit to cities all over the U.S. with strength and confidence.

I will always remember one incident that happened on the top floor of a skyscraper in New York or Chicago. Two generals in dress uniform—one from the air force and one from the Israel Defense Forces—accompanied me. A maid met us when we got off the elevator and asked us if we were the orchestra.

We explained that we were the guest speakers for the evening, and she led us into the crowded ballroom. What she didn't realize was that she had performed a valuable service. The generals were on their first speaking tour of the United States, and this was their first public appearance. They were very nervous, and the maid had managed to break the ice. We went on to have one of the best meetings of the entire tour.

Q: You were involved with legendary David Ben-Gurion in pre-state Israel when you were very young. You grew to maturity during the dramatic period of Israel's birth under his leadership. How did this visionary little giant view the UJA and the American Jewish community? Did he see it as just a fund delivery instrument? Did he believe that UJA had the potential to increase the Jewish identity of American Jews and bring them spiritually and physically closer to Jerusalem and to Israel?

A: Israel was created and grew in loneliness. The only compensation for our loneliness was Jewish unity. The relationship between America and world Jewry wasn't just a matter of financial support, no matter how critical and essential that support was for Israel's growth and development. It was like having a brother, a sister, a friend. A brother in need is a brother indeed, and UJA and Keren Hayesod were the instruments that brought the family together. What you did was and is right and justified.

Today, American and world Jewry participate in everything—in building the infrastructure of this country, in helping with security, as volunteers, and by offering political support.

The support hasn't been limited to money, but without the funding, Israel would never have been able to bring in and absorb so many immigrants.

Q: You will be coming to the United States several times this year [1996] for a number of meetings, including the General Assembly of the Council of Jewish Federations in Seattle.

A: Meetings and programs in the earlier days were more on an emerging and on-the-spot basis. On one visit for UJA, we took a small plane to fly from community to community to share our message and rally support. We almost collided one time when we went into the air space of another plane, but we had a lot of confidence because our plane was Israeli-made.

Today's meetings are planned far in advance. These meetings are important to assure the Jewish community and the powers in Washington that despite the assassination of Yitzhak Rabin and the change in government, despite the differences, Israel is still the ally of the United States and a stable country standing for peace.

Q: As prime minister, you assessed Israel's economic needs for investment, and you projected an innovative and daring program called Operation Independence to encourage investment in Israel. You reached out to Max Fisher to lead the effort. Max involved Charles Bronfman, Morton Mandel, Harvey Krueger and others at top economic levels, and most American Jewish organizations.

Looking back, how do you assess its value? Did it succeed? Did it meet your hopes? Did it have impact on Israel? If it didn't work, please tell me why.

A: I think it was a tremendous success. It brought in a lot of investment, a lot of companies. It had its ups and downs. You cannot really organize these sorts of activities. You can create an interest. Maybe the organization wasn't perfect, but the results were superb. Look how many investments have been made in Israel, with most of them coming from the seeds of this organization.

Q: You speak about UJA as a constructive organization more than you do about it as fund-raising one. Project Renewal, the Israel Education Fund, the emergency campaigns during the various wars could probably all come under that rubric. Are there other programs that we should be doing that would fit that pattern?

A: We need programs in basic education, higher education, research and development, Jewish education, Israeli education. We have to invest everything we have in education—and in peacemaking. Israel is beginning to enjoy the benefits of the investments of multinational companies, but the multinational companies also have to invest in a multinational Middle East. It will happen, it will happen. Many American companies came in and invested in Israel, but I believe Israel must be their introduction to the Middle East.

Q: You have spoken about the need to develop Jewish personalities faithful to the prophets. Do you still believe the first is achievable in the materialistic climate of the West and in an Israel that is torn by strife?

A: We must. Think of what you in UJA accomplish by holding literally thousands of individual meetings weekly. Think about what your publicity says; think about the subjects of the speeches you all make. You have to continue this process with far greater and deeper substance in your message. Remember that there is still idealism in the Western World. Take the American position in wars. Although they won, and paid in blood, they still didn't keep anything for themselves. Was this pragmatic, or was it idealism faithful to the prophetic vision of the biblical prophets?

Q: So many prominent Israelis write books. Despite your horrendous schedule, you have managed to write a number of books: *David's Sling* and *The Next Phase* among them. As a writer, I must ask you where you find the time to write, and how do you choose your subjects?

A: I choose a subject, but I also have a message. In my newest book on the Middle East, I wanted to put forth a message of peace. It must have had an impact, because the book has been translated into twenty-four languages, including Arabic.

I write either late at night or very early in the morning; I need complete tranquility so that I can concentrate. I do not type. I write by hand with a pen. I wrote *Margin for Peace* from memory, without notes. I started every morning at 4 A.M. until I finished it.

Q: My fondest memories of time spent with you and your wife, Sonya, were the Shabbat evenings at your dinner table, where world leaders would get into discussions on the issues. You were one of the very few people in leadership who followed this practice—that led to interesting relationships among those present. It was also a rare opportunity to listen to you when you were not under pressure. Do you still hold these gatherings?

A: No, we don't do it anymore because of security reasons. We are not getting younger, and Sonya and I did everything. She cooked, and I made the drinks and washed the dishes. Hopefully, we may do it again, but on a much smaller scale.

Q: In June of 1984, I left UJA to teach at Brandeis and to become active in other organizations. I became concerned with the direction of the UJA, which appeared to be lowering the profile of Israel and raising the profile of our community's needs.

There was a meeting in Jerusalem of the Jewish Agency board of governors. You may remember, you came and spoke about this change in an effective way. You warned those who were pushing in that direction and those who were letting it happen. As a member of the Jewish Agency board, I went to many ministers to try to get them involved in the process. But the only one who responded was you. Are other ministers in your government interested in what happens in the American Jewish community, especially as it relates to Israel? Are they so tied up in their ongoing responsibilities that this becomes a minor matter? I think you were then prime minister. You had enough on your plate, yet you helped resolve the problem.

A: I think all the ministers are interested in the progress and the problems of UJA. It is just that too many of us cannot see beyond our own specific responsibilities. The reason I responded is that you asked me to, and I respect your opinion. My history with UJA goes back longer than any of my ministers. Remember that I was invited to address them, and so I took the opportunity to address the issue.

Q: In 1946, Moshe Dayan was thirty-one and you were twenty-three. The establishment chose both of you to be delegates from Israel's young guard to the Zionist Congress in Basel, Switzerland. When you were secretary general of Rafi, you played a very prominent role in Dayan's life and career. How close were the two of you?

A: I was a good friend of his brother Zorik, who was killed in the 1948 war, and I would see Moshe occasionally. Our friendship really developed during '46. We became very close friends, seeing eye-to-eye on many issues. I believe I convinced Ben-Gurion to appoint him as chief of staff despite opposition within the party.

We worked closely when he was chief of staff and I was director general of the Ministry of Defense. We worked hand in hand as real friends. Together we organized the Sinai Campaign, I on the political side and he on the military side. We worked on France together.

Our happiest days were with Ben-Gurion, even when Pinchas Lavon, the defense minister, authorized sabotage units to Egypt. It ended in disaster because he never consulted with Dayan, his chief of staff. We stood with Moshe when he took the heat.

Then, after the Yom Kippur War, Moshe lost a great deal of his support in Rafi. When I became the candidate for Prime Minister, I put him seventh on the list, against the will of the party. Otherwise, he would never have been elected. Then, when Begin became Prime Minister, he asked Dayan to be his minister of defense.

Moshe called me late at night and said, "I am sure you are angry that I didn't consult you before I did it."

I told him he was right. He said he didn't call me because he knew that if he had, I would have told him not to go to Begin. Moshe said he would have gone anyway—and I would have been doubly angry with him. From that, you can see that ours was a long-standing relationship.

Q: It is no secret that in the early years, Yitzhak Rabin and you were not the closest of friends or colleagues. Yet the two of you ushered in the beginning of peace for Israel, and the Nobel Prize was awarded to both of you. As two prominent people with often differing points of view, what do you think brought you to a rare symbiotic and productive relationship?

A: We both realized that there are things greater than either of us, that together we could achieve more than we could separately. Yitzhak tended to be a very suspicious person and suspected that we might not be together on key issues. I told him that I was not interested in power, my interest was, and is, in peace. I told him that as long as the peace process continued—as long as we could avoid war—we would always be together; and if we did not work together, we would lose the opportunity for peace. I told him, "Look, you are over-pessimistic and I am over-optimistic. Unless we work together, we will never have balance."

Never did I question who did what or who would get first billing. Things we thought were impossible happened. All these factors combined and enabled us to work together. And then, when things became very difficult, we began to see the results. Ours became a very good relationship.

We also communicated directly, without the interference of aides or others. That's how we were able to develop a higher level of trust. I do not doubt that if he were here, he would say the same.

Q: How would you characterize your relationship with your colleagues from Likud during the dramatic years when you served as prime minister and foreign minister? How did you deal with issues on which you fundamentally differed?

A: We had four major issues. One was inflation. It was close to 500 percent. Shamir was my partner, so to speak, but he didn't care much about the economy. As minister of finance, Yitzhak Moda'i understood that he had to go with me.

The second issue was whether or not to pull our forces out of Lebanon. I worked with then Minister of Defense Yitzhak Rabin. Others said that we should do it in seven months, and so I insisted that it be done in seven months, and it was done in seven months.

The third issue was Taba and our relations with Egypt. Here again, we were split between Labor-Likud; therefore, I could not make demands. But David Levy, a Likud minister, voted with us and we gained a majority.

The fourth issue was relations with Jordan and the Palestinians, which could not be resolved as easily as the first three.

Q: I came to Israel at that time as the national vice chairman of Yeshiva University's centennial campaign with a group of leadership people who were knowledgeable. Yosef Burg told us you would never give up the Office of Prime Minister as you had agreed to do per the Labor-Likud agreement. Those of us who knew you well said you would do so—and you did. Would you care to comment?

A: In democracies, you govern by your word. If you do not respect your word, you cannot truly govern.

Q: You have met with world leaders from nations small and large.

Would you tell us who among them impressed you the most?

A: De Gaulle, Adenauer, Mitterrand, Kennedy, Mendès-France, Clinton, and Bush. I liked them all very much.

Q: You have at various times in your career been called an academic, an intellectual, but not a pragmatist. And yet, in your political career, you have accomplished some of the most pragmatic feats: nuclear capability, negotiating arms deals prior to the Six-Day War, overcoming runaway inflation, calming the country after the assassination, and negotiating peace agreements. How do you account for this contradiction between perception and fact?

A: I really don't know. In most of those instances I was simply the head of the people and thus a target of suspicion. They wrote I was "an intellectual without intelligence." They went from one extreme to another: "Peres doesn't know how to write a speech" and "Peres doesn't know how to write an article, everything is written for him." They called us the implementers. And I was considered the greatest of them all. Then the press went to the other extreme, calling me a visionary.

Great things are born in your mind. That's what you call ambition. If you really want to implement your ideas, you must have patience, you must overcome obstacles and crises. You must never be frightened by failure. So if you judge me by my achievements, they exceed all the descriptions of me because I really believed in the things I was doing. I never wavered once I took something in my hands. I also believed in my own concept of management as control; I never wasted my time. It was really not by controlling, but by mobilizing, that I made my life.

Q: You said recently that Israelis need more Yiddish, and Diaspora Jews need more Hebrew. What will be the nature of the partnership between Israel and the Diaspora in a post-peace world? If we could ever realize peace in our lifetime, what would be UJA's role in such a world?

A: First, we have to set a new agenda for the coming fifty to one hundred years of Jewish life. The first item on the agenda, which will reach its hundredth anniversary this year, is completely fulfilled, better than Herzl ever dreamed it could be. Now we need a new dream. After we achieve peace with our neighbors, we have to build our spiritual center. We will gather whatever is Jewish historically, universally, and intellectually and bring it to Israel. So the agenda will be to build a spiritual center for a Jewish future in Jerusalem, in Israel.

If Israel was the answer to Jewish tragedies and the Holocaust, Israel must become attractive enough for the Jewish youth of the Diaspora to want to live here. For that reason, I believe, as I have said, that the real answer to the question of "Who is a Jew?" is not whether your parents were Jewish, but whether or not your children will be Jewish. I believe education will become the major instrument in the relationship between the Diaspora and us.

Yes, we have to attract material support, but we must also attract Jewish intellectual talent wherever it is. Israel went against the tide and succeeded solely because we are a believing nation, because our moral fiber exceeded our imperial strategies. This is the same as what we have to do for the future.

When Israel was born, UJA helped us with everything from infrastructure to human resources and materials. For the future we need an intellectual infrastructure, not just a material one. Building an intellectual infrastructure will make a spiritual center. The future of Israel is not to enlarge the land but to elevate moral, ethical, and intellectual standards to make Israel attractive to the outside world and to the people within Israel itself.

The twenty-first century depends on science and technology, and what we have today will never be sufficient to succeed after the millennium. We must combine the spiritual and the scientific to stimulate curiosity, to develop new forms of development. The French described us as a people who didn't let the world fall asleep, but neither would we let ourselves fall asleep. Ours is a sleepless nation in a borderless world. Therefore, I think we have to emphasize and increase research, development, and education and try to think philosophically as well as physically.

Q: How will Israel deal with religious pluralism? Can the right-wing interpretation of Judaism bring the majority of Jews in the world back to our faith? Is religious plurality possible in Israel?

A: Without religious pluralism we shall not be able to exist. It's even written in our tradition—there are seventy facets to the Torah. Judaism is a faith, and in between the world and ourselves there is nobody the Lord has empowered to represent us. Each of us is connected directly to heaven. We simply don't have the sort of hierarchy that exists among the Catholics and the Protestants, the Muslims or the Buddhists. I don't see how we can introduce discipline or hierarchy in Jewish life. We will have to be pluralistic in our perspective.

The problem is not between right and left, but between forward and backward. You know, in the Hebrew language there is almost no patience for a present—because Jewish philosophy is that either everything has already happened, everything will happen, and nothing is happening. For that reason, I believe that the essence of Judaism is to believe in *tikkun olam* [fixing the world].

If you believe in improving the world and if you are improving yourself, you believe in the future. If you need biblical sources, there are Isaiah and Amos. All the rest is imported stuff as far as I'm concerned. So if you have a spring, you can drink the water; and if you have an orientation, you can look at the future.

Q: It was the eve of the Suez Campaign. As director general of the Ministry of Defense, you visited Moshe Dayan in the Sinai just before the attack on the Fortress Husan. After it was destroyed, as you and Dayan walked toward your helicopter, Dayan observed, "We are reaching the end of the beginning." Would you say that you are also reaching the end of a beginning?

A: Yes. We are reaching an end of a chapter and the beginning of another one—much more dramatic, with much more potential; and it would be wise to take advantage of it. As the poet Alterman, says, "I shall die, but I shall continue to walk."

Q: What is your reaction to the climate in Israel following Rabin's assassination?

A: The days go by, but the intense pain shows no signs of diminishing. In every moment that passes, we must try to grow, to mature, and overcome the tragedy that has befallen us. Somehow, from the depths of darkness that surrounds us, we must bring about reconciliation on a national scale and develop a peace among brothers. Let us summon together the courage to face our shared destiny, and let all of us extend our hands to one another.

11

MAX M. FISHER/
SHIMON PERES:
RETROSPECTIVE

M ax Fisher has been a dominant personality in the American Jewish community since the early 1950s. He is the only leader to have served as chairman of the CJF, national UJA, UIA, and the Jewish Agency for Israel, in that order.

Fisher's prominent role is due not to his wealth, nor to the level of his contributions, as there are others in the community who are richer and make larger gifts. It is due rather to his ability to grasp all sides of an issue; to present his own point of view in an objective, non-personal manner; and to work out accepted compromises. Fisher does not hesitate, when there is obstinacy on one side or the other, to let his strength be felt by all concerned—as he analyzes the "profit and loss" in any lack of resolution.

Noteworthy use of these abilities occurred in 1970, during a historic meeting to reconstitute the Jewish Agency, an effort that had failed before. Until Fisher arrived as head of the UJA, American leaders had been unable to convince community leadership to follow them to Israel.

The meeting with the late Louis Pincus, the Agency's chairman, was held in Jerusalem at the King David Hotel. Pincus was alone. I accompanied Fisher. Before our meeting, Fisher said to me, "Just listen and watch carefully. Pincus will find it difficult to agree to our right to 'advise and consent' on the appointment of the key officers of the Agency. At that point, I will put in the 'steel.' If he returns in kind, we have a problem. If he lets it slide by we are home, and the rest of the meeting will be commentary."

The discussion went as Fisher predicted. Pincus fell silent as Fisher indicated that American and world participation depended on the power to "advise and consent." Fisher then quietly waited. The silence seemed to last for an eternity but in fact lasted less than a minute. I almost interrupted but didn't, because Fisher deliberately put his foot on mine. Pincus was an *oleh* [immigrant] from South

Africa who had headed El Al Airlines before being elected chairman of the Agency. He understood both the Diaspora and Israeli psyches. He sighed and said, "Max, you are right. It will be difficult for us, but I know it will work this time."

Two years later, at the height of the Cold War, my wife and I arrived in Moscow for a five-day visit. Waiting for us at the hotel was a cable from New York: "Regret to advise you that your Uncle Louis died and your brothers Max and Eddie want you to attend the funeral and family reunion."

The signature on the message was cousin Marc. It took a little while to interpret the message. My Uncle Louis could only be Louis Pincus. Pincus was only sixty-one. He had so much to give. It was a terrible loss for *Klal Yisrael* [the people of Israel].

My "brothers Max and Eddie" were Max Fisher and Ed Ginsberg (who would follow Fisher as UJA chairman). The family reunion had to be a meeting of the Jewish Agency to determine Pincus' successor. Cousin Marc, the sender of the cable, could only be Marc Tabatchnick, UJA's office manager in New York. I tried calling New York, but was told there would be a three-day delay.

Without unpacking, we made the rounds of airlines in Moscow, beginning with Pan Am, the carrier that brought us. As soon as they heard that our destination was Israel, they froze, gave us back our tickets, and told us they could not help us. At that time, Moscow's relations with Jerusalem were practically nonexistent. To complicate matters, the Soviet Union did not belong to IATA [the International Air Transport Association]. Therefore, our tickets had no value unless we waited five days and flew back to New York on Pan Am.

Our mission seemed impossible, until a young woman at Aeroflot took us by the hand and led us from airline to airline, arguing with each, until she compelled Swissair to take us. We were convinced she was Jewish, but we couldn't get anything out of her—name, family, background—except that at the last moment, she bade us farewell with a *"Shalom."*

We arrived in Israel too late to attend the funeral but in time to participate in the meeting to select Louis Pincus' successor. He was Yosef Almogi, former minister of labor and mayor of Haifa, who had a reputation for getting things done. The Agency, however, is a complex, process-oriented entity; and it was soon clear that our choice was not in the best interests of the Agency.

Fisher's involvement with UJA began in 1953, when community leadership in Detroit and UJA's chief executive, Henry Montor, persuaded him to join a fact-finding mission to Israel with fourteen other national and community leaders. In Israel, Fisher, the least experienced of the group, was elected group spokesman. After that, an experience he describes as awkward, Fisher's national career was launched as chairman of the CJF. Then he became chairman of national UJA. He is the only person to have held both positions.

Although the two entities have similar interests, they have different priorities: CJF's primary role is in domestic Jewish needs, whereas UJA's focus, through the JDC and UIA, is on overseas Jewish needs.

In December of 1966, Fisher was nominated and elected as national chair of UJA, which was then under Rabbi Herbert A. Friedman's stewardship. Because Fisher was a leader in both the Detroit Federation and the CJF, and because he had standing in industry and political affiliations, he helped bring many people into UJA leadership on a national basis, leaders who had not previously been involved. Fisher also spent a great deal of time persuading UJA and CJF professionals and leadership to work together instead of against each other. Under his stewardship, both organizations were brought closer together.

Fisher also added a very effective and influential social component to UJA life by changing our then primary mission, the Study Mission, to one for couples. [The original Study Mission was UJA's initial mission of every annual campaign. It consisted of the larger contributors in the country and was designed to set the pace of giving for each campaign. In later years it became known as the Prime Minister's Mission.] He added a stop either in London, Paris, or Rome and brought in members of the Rothschild family, who later participated in national UJA conferences in New York City.

Fisher opened the White House and the State Department for meetings of UJA leadership and brought speakers from the political hierarchy to UJA meetings in and out of Washington. But his most significant contribution, because of his roles in both CJF and UJA, was his ability to lower the decibel level of the arguments between both organizations, which allowed for a more cooperative and productive approach.

Fisher also established an excellent and productive relationship with Edward Ginsberg [chairman and president, national UJA; chairman of Cleveland Jewish Federation campaign; chairman, JDC], who was being groomed to succeed him. The two worked very closely together when Fisher became president of UJA and Ginsberg became national chairman. Their constructive continuity of leadership accelerated fund-raising and UJA's impact on the Jewish community, the Jewish Agency, and the government of Israel. Fisher was the Jewish community's diplomat; Ginsberg its principal fund-raiser.

One of Fisher's first tasks was to reorganize the United Palestine Appeal (UPA), which together with the JDC had formed the UJA. The UPA was our Zionist partner and negotiated with JDC regarding the distribution of UJA funds for its programs. The reorganization was necessary for legal reasons, since we were now dealing with the State of Israel, not an area called Palestine. It was also critical to develop a board with greater communal credibility.

Fisher and others on the UPA board—together with the leading Zionist, Dewey D. Stone, and Hadassah leaders Rose Halpern and Charlotte Jacobson—were the driving force behind the changeover. It took two years to negotiate due to historic prejudices between Zionists and non-Zionists.

Fisher comments that neither Edward Warburg nor William Rosenwald would agree to serve on the UPA board because of its Zionist membership. Their view was a holdover from their earlier years as non-Zionists. Today, such an invitation would not be rejected. During that same era, at my behest, an institute for training fund-raising professionals for UJA, federations, and Keren Hayesod was founded in Jerusalem and played a key role in orienting professionals to Israel's needs.

How does one explain Fisher's personality and his impact on Americans and Israelis, especially when the initial perception of him is often contradicted by reality?

Fisher is six feet two, with the build of the former football and basketball athlete he was at Ohio State. He is a good listener. In private conversation his voice is low, soft, and at times difficult to hear. And yet in moments of crisis or decision, he rises to the occasion and uses a strong, articulate, persuasive style and voice. The greatest contradiction of all is that for one who had no formal Jewish education and no Jewish fellowship in his youth in Salem, Fisher has been one of the twentieth century's most active proponents for Jewish education and Jewish unity.

I first met Max Fisher in the fall of 1958, when I was UJA's regional director on the West Coast and Fisher came to speak in San Francisco at the home of Ambassador Madeleine Russell, a prominent member of the Levi-Strauss family. Fisher, then, was not as adept in public speaking as he is now, and came in with his remarks written on three-by-five index cards. He asked me to arrange for a setting in which he would not have to shuffle the cards openly.

With the ambassador's help, we arranged a desk with a jade box against which he could lean his cards. His address was adequate in terms of substance and presentation, but was not yet up to his potential. But Fisher had the rare capacity to learn from his faults. Ever since his student days at Ohio State, he kept personal notes of his inadequacies and listed ways to avoid them.

His growth was evident at a 1993 meeting at Brandeis University. Over four hundred academics, students, and Boston community leaders came for a *Meet the Press*-type interview with Fisher, based on his biography, *The Quiet Diplomat*, written by historian Peter Golden. The two interviewers were Shoshana Cardin and I. We questioned him for thirty minutes and followed with questions from the audience.

Shoshana and I were determined to be credible and ask Fisher difficult, even personal, questions. I planned to ask about the accusations leveled at him in the 1970s and '80s that he was the Republican's "court Jew."

Because of the sensitivity of the question, and the open nature of the Brandeis meeting, I asked Max if I could brief him on the questions. To my overwhelming surprise he said, "No, just fire away."

Shoshana and I, like our counterparts on television, threw everything we could at him. He was consistent in his replies, never defensive—frank, open, personal in explaining his point of view and also the views of those who disagreed with him. The same pattern of question and answer continued when the moderator, Professor Bernard Reisman of Brandeis University, opened the floor to the audience. Fisher spoke for two hours without a note or document.

At the end of the two hours, despite his being the epitome of conservative republicanism, Fisher received a standing ovation from the largely liberal, overwhelmingly Democratic audience.

Through the twenty-eight years of Republican control of the White House—under Eisenhower, Nixon, Ford, Reagan, and Bush—Max Fisher had entrée to the Oval Office and the Departments of State and Defense. The scarcity of such access must be measured against the fact that the largely Democratic American Jewish community rarely had such access during the Democratic administrations. Two exceptions were Abe Feinberg during the Truman administration and Philip Klutznick during the Kennedy years. Still, neither had as much influence as Fisher did in both the Jewish community and the administration in Washington.

Fisher's influence in Republican circles is neither a birthright nor a gift. It was earned through years of hard work, by raising funds for the Republican Party and offering solid advice and guidance. Fisher was also sensitive enough not to accept prestigious cabinet and ambassadorial appointments, knowing that if he did, his opinions and advice would not have the same value. In 1996, he was Republican Party presidential candidate Bob Dole's chief fund-raiser.

Fisher's affiliation rarely, if ever, created conflicts with Jewish lay or professional leadership—and most are registered Democrats. Fisher believes it is essential for Jews to be active politically in all parties in order to assure Jewish stability. Among Fisher's significant assets are his personal and business relationships with, and access to, the captains of American industry and commerce.

Fisher believes that his ease in the non-Jewish world stems from his small-town experience. He also feels it has something to do with his interest and involvement in the oil industry—in which there are few Jews.

Through his associations to improve conditions in Detroit, Fisher met Henry Ford, and the two developed a very close relationship. Ford, who marched to the beat of his own drummer, followed the axiom, "Never complain, never explain." An intelligent, able man, he was also outspoken and direct about his beliefs and personal convictions.

Ford was only twenty-three when he took over the multimillion-dollar Ford Motor Industries complex. He held his position there for forty years. In spite of his grandfather's virulent antisemitism, Henry Ford was without prejudice. He regretted and was shamed by his grandfather's activities [printing *The Protocols of the Elders of Zion* in the *Detroit Free Press* in the 1920s]. Ford's involvement and contributions to Jewish causes and Israel, especially to the UJA, for whom he was also a spokesman, were based on his own personal values and not shaded by his family's past.

Although politically Ford was an Independent and Max was a Republican, the interests they had in common were far greater than their differences. Walter Hayes, Ford's biographer, describes this unique symbiosis:

> Both were pragmatic men who liked sitting at the fireside, considering the affairs of the day late into the night. Apart from friendship, there was another bond. Leaders of large companies and small ones, like tennis players, need walls against which to practice and see if their ideas rebound. In the larger company, it is very often difficult to bounce some ideas against working colleagues, particularly if their own futures are involved. Max Fisher was such a wall [for Ford].

The two met socially in Detroit, New York and Palm Beach and chartered a yacht together in the Mediterranean during the summer months. Fisher, nine years older than the charismatic Ford, was a father figure to him.

Ford respected Fisher's devotion to the totality of community service: the city of Detroit, politics and the national good, and the Detroit Jewish community. He admired Fisher's pride in his Jewish faith and tradition, in the people and the State of Israel, and in physical and spiritual Jerusalem. Because Ford regarded Fisher highly, he forced the restricted Detroit Club to accept Fisher. Once the barrier was broken, other Detroit Jews were invited to become members.

Fisher and Ford entered into business deals, sometimes with Al Taubman, another leader in Detroit's Jewish community.

Together, they purchased Sotheby's, the world-famous auction house. They outbid Mobil Oil for one of the largest and most valuable tracts of land in the United States—the Irvine Ranch in California.

In 1973, Israeli Finance Minister Pinhas Sapir asked Fisher to find out if Henry Ford would come to Israel to counsel the government about its fledgling automobile industry, which basically consisted of assembling compact cars. Although his advisers warned him that the Muslim world would boycott his products, Ford immediately agreed to make the trip.

The boycott went into effect while Ford was in Israel. He had disregarded his advisers by allowing his presence in Israel to be publicized. The boycott lasted fifteen years, and I will never forget what Ford told me when the news of the Arab League's boycott hit the media. Although he, like any other corporate leader, did not relish losing customers and income, he said that the real hurt was the human factor, since most Ford franchises affected by the Arab action were owned by families who had passed the franchise down from generation to generation. That bothered Ford greatly, but it did not stop him from doing what he thought was right.

Since the Fishers and Fords were spending some time together in London in 1972, Judy and I, with Max and Marjorie Fisher and Henry and Cristina Ford, flew together to Israel. Cristina had never been to Israel before, so Marjorie and my wife traveled with Cristina, touring the land and visiting institutions and programs funded by UJA.

At the same time, Ford, Fisher, and I had meetings with Pinhas Sapir and Joe Boxenbaum, who headed the automobile assembly plant. We also planned to visit the Suez Canal so that Ford could see the Bar-Lev Line protecting Israel against Egyptian attack.

Ford's assessment of Israel's attempts to build automobiles was straight and direct. He told them that it was a waste of labor and capital to begin an automobile industry because Israel could purchase the same cars overseas for less than they would cost to manufacture. Since Israel had virtually no railroad and was dependent on trucking, Ford advised the Israelis to invest in assembling trucks and buses.

Sapir listened carefully; agreed; and, as only Sapir could, then asked Ford if he would provide consultants. Ford, to his credit, didn't hesitate and replied, "Yes, I can." Sapir, without batting an eye, asked, "When?" Ford, enjoying the encounter, answered, "In two weeks." They shook hands, and in two weeks Ford's people were in Israel.

The next morning, Ford, Fisher, and I traveled to the Suez Canal by helicopter accompanied by an army spokesman; my twenty-year-old son, Bob, [who was spending a year on Kibbutz Yifat]; and Walter Hayes, Ford's biographer and the public relations director for the Ford Motor Company in Europe.

Although Fisher and I had often been to the Suez Canal, it was exciting for us to experience the event through Henry Ford's eyes and reactions. We were all standing, moving around to see as much as possible of Israel and the Negev, when suddenly the helicopter lurched sharply to the right and then to the left, with both the young pilot and Ford shouting simultaneously, "Seat belts! Seat belts!" We quickly belted ourselves in. The helicopter seemed to be doing its best to turn over while we, with bated breath, were silent, trying to be brave, I holding my son's hand tightly. We sighed with relief when the helicopter slowly settled in the sand—and evacuated as quickly as possible.

The pilot showed us the problem—a large piece at the end of one of the rotor blades had broken off, throwing the rotor out of sync. We shook his hands warmly, hugged him and slapped him on the back, because his skill had saved our lives. We didn't think about the alternative.

After a few moments, Fisher wandered into the desert. Alarmed, I asked him where he was going. Ford replied, "Don't bother him, he's looking for oil." And of course we all broke up laughing, melting away our tension.

As the pilot was bringing the helicopter down, he or his copilot had radioed "May Day, May Day," and when we set down we could see planes flying over us. We were told that another helicopter was on the way. It was very hot in the desert, and our pilot took off his helmet. We could see he was wearing a *kippah* [yarmulke]. When the other helicopter came for us, Ford called me aside and said, "Irving, I have done everything you and Max asked of me. I have never complained when things went wrong. Now I want you to do me a favor—ask the other pilot with the new helicopter to take off his helmet."

Since I didn't want to do that personally, I went to the army spokesman and repeated Ford's request. Reluctant at first, after I insisted, he did so. The pilot took off his helmet. His head was bare. Then Ford came to me and said, "Irving, you know that I know what a yarmulke is, as I have been in more synagogues and temples than I can even remember. But I am not flying with the new pilot, only with the one who saved our lives, as it just may be that he has a straighter line to God."

Back I went to our spokesman with this new request. He rightfully said, "Helicopters are not like cars—pilots are assigned and I can't make the change here. We have to call headquarters." So, through our helicopter's radio, through Bir Gafgafa, the former Egyptian airfield in the Negev, we got through to the *Kirya* [HQ] in Tel Aviv. Luckily, Ezer Weizman, now President of Israel and then commander of the air force, was there. When he first heard my voice, he was angry beyond words, since I had no right to be on a military channel. But when I told him the story, he exploded with laughter, forgave all my sins, and approved the transfer of planes and pilots.

Off we went to the Canal in the new helicopter with our old pilot [he was twenty]. Behind us, we left the damaged helicopter and the forlorn pilot who had come to rescue us.

There were formal receptions to attend, which Ford enjoyed, particularly since the discussions at those events were very informal, personal, and humorous. The most memorable of all was one with David Ben-Gurion. He had come all the way from Sde Boker to his house in Tel Aviv to pay tribute to Ford. It was a very moving experience, and best described by Walter Hayes:

> The one encounter that has remained in my mind, and has come back to me with an almost immediate presence many times in later years, was our meeting with David Ben-Gurion in the house he built in 1913 in Tel Aviv and later gave to the state. His hands were crippled, but his eyes had not lost their twinkle. The house was one vast library—with one room full of books on the Greeks and others filled with shelves of Russian and Chinese texts. He could read in eleven languages.

He talked, as we wanted him to, about the creation of the Jewish State and predicted that at least five million more immigrants would come. He was alert to current events—but feared the next war would be about oil and that Israel's fight for survival would last for generations. Old age does or does not always bring serenity, but it evidently had for this white-haired prophet in sandals and open-necked shirt. He had no regrets about the past and no impatience with the future. Hadn't the Jews waited centuries to return to their land? Why expect a less patient tomorrow?

The meeting with Ben-Gurion ended on a humorous note when Ben-Gurion, after praising President Nixon for opening the doors to China, said, "I told that other fellow in the White House years ago that he should have done it then." Fisher and I mentioned names of Presidents, trying to identify "that fellow" in the White House while Ben-Gurion continued to shake his head saying, "No, no, no—that other fellow," until Ford came to the rescue with "Eisenhower," and Ben-Gurion smiled and shook Ford's hand.

One year later, Fisher and I were in Israel for meetings with the Jewish Agency. As I usually did, I called Moshe Dayan for a meeting to brief the two of us on Israel's military, geopolitical, and strategic situation. "Strange," he said, "I was just on the phone trying to reach you. I have to see you."

We set up a time for the next day because Max and I were scheduled to return to New York the following night. We met Dayan in a booth at the Casbah, his favorite restaurant, where Dayan asked Fisher if he could get a message directly to President Nixon without going through Kissinger and could he do it quickly? Fisher said he believed he could.

Dayan told us that in his opinion there was only one way to avoid war with Egypt, and that was for Israel voluntarily to withdraw to a point several miles from the Suez Canal, on condition that Egypt would cultivate the land with farmers, not soldiers. Dayan's theory was that if Egypt developed the land with productive villages, homes, schools, farms, and agricultural growth, Egypt would never invade, because it would be self-destructive. We asked if Golda Meir [then Prime Minister] was aware of his proposal. Dayan did not believe Golda would favor it but felt that if it had Nixon's support, it had a chance of being accepted by both Egypt and Israel.

Instead of leaving for New York, Max and I flew to Athens to see Henry J. Tasca, the American ambassador to Greece and Fisher's personal friend, who would send the message so that it would go directly to Nixon and bypass the State Department.

The next morning, Fisher and I set off for New York. On our arrival, to our consternation, we read in *The New York Times* that Golda had heard about the concept Dayan was floating [she was not aware of Dayan's meeting with us or of Max's effort to get the message to Nixon]. She ridiculed the idea and refused even to consider it. The end result? Nixon shelved it.

Fisher's role in Israel has been and continues to be multi-dimensional. He was an early investor in petrochemicals, oil, and energy development. He was called to chair and launch Operation Independence, the ambitious project to increase investment in Israel. He is still politically involved as an interpreter between Washington and Jerusalem.

Each new Israeli Prime Minister at first questioned Fisher's role in Washington and in the American Jewish community, but all soon learned that Fisher had no other motive than to maintain the integrity of the Israeli-American relationship. They realized that he played a significant role in Washington on Israel's behalf during the tenure of Republican Presidents.

Golda Meir wrote him this letter on December 19, 1967.

> Dear Max,
>
> I am writing to you [because you are] one of Israel's proven friends. I am sure you understand we are going through difficult days, attempting to carry on in the face of the enormity that surrounds us. If it were possible for you to come to Jerusalem, I would be delighted to receive you in person and tell you in detail the problems facing our people. Since that may not be feasible and time is urgent, I would send you my personal emissaries with confidential material. I know you will listen to them as [though] you were listening to me.

The emissaries brought information about the Soviet Union shipping military supplies to Egypt. Golda knew Fisher would share it with the White House.

Since 1970, Fisher has played a unique role in preserving the unity of the Jewish Agency. He made sure that its Zionist and fund-raising partners would work together on the historic rescue and absorption of threatened and troubled Jews from the former Soviet Union, Ethiopia, and Syria.

This effort to preserve unity, and to keep important Diaspora leaders involved, has not been an easy task. Despite the fact that both Max Fisher and Louis Pincus invited Diaspora leadership, the alliance has been an uneasy one because of fundamental differences between the two groups.

The problems stem from the structural differences and constituencies in the political systems of the two countries. For the Diaspora community and campaign representatives, it is incomprehensible that Zionist bodies are linked to political parties in Israel. Americans in particular think that the Zionists who follow an Israel party line lack the ability to make independent decisions. The Zionists are not happy about this. In this perennial dispute, Fisher is the ameliorating and unifying force. His persona epitomizes the problem and the solution, and he continues to be the most important factor that has kept both sides together—even though three Diaspora leaders have succeeded him as chairman of the board of governors of the Jewish Agency.

His point is that although many community leaders do not belong to Zionist organizations, they may well be Zionists anyway. Fisher says he and his colleagues are lovers of Israel no less than the organized Zionists, but they do not want to belong to Zionist entities because of those entities' political affiliations in Israel. Fisher calls himself a "new Zionist," as do many of his followers. Although it has created greater understanding between the two groups, regrettably this concept has not been developed beyond Fisher's personal philosophical voice.

Fisher's credo was, and is, that the Diaspora needs a strong Israel and Israel needs a strong Diaspora. This expression of interdependence is rooted in the unity of the Jewish people. In this sense Fisher is a true ideological Zionist. His overarching reality is "The House of Israel," the title of one of his better speeches, delivered in the Chagall Hall of the Knesset at the end of a Jewish Agency assembly. Fisher never believed there were inherent differences and conflict between Zionists and fund-raisers—or between local and overseas needs. To him, they were one and the same.

In 1973, some members of the Conference of Presidents of Major American Jewish Organizations accused Fisher of being a "court Jew" in the Republican administrations. [They believed he followed the leaders of the Republicans and did as they asked; that he was being advised instead of being the advisor.] This accusation was one of the most significant factors in Fisher's growth and his being accepted as a world Jewish leader.

He points out that there was never an "open White House" for the Presidents' Conference in either Democratic or Republican administrations. Although occasional meetings were held, it was usually when they served the administration's purpose. Fisher was the first American Jewish leader, Democrat or Republican, who was able to arrange such meetings when it was deemed essential by the Presidents' Conference to express the will of the Jewish community, whether the administration in office liked the timing or not.

The whispered charges of "court Jew" came from those conference members who suffered wounded pride and did not want to depend on Fisher because they were suspicious of his Republican affiliations. They wanted the Presidents' Conference to schedule such meetings through its own power, right, and will. No matter how laudable their aspirations, the reality of the political situation was that Republican administrations depended on Fisher as their liaison to the Jewish community. It was Fisher who influenced Nixon to invite the Presidents' Conference members to the White House for a meeting. Now U.S. Presidents invite them on a regular basis.

The negative voices, however, were not stilled. The accusations were made to personnel at the Israeli Embassy, from where they were passed to Ambassador Yitzhak Rabin. Since I knew from long and intimate experience that the charges were baseless and counterproductive, I called Rabin and asked for a private meeting with him, Deputy Ambassador Shlomo Argov, Fisher, and Edward Ginsberg [then president of UJA and its former chairman].

Rabin, being the direct person he was, immediately agreed because he was already dealing with both the Republican administration and Fisher. The meeting was scheduled for 5:30 P.M. in a private room at the Madison Hotel in Washington.

I knew that if the charges were allowed to fester, it would be detrimental to UJA and Jerusalem-Washington relations. After some preliminary and unrelated discussion, I began the meeting, raised the issue of the accusations, and said that if left unresolved, the accusation could undermine the embassy and Israel's efforts. Argov, later Israel's ambassador to London who was shot in the head by the Arab-sponsored terrorist Carlos, spoke for the embassy. [To this day, Argov remains alive in Hadassah Hospital.]

Then Ginsberg explained that although most Jews were Democrats and not Republicans, the American Jewish community had almost never had an important Jewish leader who could see the President or the Secretary of State at any time to discuss American Jewish domestic interests and Israel's interests. He said that Fisher was a rare phenomenon, and nothing should be done to weaken that unique resource.

Rabin and Fisher sat silently and listened. When Ginsberg finished, Rabin said that we hadn't heard from Max and that he would like to hear from him. Fisher hesitated, then spoke quietly, first of the tiny Jewish community in Salem and his own limited Jewish education. Then he explained how long it had taken him to gain a foothold at the highest levels of the Republican Party, and how he had turned down honors and appointments so that he wouldn't lose access to those in power in Washington. He spoke of his involvement in Jewish life in Detroit, beginning in 1950. He spoke about his devotion to UJA and the CJF, his interests and involvement in Israel—both through investment and philanthropy—and his leadership in the Jewish Agency.

How, he asked, could he be a "court Jew"? How, he asked, could his concern not be for the best interests of the American Jewish community and Israel? Hadn't he opened the White House doors to the Presidents' Conference—after they had been closed for so long? Was it wrong if the White House wanted him to be the intermediary with other Jewish organizations? He had the trust of Washington officialdom. Didn't that strengthen his role on behalf of Jews everywhere? If he was a court Jew, how could he retain their confidence?

The room was silent. Rabin said, "I believe Max. The meeting is over." We all shook hands. Rabin and Max left together—friends and allies to the end.

It is fortunate for American-Israeli relations and Israeli-American Jewish relations that Fisher has always had an intimate relationship with Rabin's successor, Shimon Peres. Beyond their knowledge of each through Fisher's leadership of UJA, CJF, and the Jewish Agency board of governors, they also worked closely together on the Washington-Jerusalem political relationship when Peres was defense minister, foreign minister, and prime minister.

It was Shimon Peres who asked Fisher to head Operation Independence, the project to bring economic investments to Israel. It was a mark of the respect both men had for each other that Peres asked Fisher, and Fisher accepted the challenge. Fisher enlisted the leadership of the American and Canadian Jewish communities [Charles Bronfman in Canada, Morton Mandel of Cleveland, and Harvey Krueger of New York City] and most of the major Jewish organizations. Thus, he stimulated an unprecedented surge of investment in Israel by creating business relationships between the Diaspora and Israel.

The relationship between the two men is best summed up by the tribute Peres wrote for Peter Golden's biography of Fisher, *The Quiet Diplomat*. "The establishment of the State of Israel was an unprecedented event. Similar in magnitude to this event were the people who precipitated Israel's renaissance. Max Fisher is one of these unique people. Without his vision, many things we take for granted would not exist."

Fisher is proud that his entire family is involved in UJA/Federation and Israel. He knows that despite the success of UJA's Young Leadership program, too many of the sons and daughters of leaders opted for secular outlets. His daughter Jane is a long-term member of the Jewish Agency and the UJA and has chaired several programs. His son, Philip, and daughters Julie and Margie and their husbands are all active in their local communities.

His pride and pain concerning his daughter Mary is rarely mentioned publicly because Fisher is a very private person. Mary spent many years in Israel. She is a creative artist. After she had her second child, she learned that she had been infected with the AIDS virus by her ex-husband. Fisher went public about Mary, and persuaded the Republican Party to let her speak at the Republican National Convention in 1992. She spoke with such eloquence and directness that editorials all over America, including one in *The New*

York Times, praised her and thanked her for the message that alerted and educated all Americans. It may very well be one of the factors that keeps Fisher so busy building and saving lives when he is old enough to have earned the right to sit back and relax and let his deeds and followers speak for him.

In 1987, at the young age of seventy, Henry Ford died of Legionnaire's Disease. His sudden and unexpected death was a deeply personal loss for Fisher, who couldn't help him this time. Ford's death also meant the loss of a loyal friend and generous supporter of UJA and of the people and State of Israel. Fisher himself remains continually active in UJA.

Irving and Judy
Bernstein.

Henry Montor, the first professional director of National UJA
(1939–50) and Bernstein greet each other in
Jerusalem in the 1970s.

In 1961, when Bernstein returned to New York from Los Angeles, Kirk Douglas presented him with this photo, signed in Hebrew.

(l-r) Danny Kaye, Gen. Ahron "Arele" Yariv, and Bernstein, guest speakers at a major Los Angeles event during the Yom Kippur War in 1973. Yariv was head of Israeli Military Intelligence.

(l-r) As Jerusalem Mayor, Teddy Kollek was instrumental in bringing great artists to Israel, including Leonard Bernstein and Isaac Stern.

Golda Meir embraces Bernstein after a very emotional speech at the This Year in Jerusalem mission in 1977.

Chairman Frank Lautenberg and Bernstein greet Golda Meir as she arrives at the Jerusalem Hilton. They burst into laughter when the prime minister mistakenly kissed a man next to them, who turned out to be a Christian tourist from Wichita, KS.

Menachem Begin, Judy and Irving Bernstein in the prime minister's office during a UJA Study Mission in 1981.

Judy Bernstein greeting Ethiopian immigrants who arrived in Israel via Operation Moses, 1984.

(l-r) David Ben-Gurion, Paul Zuckerman (UJA Chairman), Golda
Meir and Bernstein waiting to enter the auditorium at the This
Year In Jerusalem Mission in 1977. It was the first time the two
former prime ministers had spoken to each other since a
political falling out in 1965.

(l-r) Sylvia Hassenfeld (Women's Division chair), Elie Wiesel,
Golda Meir, Bernstein, and Frank Lautenberg (UJA Chairman) at
a National UJA Conference in New York, 1977.

(l-r) Former chairmen Max Fisher, and Eddie Ginsberg, and
executive vice chairman Bernstein greet incoming 1971 chairman,
Paul Zuckerman.

(l-r) Max Fisher, Henry Ford, and Bernstein at
the Suez Canal, 1972.

(l-r) Bernstein, his son Bob, Henry Ford, Max Fisher, and their Israeli army escort wait for a rescue helicopter after their forced landing in the desert, 1972.

(l-r) Irwin Field and Max Fisher present Henry Ford with an award for distinguished leadership in New York, 1978.

An intimate moment that defined the relationship between
Prime Minister Shimon Peres and Max Fisher, 1984.

Sylvia Hassenfeld and President George Bush in the Oval Office
on the 75th anniversary of the Joint Distribution Committee, 1989.

Israeli Finance Minister Pinchas Sapir and Bernstein, 1972.

Bernstein and Prime Minister Yitzhak Rabin covering their heads
with napkins at a UJA event in the Chagakk Hall of the Knesset,
1976. There were no *kippots* on the tables.

(l-r) Irving Bernstein, Yeshiva University president Dr. Norman Lamm, and Prime Minister Shimon Peres, on the day they received their honorary doctorates from YU, 1987.

The Bernstein Family, 1995.

Bernstein and one of the leaders he groomed, UJA/Federation, New York vice president emeritus Ernest Michel.

Bernstein accompanies Michel on a visit to Auschwitz in 1983. Sitting on the railroad tracks, they gather strength to enter the camp for Michel's first return since The Liberation.

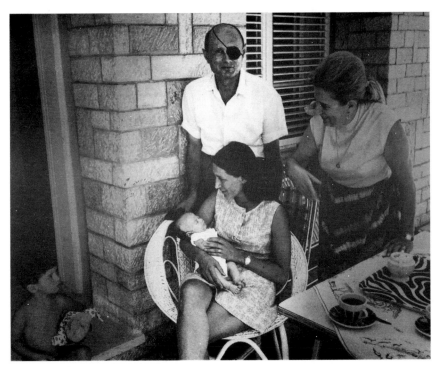

Moshe Dayan, his first wife Ruth, their daughter Yael, and her children in the famous garden in Zahalah.

Bernstein and Dayan share a private moment, 1979.

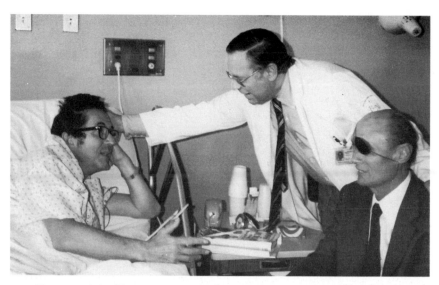

Dayan visits Bernstein at Beth Israel Hospital in New York after his heart attack in 1978. The doctor is Bernard Weiss.

Yael Dayan, war correspondent, with Moshe Dayan, minister of defense, during the Yom Kippur War, 1973.

Elie Wiesel and Irving Bernstein at UJA's National Conference in New York City, 1975.

On the *bimah* of the Chorale Synagogue in Moscow with Elie Wiesel and Frank Lautenberg in 1979 during a study mission for the U.S. Holocaust Commission.

Marvin Lender, chairman of Operation Exodus, greeting the first Jewish immigrants from the former Soviet Union in Israel, 1990.

(l-r) Bernstein, Max Fisher and Prof. Bernard Reisman at the dedication of the Fisher-Bernstein Institute for Leadership Development in Jewish Philanthropy at Brandeis University, 1997. Prof. Reisman is the Institute's director.

12

THE WOMEN'S DIVISION: SYLVIA HASSENFELD

B orn in Philadelphia, Sylvia Hassenfeld has long been active in Jewish affairs and philanthropic causes and has had forty years of leadership experience in international communal service. She is the immediate past chairman of JDC and served as its first woman president from 1988 to 1992. The liberalization policies in Eastern Europe coincided with her presidency. Her skillful diplomacy with heads of state, government officials, and leaders of non-governmental organizations in the former Soviet Union and its dependents contributed to the protection of Jewish civil and religious rights in those lands, as well as the provision of social services to Jews in need.

In October of 1989, in honor of JDC's seventy-fifth anniversary year, Sylvia Hassenfeld led a special JDC leadership mission to Israel, Eastern Europe, and the former Soviet Union. This mission focused on an assessment of needs and strategic planning for JDC's current efforts on behalf of Soviet Jews. She has made many return visits to Poland, Romania, Czechoslovakia, Yugoslavia, and Hungary, and a first visit to Bulgaria to determine JDC's ongoing programs in central and Eastern Europe in the aftermath of revolution.

Hassenfeld was the first member of JDC to visit India, where she traveled to meet with the Jewish communities of Bombay, New Delhi, and Cochin. There followed many visits to Morocco, Tunisia, and the island of Djerba to visit the Jewish communities in North Africa.

Hassenfeld was a national vice chairman of the UJA and serves on the board of the UIA. She served for many years on the Board of Governors of the Jewish Agency and chaired that board's Committee for Rural Settlement.

Sylvia Hassenfeld's commitment to the improvement of the human condition spans a broad range of national and international philanthropic and voluntary activities outside Jewish communal life.

She serves on the Board of Trustees of the New York University Medical Center; the Hasbro Children's Foundation; the Appeal of Conscience Foundation; and is an associate member of the Board of Trustees of the Paul Nitze School of Advanced International Studies at Johns Hopkins University. President Reagan appointed her to the U.S. Holocaust Memorial Council.

In the world of commerce, Sylvia Hassenfeld serves on the Board of Directors of Hasbro, Inc. and as chairman of its nominating committee.

Her honors include the Emma Lazarus Award for "contributions to improving the human condition," awarded by the American Jewish Historical Society; honorary citizen of Jerusalem; and the Gold Medal Award from the Israel Bond Association. In May 1997, she was inducted into the Rhode Island Heritage Hall of Fame.

Interview by Irving Bernstein
August 1995

Q: You and your husband, Merrill, were UJA's first husband and wife to serve as national chairs. How did it happen?

A: I became involved because Merrill was involved. At that point in time it seemed to be the organization with the greatest need, so it was never a matter of competition between us. The Women's Division and the Men's Division were much more separated than today, so he went along with the men and I with the women.

Q: Way back in Henry Montor's days—1939, 1940, and 1941—the Women's Division was considered supplemental giving. But today it seems to be that women's giving in many ways equals men's giving, sometimes even surpasses it. How did that develop, and do you think that trend will continue?

A: Originally women didn't think of giving. Their husbands gave for both of them. Women's giving started at a low level. We went to every woman who had any kind of capacity to give, and whatever she gave was acceptable. It was indeed supplemental giving. Women later began to take on different roles in society, and as they became educated and aware of the need, it was natural that their giving would be more commensurate with their ability to give, unrelated to what their husbands did. Women wanted to give as individuals.

Q: The Women's Division created the Lion of Judah concept with its various levels of giving. [The Lion of Judah program offers a piece of special jewelry to all the donors who reach a certain level of giving.] If I'm not mistaken, it happened during your tenure. How did it turn into such a badge of pride among American Jewish women?

A: Irving, I can't take any credit for the Lion of Judah. As a matter of fact, I was against it. I didn't feel that women needed to have a token for their giving. The concept came from a group of women in Miami who realized that there could be a bonding between women who wore this pin. It was not a concept they initially cared to share.

I remember long discussions at the national Women's Division board before we were willing to accept the fact that it creates a common feeling and recognition among women who wear the Lion of Judah pin. They know they have a common bond, and it is incredible. As I said, I laughed at it at first, because four or five of us on the national board thought it was quite horrendous to have some thank-you token. We were certainly proven wrong. It's been most wonderful and most successful. The minimum level of giving to earn the right to wear the Lion of Judah is $5,000, and then it rises to various levels as different stones are added—$10,000 for a ruby, $18,000 for a sapphire, $25,000 for an emerald, and $50,000 for gold and diamonds.

Today there are seven thousand women wearing the Lion of Judah. At the last Lion of Judah Conference in 1993, eleven hundred women attended and contributed $16 million. We anticipate that at the next conference even more will be raised. Furthermore, in the Lion of Judah Endowment Program (LOJE)—started nineteen months ago— three hundred women have pledged $55 million to ensure their levels of giving for the future, no matter what may happen to them.

Q: Even I had questions in the beginning as to whether it would be widely accepted.

A: It could have been dismissed as another gimmick. We could not have been more wrong. It has really been a catalyst and has driven the Women's Division to greater heights of fund-raising.

Q: Women do wear it, everywhere.

A: I walk into a room, and I will see women wearing it who walk over and talk to one another because they have this pin in common.

Q: Men don't have anything like that.

A: You asked me earlier if I thought the Women's Division provides supplemental giving. Not anymore. Now it is meaningful giving. I think that women, in many cases, may have more time and have become more immersed in their communities and more knowledgeable generally. I think that women are less susceptible to peer pressure than men are. I think many men know little but give much. I think that most women don't give much unless they know more.

Q: I have always said that when you walk into a men's meeting and bring up a problem, they say, "Don't tell us the details; give us the bottom line." To the women's credit, they begin at A and end at Z, and once they come to an agreement, they will follow through, while the men with their bottom-line talk may not completely follow through. As the national chair of the Women's Division, you served both on the UJA board and the executive committee. Did you in any way find it difficult to express yourself and influence direction at these meetings since the great majority of the members were male?

A: I didn't find it difficult to express an opinion, but I'm not sure I was able to influence opinion. In those days the men were much more chauvinistic than they are today, but to express an opinion? I was never hesitant.

Q: You had a wide influence because of your internal strength, courage, and integrity. You never failed to speak up on an issue you believed in. You and some of the women who preceded you— for example, Elaine Winik of New York—went on to play greater roles in the organized Jewish community. You became chair and then president of JDC, the first woman to serve in that role. Yet at the UJA, I failed in my effort to have you elected as national UJA chair. It wasn't because the men didn't respect you— they just believed it wasn't the role for a woman to play. Is UJA different than other organizations? Have times changed for women?

A: Yes, UJA is different, because it's fund-raising. You must remember that JDC is not a fund-raising organization. And you know better than I do, Irving, that it was not easy for me to become chair of the JDC. There were those who did not think that a woman could chair a national organization composed of many men. I think also there is a time lapse of perhaps ten or twelve years, when women were not accepted because the men did not feel a woman could go out and solicit large gifts. Today, I'm not sure that's the case. But I wouldn't want to see a woman be chair just because she is a woman. It would have to be someone who earned it and somebody who could handle it.

Q: Can you describe your relationship with the professionals during your tenure at UJA and at JDC? Were you treated any differently than the UJA general chairman and the JDC chairmen who preceded and followed you?

A: At JDC, absolutely not. I really had a perfectly wonderful relationship with the executive director and I never, at any moment, felt that I was being mistreated in any way.

Q: And then at the UJA?

A: I didn't have that kind of a leadership role in the UJA, although I did with the professional women who were the executives of the Women's Division. I did enjoy working with Eve Weiss, who was Women's Division executive chairman at that time. She was a great partner.

Q: As you grew up in Philadelphia's main line, was your family involved in Jewish communal life? Did you have any role models to connect you to UJA?

A: Not really. I think I never really had a role model until I married Merrill—and Merrill and his father were my role models. They were so deeply immersed. Don't forget this was during the Holocaust. It became all consuming.

Q: Did you find that coming from Providence, Rhode Island, was a handicap? You came from a relatively small community, and most leadership stems from the twenty or so larger communities in the United States.

A: As a matter of fact, I think it was easier. Because I came from a small community, I was able to rise in that community and deal effectively with leaders. I was invited to speak on the national board and there everybody is equal—it's just a matter of asserting yourself.

Q: From your own experience, how do you see the role of the UJA Women's Division today, and how would you envision it in the years to come?

A: That's a difficult question, Irving. To say this without denigrating any other division, I think Women's Division probably is more steadfast, concerned, and more knowledgeable than other groups. I think the whole business of projected change in the national structure could affect the whole dimension of Women's Division. It worries me very much.

Q: This is just a digression, but I am concerned. I think leadership may be headed toward disaster for UJA and for Israel. I have been in touch with many of our leaders. I don't think they realize the consequences to fund-raising if the fund-raising campaign ever loses its independence.

A: They are opening a Pandora's Box by not knowing where they want to go. It is vital that UJA and Federation work together but that each maintains a separate identity. They aren't aware of what it would do and it really frightens me. I think that Women's Division is still as strong as it is because they still are not questioning our structure. This kind of self-doubt harms the campaign. I also believe our women have been very fortunate in having superb leadership over the years. I really do.

Q: You have been to Israel countless times, on missions, with your family, with friends, and by yourself. What were some of the more dramatic moments? Could you say something about the perception of the Israeli leadership toward the Women's Division?

A: I was head of Women's Division from 1976 to 1978. I think probably one of the highlights was the "This Year in Jerusalem Mission." Frank Lautenberg was chairman, and you were the chief executive. It affected everyone who was there. I remember marching in Jerusalem, and the emotional response of all the Israelis. It was the first time they realized there was a kinship—that we didn't just come as benefactors—that everyone was with them and that we were all one.

During Elaine Winik's tenure as national chairman, the Yom Kippur War began [1973]. Some of us were eager to go, but there was no way anyone would give us clearance—you, Irving, were the culprit. Like good soldiers, we listened and remained in the United States. But we were on the first plane to Israel the day the war was over. I remember the emptiness in the King David Hotel. The lobby was empty. All the guests were on one floor. The first question the Israelis asked was, "Where were you during the war? Nobody came." We felt so guilty.

On that trip, my memories of Tel Hashomer Hospital are most vivid. It was a horrible sight—ward after ward of young soldiers, all burn victims—and their parents, helplessly watching, patiently waiting. Seeing them tore us apart.

Many years later, during the Persian Gulf War, when I was president of JDC, I didn't wait. I went when the people had to wear gas masks, and Iraqi SCUDS were targeted at Israel. I was the only woman on an El Al flight filled mainly with returning Israelis and Hasidim from the United States. I sat on the upper deck with Isaac Stern. He was going to perform with Zubin Mehta, helping in his way to relieve the tensions in the country. I was going to see what JDC could do to help. I refused to wait or to question—I went, and I went alone.

Q: It is to your credit that you flew over at that frightening time to be in Israel. I was also there. I was the only one on the sixteenth floor of the Sheraton Plaza in Jerusalem and it was the first time I was issued a gas mask since I served overseas in World War II.

A: I remember Israel in the days of the *Ma'abarot* [the transit camps]. I remember the Moroccans and Yemenites coming, and the questioning, "Should these 'different' Jews from various countries be placed in settlements with the Eastern European Jews, or should they be segregated?" There were visits with Cochini Jews from India. It was UJA that brought them, and it was UJA that cared for them. I remember Israel in the days of food rationing. I visited the bomb shelters at every settlement and at every school. I was there when bus bombings killed many children; there were so many tragedies. It was a different time with different priorities. How far we have come! How much we did!

A few years later, Irving, as a member of the board of governors of the Jewish Agency, I was chairman of a settlement department of the Agency, and I traveled the length and breadth of the country, visiting the agricultural settlements—the successful ones and the unsuccessful ones. I learned about soil and water and quotas and bank loans. It was so fundamental, but it gave me a picture of the country. I was under the tutelage of Ra'anan Weitz, a world-renowned expert in agriculture, a Sabra [native-born Israeli], a decent, knowledgeable, and caring man who taught me so much, a true hero of Israel.

Q: Do you recall how much the Women's Division raised during your tenure?

A: I think it was $90 million, because I remember that everyone felt we had accomplished the impossible.

Q: Do you recall what they are raising now?

A: Their last campaign raised $130 million. I don't think that in those days we had many women giving $100,000 and over, and today there are a large number of women who give that and more: the Palm Beach luncheon alone raises $9 million.

Q: It is a magnificent tribute to the women.

A: They really stayed with it and it's interesting. They brought along a lot of young people. You see many young women wearing the Lion of Judah today.

Q: You and Merrill developed very close relationships with many Israeli leaders, among them Teddy Kollek and Yigael Yadin. I think you were closest to them. How would you describe them? Did they understand the Women's Division?

A: I don't think they understood it at all. Yigael was not a person who thought in terms of money; he was an academic. Teddy, as you know, didn't think about the Women's Division. Teddy thought only about Jerusalem. And thank God he was there at that time, because he did wonderful things nobody else could have done. Yet both men were aware of the Women's Division and respected both our active involvement with Israel and our leadership.

Yigael's wife, Carmela, was a good friend. Their only daughter, Orly, was married at our home in Providence when Yigael was on sabbatical at Brown University. The airport in Providence was closed for a few hours on the day of the wedding. The Ebans, Dinitzes, Dayans—they all came. These were special friendships for me. Carmela's father was Arthur Ruppin, a pioneer of Israel, and the family was interrelated with the Dayans, the Weizmanns, and the Dinsteins. We also became friends with the Herzogs when he was the ambassador to the United Nations. I would also list among my friends President Katzir, as well as the late Yigal Allon and his wife. I spent many pleasant days with them on their kibbutz.

Q: Did you find a willingness on the part of most Israelis to relate to you on issues and programs in the same manner in which they dealt with our male leadership?

A: I can remember meeting with Katzir a number of times. These were my friends, so I could call and talk on a one-to-one level. I never had a problem. The same thing was true of Rabin when he was prime minister. No difficulty at all.

Q: There have been many Hassenfeld contributions to Israel, some of them very dramatic. I know, from my own experience and from what people tell me, about the magnificent Sultan's Pool in Jerusalem. It obviously took a major commitment from you and your family. How did it begin, and what does it mean to you today?

A: It means a great deal. It is probably one of the gifts that have given us the most joy. We wanted to do something in Merrill's memory. Steven, Alan, and I went back and forth to Israel many times, and finally we spoke to Teddy. He drove us around Jerusalem, pointing out what was needed, and then he mentioned the amphitheater. It clicked with us immediately, and we're very proud of it. The opening event of Jerusalem 3000 was held at the amphitheater with the Berlin Symphony Orchestra led by Daniel Barenboim.

Q: It took a lot of imagination on your part and the family's part, because most of us didn't think it would turn out that way.

A: We were able to envision it. Teddy is a great salesman and he was enthused about it, very excited, and his enthusiasm generated enthusiasm in us. Steven, Alan, and I knew Jerusalem well, and we believed it would become a major cultural center.

Q: If you had it within you to change the past at UJA, especially in the Women's Division, what would you do?

A: In the Women's Division, nothing. They really did do a fine job. I don't think you could do a better job. I think that we have had chairmen who were stronger than others, but I think everyone has done well. I would not in any way change the Women's Division.

Q: Would you say that the Women's Division has more of a democratic process and involves more leadership in their decisions than men do?

A: Very much so.

Q: Your Israel relationship has developed far beyond just Israel-American Jewish relations. Besides UJA and JDC, you have been involved in a broader field. If I'm not mistaken, you were the chair of the Washington Institute for Near East Policy directed by Martin

Indyk, who is now the American ambassador to Israel.

A: I wasn't chairman. I'm on the board of the Washington Institute and very much enjoy dealing with the major issues of the day. I have full opportunity to express my opinions.

Q: Didn't you chair a session in Palm Beach? How were you chosen for that board? Are there many women on that board?

A: Yes, there were others. When Larry and Barbie Weinberg of Los Angeles became involved in the America-Israel Public Affairs Committee (AIPAC), they founded the Washington Institute.

Q: Did you have a close relationship with Martin Indyk ?

A: When I was in Israel in June, I had dinner with him. We respect each other and we relate well. I believe he will be one of our country's best ambassadors to Israel and that he is a friend of American Jewry.

Q: Of all the personalities you met on the American scene, who are those you will always remember? Were there people who inspired you? Were there people who supported you?

A: I think Bill Rosenwald was always a hero to me and to everyone. Being able to see what he did and was able to do, how much of himself he gave, was certainly very exciting. On the American scene there were you, Herb Friedman, and of course Mathilda Brailove—who was in a class by herself. I never knew Adele Rosenwald, but Mathilda was very gifted and devoted. I think she really was the goad for many of us. She was the Pied Piper for the Women's Division for a number of years, and she never received the national recognition or acclaim that she should have gotten. She was outstanding.

Q: She was certainly beloved.

A: More than that, she was articulate and tremendously capable, very committed, and knowledgeable. Sarah Goodman [of

Indianapolis] was wonderful as well. She was a wonderful woman. A new generation comes along, and people forget the old names. It happens to all of us.

Q: Is there anything you would have done differently in the Women's Division as you look back? Is there anything you would have done that you didn't do?

A: Not in Women's Division. You said before that you would have liked to see me as the national chairman. I think perhaps I didn't care enough. I think if I had wanted it more, if I had been willing to really go after it and fight for it, I might have been able to do it. I think it's true. I didn't have that driving ambition. It would have been nice, but I didn't have great ambition, because almost anything else I wanted I got in the course of community life. As you may know, Irwin Field and Irving Kessler asked me to be executive vice chairman of UIA when Irwin was completing his term of office. I didn't want it, and I was the one who recommended Henry Taub, who was elected. I am proud of that—since Henry represents the best in American Jewish life.

Q: You traveled on behalf of Women's Division and JDC to practically every corner of the world. You may be the most traveled organizational woman in America and the world. Would you comment on some of the more dramatic experiences?

A: Certainly. There was that first trip to Auschwitz. No matter how many years, no matter how much time, no matter what else I would ever do, nothing would quite erase that first trip to Poland. It was the first women's mission to Poland. That was during my leadership. Then we went to Israel, and of course the contrast between death and renewal of life was deeply moving, dramatic, and unforgettable. Everyone, Jew and non-Jew, should make that same visit, Auschwitz to Jerusalem. If they did, there would be no hatred and discrimination in the world.

And how could I forget my visit to Romania, when I walked the streets with Rabbi Moshe Rosen. (We knew that everything that he had was bugged—his car, his apartment, his study.) We'd walk, even in the rain, and he prepared me for my meeting with Romania's

President Ceausescu.

I believe I was the first one to go into Hungary. I took a mission into Budapest before the JDC was invited back, and I went with instructions from Ralph Goldman [CEO of the JDC] to find out all kinds of things. I got to Argentina the day Eva Peron was overthrown. Nobody met me at the airport. I didn't know what was happening, and I finally took a cab to town and sat in the hotel for three days. Nobody called me, because the Jews were afraid to come out and welcome me—but I did meet with them before I left.

Q: During those visits to Hungary and Romania and Eastern Europe, did leadership have difficulty relating to you as a woman?

A: No, interestingly enough, not at all. They had their own agenda. It almost didn't matter who I was. They had a story they wanted to tell and have it conveyed back home. As a matter of fact, if anything, it was easier. They were as polite to me as they would have been to a male, maybe even more so.

Being chairman of JDC when *perestroika* came to the former Soviet Union and being there and meeting with government leaders was an experience I'll never forget. I said to them that in America we could be good Americans and good Jews and that was what we sought there. In no way did we want to affect Russian Jews' relationship with their government. All we wanted to do was make their Judaism stronger.

When I arrived in Baku in Azerbaijan, there was a huge sign at the airport that read "Welcome to the lady president!" The President of Azerbaijan met with me and wanted to discuss economics while I wanted to talk about the revitalization of the Jewish community. I did meet with the Jewish community in the synagogue. The people cried, and I cried as they told me they hadn't had a rabbi in seventy years.

I promised them a rabbi would come, and he did. At Kishinev in Moldova, I again met with the president of the country and left with the promise that JDC could open an office, that there would be a day school, and a synagogue would be allowed to function. And it happened.

There were trips to Addis Ababa to see the work of the JDC in Ethiopia and to see the way the Jews were living. We went to see the schools and the feeding stations we had established, and to see what we were doing to help prepare the people for the transition to another century. I remember when the twenty-four-hour alert notified them that they would leave Addis for Tel Aviv. It was a tense time, a time of waiting and praying that it would be a successful mission.

On one of my trips to Turkey, I flew from Istanbul to Adana to Insirlik [the U.S. Army base]. We flew by Black Hawk helicopter to the Syrian/Turkish/Iraqi border, and there we presented a field hospital for the Kurdish refugees, made in Israel, to the Turkish Red Crescent. It was a first. As president of JDC, I went to Bombay, to touch the B'nai Israel—to let them know we cared.

Strangely enough, they wanted to know about the Soviet Jews who were coming to Israel, and they were so happy to know we hadn't forgotten them. I am happy to say there are JDC staff and volunteers now working with the community in India.

I was in Zagreb just a few years ago—already a war zone—with refugees coming in from Sarajevo. The Joint bused Muslims, Serbs, and Jews out of the area. I went because the Jewish community had just opened a new community center with a kindergarten for youngsters in the community. Imagine! A new kindergarten in a war zone.

I had experiences in the former Soviet Union. In St. Petersburg, on my first trip, finding the synagogue was difficult. No one would direct me. The main building was closed, and I found only a few men praying in a small, adjacent building. A few years later, thanks to the work of the Joint, I saw children playing in the yard of the synagogue; and children filled every aisle inside, studying and learning. I found myself worrying about the crowded conditions and what would happen in case of an emergency. Would they be able to get out? Strange, what happened in a few years.

I had a wondrous and unique experience at the Grand Synagogue in Moscow on *Simchat Torah*, as I spoke from the *bimah* [altar]. The people crowded into the synagogue until it was so full no one could move and crowds overflowed outside, closing the street—a moment in time I will never forget. And I did meet with the community. I met with them in the synagogue.

I could tell stories about Morocco, Tunisia, the island of Djerba, and yes, even Iran when the Shah was still in power; stories about all of Eastern Europe—Poland, Bulgaria; Hungary and Yugoslavia; Czechoslovakia and Greece; Lithuania and Estonia. I was there. Dr. Ruth [Westheimer] tells me I should write a book, but this is as close as I will ever come to doing that.

Irving, you have opened a storehouse of memories: Rome, Ostia, and the transmigrants in Vienna—working with the Austrian and Italian governments. I could go on, but I won't. One last thought, however, comes to mind: an El Al flight from Tel Aviv to Yervain in Armenia after the earthquake in 1989. It was the first flight ever to land in the Soviet Union from Israel. It was the flight taking the injured to Israel for prosthesis fittings and rehabilitation. What a treat it was to see Aeroflot steps attached to an Israeli airplane.

Q: Were there any experiences in the Soviet Union that were difficult for you?

A: In Kiev I went to see the head of the local government and asked him to do something. He said that under *perestroika* they don't do that. We were caught in the transition between the past and the present. The first time we came to Russia, the red carpet was out for us. Everything was wonderful. And then, under *perestroika*, it wasn't so wonderful. Everybody did his or her own thing. I don't have to tell you, you know, it was a very different experience. I can remember another bad experience in Kiev. I was trying to hail a cab, and the Russian who was taking us around was wearing a *kippah*; the cab driver wouldn't stop.

Q: Besides the emphasis on fund-raising, has the Women's Division highlighted Jewish identity and consciousness among its participants, and if so, by what process?

A: By education. Men don't have time to be educated. When you take men to Israel, you take them to an airfield; you take them to see machinery. But when women come over, you take them to see children, the aged, and the things their money is doing. Men don't do that to that same degree.

Q: The Washington Women's Division Conference has become a major event in American Jewish life. First Ladies and major political leaders of America and Israel have addressed that conference. Hillary Clinton was one of the featured speakers this year. How did the Washington Conference develop, and how did it develop such dimension and importance?

A: I think you have to give Carole Solomon credit for that. It developed during the time that she was national chairman. She and the women on the board realized that Washington was where the power was. That's where the senators were, where everybody who influenced policy in some way resided. It would be the easiest place to get a large turnout of influential, knowledgeable speakers, and they did it four years ago. It turned out to have a multiplying effect. Every community wanted to send as many of their people as possible.

I can remember sitting at a meeting with women senators present. Not one of them said no; every woman senator was there—Republican, Democrat, Jewish and non-Jewish, black, white—they were all there. It was beneficial for them to speak to a group of articulate, well-informed, financially able women. So they would not say no. The same thing is true of Hillary Clinton. Where can she find three thousand women to speak to? The only limitation on the number of women who would come was the number of accommodations the Women's Division was able to secure in Washington.

Q: Many years ago, when I ran into difficulty with my own leadership, you and Merrill called me on a Sunday and insisted I fly to Providence. You were the only ones who told me what was going on, at some risk to your status within the organization. I was not aware of efforts by a dissident lay leader who opposed my leadership—just another instance of the ongoing clashes between lay leaders and Jewish professionals. Yours was an act of courage which I will remember all my life and be grateful for. But why did the two of you speak up when others were silent? Even people closer to me than you and Merrill remained silent.

A: As I said before, I wasn't that ambitious, and certainly Merrill was not ambitious. We knew what was right and were shocked at what was happening. We felt it was the only decent thing to do. It never dawned on us that we were jeopardizing our influence in the organization. I don't even think along those lines.

Q: I must tell you that it was to the everlasting credit of both of you, just a remarkable act of decency. Because I found out early enough, I was able to bring together others who eventually resolved the issue in my favor.

What were the moments in UJA in the Women's Division that disappointed you most and those moments in which you take the greatest pride and felt the most rewarded?

A: It goes back a lot of years, Irving. I was chairman three years: '76, '77, and '78. We're going back almost twenty years. The disappointments were minor; things that seemed major at the time were really not disappointments. Exhilarating experiences, yes. Having the ability to go to Israel and meet with Golda and the people in the Israeli leadership was incredible. I was young enough to be tremendously idealistic, and it was a very challenging and certainly rewarding experience for me.

Q: Since you gave of yourself to UJA and the American Jewish community and Israel, often at great personal sacrifice of time, effort, and funding, what do you feel has been the gain to you and the Women's Division?

A: It certainly has been a wonderful teaching and learning experience. I met great people, and I was exposed to things I otherwise would never have been exposed to. I certainly gained a great deal more than I ever gave. Really, I got to know wonderful people in the United States. In many communities I go into today, I now know people, lovely people, I otherwise would not have met. I think that my good fortune in having been chairman of JDC gave the women a feeling that now they too could strive for leadership in a national organization.

There are very few women who have dropped out. I may not go to all the meetings, but everybody knows that if they need me, I will be there. For example, they were dropping one program and forming another and they called me in to help. Whenever there is a problem, they always know that I am with them. I think that's been true of almost all of the past leadership. It's not as though I haven't gone on to do other things because I have nothing else to do, but I believe a closeness has developed in the Women's Division. I don't know all the new board members, but I do know the leadership, and I'm constantly in touch with them.

Q: During your period of leadership at JDC, have you steered some of the women you met around the country to the Women's Division?

A: Of course. Many of them. I have brought a whole different group of people to JDC because of my involvement with UJA. Many such women serve today on JDC's board and executive committee—and they also chair committees.

Q: Sylvia, if you had to do it over again, would you have accepted when you were invited to join the Women's Division?

A: Without question, Irving, it was one of the most important decisions in my life. It gave me a public platform to express my opinions as a Jewish woman. I met some of the most wonderful women from all over the United States whom I never would have met. I had the opportunity to meet and get to know the leaders of Israel and other countries. In the process, I grew as a Jew, a woman, and as a leader.

13

TEDDY KOLLEK

T eddy Kollek was born in Vienna in 1911. He settled in Palestine in 1935 and joined Kibbutz Ein Gev in 1937; in the same year he married Tamar Schwartz.

A war hero, in 1943 he opened the Jewish Agency office in Istanbul and worked with both the OSS and British military intelligence while furthering illegal immigration from Europe and organizing Jewish resistance against the Germans.

In 1947–1948, Kollek headed the clandestine Haganah operations in the United States and the first Ministry of Defense mission there. By 1949 he was in charge of the U.S. desk at the Israeli Foreign Ministry, and by 1950 he had become Israel's Minister Plenipotentiary to the United States. In that capacity he helped negotiate American foreign aid for Israel and organized the first Israel Bond drive.

In 1952, Ben-Gurion called him back to Israel to be director general of the Prime Minister's Office. In that capacity, he was responsible for the Israel Broadcasting Authority, the Department for Applied Civilian Scientific Research, the Bureau of Statistics, the Press Office, and Israel's aid programs to foreign countries. He was in charge of everything from minting coins to desalinating water and developing tourism. He was also in charge of the celebrations of Israel's tenth anniversary.

At Ben-Gurion's insistence, Kollek ran for mayor of Jerusalem in 1965, a post he held until 1993, when he was defeated by Likud member Ehud Olmert.

Often described as the force that kept the city whole, Kollek was also chairman of the Israel Government Tourist Corporation between 1956 and 1965 and was instrumental in raising funds for the Israel Museum, of which he was a founder and chairman. In 1966, he established the Jerusalem Foundation to beautify the city.

Kollek has won numerous awards, among them the United

Nations Human Rights Award; the Bavarian Order of Merit; the Jabotinsky Prize; the Israel Prize; and the Ben-Gurion Prize. He has also received honorary doctorates from a myriad of international universities, and the Dutch flower growers' association even named a tulip after him.

Kollek has written many books. Among them are: *Jerusalem, City of Mankind*, with Moshe Pearlman; *For Jerusalem: A Life*, with his son Amos; *My Jerusalem*, with Shulamit Eisner; *Teddy's Jerusalem*, with Dov Goldstein; and *Jerusalem, Policy Papers*, published by the Institute for Near East Policy.

**Interview by Irving Bernstein and
Ralph Goldman in Jerusalem
June 26, 1996**

Q: We want to ask you about your role with the UJA. When did you start with UJA?

A: Probably in 1939, at the request of Henry Montor, who was UJA's first executive vice chairman. I was there before there were two different organizations, the United Palestine Appeal and the Joint Distribution Committee. In 1939, on the eve of World War II, they came together to establish the UJA to raise money for JDC and UIA.

Q: Tell me about your experiences in London.

A: I was asked by the Keren Hayesod in 1940 to go to England during the Blitz to try to convince them that even during the Blitz you could raise money for Israel. The leaders at that time were Simon Marks and Israel Sieff. At that time it was very difficult to bring people together. At night they were afraid of the Blitz, so instead of going out to dinner, they went to the bomb shelters.

Therefore, we held our meetings at lunch. And people came because they were attracted by the notion that I came from a country in the middle of the war that was still doing constructive things in terms of defense, while trying to absorb refugees from countries where they were being persecuted. Therefore, people responded when asked for contributions. I don't remember exactly how much we raised, but it was an extraordinary success. That's when my fund-raising career really started—even before my involvement with UJA, but it's all part of the same story.

Q: How did you get there, Teddy, during the war?

A: I went from Jerusalem to Tiberias. There I boarded a plane to Turkey, and from there we joined a convoy of ships and forty-five days later ended up in Glasgow. We campaigned for about six weeks, and then we got stuck because it was very difficult to book passage home.

I stayed there for a few months until I was able to go back with a convoy from Liverpool. The night before we left for Liverpool, Glasgow had the heaviest air raid that they ever had during the war, and if I could raise money after that air raid, I knew I could do it anywhere. I thought I should mention it, because it fits into our story.

Q: When you were in Istanbul, you got involved with Joe Schwartz of the JDC, didn't you?

A: Yes, because he was spending UJA money. That was in 1943. I was in Istanbul for a year. I had deep impressions of Schwartz, and I'm sorry he's practically forgotten. I think he was a great man. Our task was to find some kind of connection with the Jewish Underground. We really didn't spend a great deal of money.

Some money we were able to transfer to Antek, our Jewish Agency representative in Warsaw, who was trying to save people from the Warsaw Ghetto. We were stationed in Turkey only by the grace of British intelligence. The Americans were not yet playing a big part. We got a few people out from time to time, sometimes even some British prisoners of war. The British were particularly interested in pilots who had been shot down because pilots were a very scarce commodity. It was a terrible situation. We were amongst the first to hear about the Holocaust; and we were not able to do very much about it. It was a very frustrating experience.

Regarding Joe Schwartz, I just want to say that the only place where there is recognition of Joe Schwartz in Israel is at Hebrew University, where the JDC established a Schwartz program for training community leaders and organizational managers.

Q: The money that you sent to Antek, where did it come from?

A: We got the money from the UJA funds through the JDC. I didn't know what the source was at that time. Joe Schwartz, by the way, went around in a colonel's uniform, courtesy of the U.S. Army. It made it easy for him to move around. We didn't have any advantages of that kind.

Q: But the minute you arrived in the United States to represent Israel, you had contacts with the UJA, with Eddie Warburg, with Bill Rosenwald, and Henry Montor. Those were the people you had dealings with as soon as you arrived in the States. Isn't that right?

A: Absolutely.

Q: Do you remember your first contacts with them? Was there anything special?

A: Well, there was a group called the Friends of the Haganah. They used to meet at the McAlpin Hotel. They included Abe Feinberg, Rudolph Sonneborn, and Sam Rothberg. They met every Thursday for lunch.

Q: Did you know any of them before you met them at that time?

A: Sam Rothberg I had met before. We first saw each other in Jerusalem at the end of 1945. He came to Israel directly from the camps in '45. This was his first visit to then Palestine. I remember I met him at the Eden Hotel. I was told who he was and I went to speak with him. The group at the McAlpin Hotel wasn't really the UJA leadership. They were involved in other dealings for Israel, and not in getting contributions to save immigrants.

Q: Tell us a little more.

A: Have a little patience. If I have patience to see you, you can have patience with me. Well, I started in many ways. Our army was established by then. We had sent a group of soldiers and officers to the United States to speak for UJA, I believe in May '48 or the beginning of 1949, soon after the declaration of the State. And this was something, as you know, that was entirely new. The great majority of Americans had never seen Israeli soldiers. We sent some of the paratroopers, and I joined them. I was there at the end of '47. I remember that I had the great luck of being at Lake Success when the UN voted for the State of Israel.

There was great jubilation in the streets when we got the majority vote. Some of the names I have forgotten, but maybe they'll come back to me. There was a very famous dentist who got votes at the UN by filling the teeth of some of the delegates in the Latin American countries, and while he was drilling, he talked to them, and exacted a promise from them to vote for the State.

Q: But in terms of the UJA, your contact was with Montor?

A: Montor was an astonishingly effective person; really a great organizer and a great speaker.

R.G.: But weren't you also active with the UJA, Teddy, especially when you were the director general of Prime Minister Ben-Gurion's office? In October 1953, I was appointed director of the U.S. Point-4 Program and the UN Technical Assistance Program.
[The "four-point program" was an American technical assistance program that helped emerging nations develop their economies. The UN had a similar program for technical assistance. In Israel, both programs came out of the Prime Minister's Office. Teddy appointed Ralph Goldman to coordinate them.]
While in Jerusalem I found a cable from you telling me not to get started because a UJA mission led by Max Fisher was coming to Israel. You wanted my help with that mission and were anxious for me to work with Fisher. In those days you were responsible for all UJA missions arriving in Israel.

A: Yes, that was a very important mission, that's why I cabled you as Max Fisher was, even then, a very significant leader in the United States. Missions of American Jews, especially from the UJA, were very important to us, not only for the funds they would raise to bring the immigrants and settle them, but also for the influence they would have in America on our behalf.

I was the closest person to Ben-Gurion at that time, and all the arrangements for missions were being made through the Prime Minister's Office. Since everybody wanted to see the prime minister, and Ben-Gurion was interested in seeing important American leaders, I made all the arrangements for the UJA people.

I.B.: When I was the head of the UJA, we brought three thousand American Jews to Israel after the Yom Kippur War. It was the largest mission to ever arrive in Israel. How did you feel when you stood at City Hall and at the Wall and looked out at those three thousand people wearing blue jackets printed with "We Are One" and waving American and Israeli flags?

A: It left a tremendous impression. I will always remember that moment. Some people thought that it was Independence Day all over again. We measured many of our programs by what the UJA did and how we could, on the one hand, interest them more and, on the other hand, get the most out of them. The UJA was always a much more meaningful group than other groups because of its deep connections to the American Jewish community, as well as to Israel. Therefore it was obviously very important to us.

And we, in turn, always tried to do something unique in Jerusalem for UJA missions. We tried to provide different programs to make it more attractive and interesting. We once provided a concert with Yehudi Menuhin at the Wall. Isaac Stern, over the years, has helped a great deal, and still comes to Israel regularly. Others from the classical music world who have helped us are Itzhak Perlman, Arthur Rubenstein, and Pablo Casals.

Q: As you look back over the decades, how would you analyze the significance of UJA to the people of the State of Israel?

A: Since 1939, there has been a continuing relationship between American Jews and Israelis. It is true that those who had gone through the Holocaust and through World War II had been, in a sense, participants in creating the State of Israel and at the same time had been involved with us during our War of Independence. There was almost a visceral relationship between American and

Israeli leadership in those days, not with all people but with those of us responsible for the conduct of the State.

Today, people know all this only through books, newspapers, or from hearing the story from the UJA. And it's a basic problem for UJA, because people today are dealing with those who haven't gone through the same heartrending experiences.

But meeting with Jews from the Diaspora is always a very moving experience, and this particular UJA mission you are talking about, this mission of three thousand after the Yom Kippur War, which you refer to as "This Year in Jerusalem," meant much to us. We really felt we were in danger, and your presence gave us a true feeling of solidarity. It was a mission and a statement of great importance, which only the UJA could have accomplished. Your colleague, Ernie Michel of the New York City UJA also brought a moving and memorable mission to Israel—one of survivors like himself and their children. [The World Gathering of Holocaust Survivors and Second Generation in June 1981.]

Q: Teddy, you are one of the few people who has had a clear vision of how to use the resources, experiences, and the people of the UJA. What do you think today? What should the role of the UJA be? In the States we are struggling to juggle the priorities between the needs of our local communities and the needs of those abroad.

A: First of all, some of the great stupidities committed by some politicians and writers in Israel are the statements that say we don't need your money anymore. This is totally and entirely wrong. It may be that because we now have large amounts of money put at our disposal by the American government, we don't need your funds for the government part of it. We were never able to use it for that part anyway. But we still desperately need to absorb immigrants, and we're still bringing sixty thousand immigrants into Israel each year, almost six thousand a month, with a goodly number of them here in Jerusalem.

We need UJA very badly for deepening and heightening their level of education, as well as increasing the ability of all these immigrants to be absorbed into the fabric of our small nation. Without you, we cannot do these things and still have programs like Project Renewal and the Israel Education Fund to build community centers and to teach art and music and other fine points of our culture.

There's so much that they missed during the last few years of their travail in Eastern Europe. Yes, I think we have to educate Israelis to give more than they do at the present time. It's something that we have delayed. They will. But there are individual cases of Israelis who do give a great deal to Israel causes. Please remember that Israelis are among the highest-taxed people in the world, therefore that isn't the easiest task for us.

Q: Teddy, what are your comments or thoughts about what Israelis feel about American Jews not making *aliyah*?

A: The fact is that many American Jews come here to follow their money to see what's happening in the country. That has created a better relationship with Israelis, as well as greater support. But individual Jews can't do much else, even if many of their children do come to settle in Israel. The critical fact is that the majority of American Jewry has remained Jewish and identifies with the UJA, that is the great thing. Even if they give on the side—to Hadassah or Technion, Hebrew University, Israeli Arts and Science Academy, or to museums or the Jewish foundations or to many other institutions that require support—the UJA is still the main factor in their giving. And when they make those gifts through their local Jewish communities, they reinforce their ties there as well.

Q: Let me go back for one moment. You were the closest, probably of any Israeli, to Ben-Gurion, because you were with him all the time. How did he feel about the American response through the UJA, and what was his own personal reaction at that time?

A: I believe he had a very positive reaction to the UJA. His problems were sometimes with the Jewish Agency, because he thought they interfered with matters of government. However, the UJA in his mind was most important, because he felt those Jews who gave through UJA did so as a symbol of identifying with Israel. That, to him, was the most important thing.

Q: Since we're talking about linkage, Teddy, among the leaders who came here in the early days were Sylvia and Merrill Hassenfeld. You had contact with them, I believe, from the very beginning, when they came to Israel in 1952 on their honeymoon.

A: The real beginning, the real contact came after Merrill tragically and suddenly passed away. It was a terrible loss for the family, and also for the American Jewish community and for Israel. I remember traveling all over Israel, and especially in Jerusalem, with Sylvia and her children. We walked and drove through the city of Jerusalem for an entire day trying to think of an idea that would appropriately preserve the name of Merrill Hassenfeld, Sylvia, and the Hassenfeld family.

Finally we settled on a theater in Jerusalem, which was really a rough stage and had not yet been developed. Isaac Stern would tell you that we used to have concerts there with no easy access, when there was still shelling going on and when the city was still divided. I remember talking to Zubin Mehta just before a concert in those days. He said that the concert would go on and that my role was to direct the public to safety if the enemy were to fire at us during the performance.

He asked me to be master of ceremonies, and since I really didn't know what they were going to play, he wrote it all out for me on a piece of paper. It all went quietly and peacefully, and there were many people there. But potentially, there could have been some serious injury. It was Mehta who gave us the incentive to do something about the building and adapting the Sultan's Pool into a new concert hall with a stage and all the appropriate amenities. Sylvia and her children fell in love with the idea as soon as they saw it.

Q: Did you know Merrill's father and uncle when they opened a pencil factory in Jerusalem in 1949? It was one of the first industries in Jerusalem at that time.

A: I was at the ceremony, but I was quite young and really didn't know them that well. However, I knew Merrill and Sylvia intimately for many, many years and have always had the greatest respect and affection toward them and their families. And I am very pleased that Sylvia and her family are very proud of being associated today with the Sultan's Pool concert facility.

Q: This relates to the Israel Education Fund. Were you involved in it from the beginning? Didn't you come to the United States with Louis Pincus and Pinhas Sapir to convince the UJA to undertake the program?

A: Well, it started with me. We raised some money, and then Lou Pincus came and insisted that it should be included in the UJA, because they could raise more money and it would help the UJA. The idea, however, belonged to Prime Minister David Ben-Gurion, who was despondent because we simply didn't have the state funds to give new immigrants in new towns the kinds of facilities they needed to lead full lives. Whether these were community centers or senior centers or any other kind of community programs, he believed the UJA Israel Education Fund would have to build them.

Sam Rothberg, a UJA and Israel Bonds pioneer and Hebrew University leader, wanted at that time to set up an independent campaign for the Israel Education Fund. He wanted to set up a separate entity to raise money for private high schools, which at that time the State of Israel by law couldn't build. So it became part of the UJA and was named the Israel Education Fund by UJA in 1964.

I believe Joe Meyerhoff was the first chairman, and he was followed by Charles Bensley. The Israel Education Fund has raised almost $200 million to date and has had tremendous social impact on probably more than a hundred communities in Israel.

Q: What is the impact of the Israel Education Fund on Jerusalem?

A: We built at least twenty-three high schools in Jerusalem, and the first community center, which has had such great meaning for us. We opened the center just before the Six-Day War. After the Six-Day War, the city suddenly grew to the point where we had to absorb a great number of people and we really didn't know what to do. There were no schools for Arabs. There were 70,000 Jews in Jerusalem before the Six-Day War, and today there are almost 450,000. The education fund was truly something that saved us.

Q: Wasn't the Denmark School one of the first schools built here? The Denmark School was, as I recall, a complex with a library and a community center.

A: Let me tell you a story. As prime minister, Ben-Gurion came to the United States for the first time in 1961. I believe you and Ralph were the technical organizers of this trip. The first stop we made was a visit to West Point, to pay our respects at the grave of Mickey Marcus. He had played such an important role during the War of Independence.

[David "Mickey" Marcus was a U.S. Army colonel who served as commander of the Israeli soldiers on the Jerusalem front during the War of Independence. He was shot accidentally on June 10, 1948 by friendly fire—he did not know the password. He is buried in the military cemetery at the U.S. Military Academy in West Point, New York.]

From there we traveled to Baltimore, to the home of Joe Meyerhoff, truly one of America's outstanding Jewish leaders—for UJA and all causes on behalf of Israel. On the way, we passed through Princeton, New Jersey, and spent an hour with Albert Einstein. Not that this is important, but I seem to remember that what Ben-Gurion and Einstein talked about was whether there was a universe and how this universe is being ruled. I remember noticing that Einstein wore his shoes without socks.

Q: Didn't Ben-Gurion go to UJA and also speak for Israel Bonds?

A: Yes. I remember I went to Chicago with him for the UJA meeting and the Bond meeting.

Q: You have seen what the Israel Education Fund has done. If you were speaking for the UJA, what would you say we ought to do for Jerusalem and for Israel today?

A: For Jerusalem, first we need to improve education for our children by adding classrooms and hours of teaching. And I would add teacher training, because our teachers aren't really good enough to handle the problems that they face.

Q: Weren't you involved in seeing to it that JDC in Israel received land in order to build an office building to house their administration?

A: I was very supportive, even though they received the land from different sources. I made sure that you could see the JDC building from the outside and also arranged for its very beautiful public garden. It is truly a beautiful place to work and one of the most important offices we have in Israel today.

Q: Teddy, I think it's important, since JDC gets its money from UJA, for you to comment on some of the important things JDC has done for Jerusalem—like the Minhalot Program.

A: As I said, after the '67 war, the city suddenly started getting a terrific number of immigrants. The social problems in this melting pot were difficult, because many of the immigrants did not grow up in a democracy. Many had been culturally deprived for so much of their lives. Therefore, it was terribly important not to let untrained local people run the programs in the community centers.

Obviously, we had to turn to somebody, and therefore we turned to the JDC. JDC set up the Minhalot—local neighborhood organizations, which are democratically elected. The JDC has trained leadership and lay people to deal with the social programs that are necessary and essential for integrating the immigrants and to get the maximum value out of the community centers.

JDC also got involved with a very critical program, the Eshel Program, because of the high percentage of aged people in Israel. The Eshel Program enables people to conduct their own affairs in old age homes. The Beyer Home for the Aged in Jerusalem was a magnificent gift from the Beyer family. I want to congratulate Ralph Goldman again, because he was the one who obtained this magnificent gift for our city.

The Beyer family provided us with a lesson in fund-raising: that we should never give up and should never forget. I believe Jake Feldman of Dallas, one of the great heroes of the American Jewish community and of UJA, sent Ralph to the Beyers. They said Ralph should come back to them after the Jews of Russia were free. Ralph remembered, he didn't give up, and he went back to them, and that's how the project started. The eventual gift was $45 million dollars, one of the largest ever received by the UJA as a legacy gift.

Q: Teddy, I don't know whether you realize it—maybe deep in your heart you do—you are a living legend because of everything you stand for and for everything you've done.

A: Don't ever believe legends.

Q: Well some legends you have to believe because of results. You began with Ben-Gurion. Your name is synonymous with Jerusalem. You were the mayor for twenty-eight years. Is there anything else besides education that should be done for Jerusalem and other cities in Israel?

A: I can't spell it out in detail, but the real need is education, education, education. It is the only way we can get our people together. The parks UJA created and UJA helps subsidize, the centers, and all the other buildings and institutions help people create friendships and help create society. But for the sake of the future, what our children and adults need most is education.

Q: One last question: Is your role in the Jerusalem Foundation now to work with the Israeli-Arabs in Jerusalem to make them feel part of the society?

A: The Jerusalem Foundation is building a community center in Bethany for the Israeli Arabs there. It's not the first. There are already two. The Arab population in Jerusalem has increased from 70,000 Arabs in 1948 to 170,000 today. Therefore, neighborhood organizations are vital to bring the Jews and Arabs together to help them create a sense of partnership, belonging, and citizenship. Jerusalem should be, and can be, the example of a working peace, but still has a long way to go to be a model for the rest of the country.

14

SYLVIA HASSENFELD / TEDDY KOLLEK: RETROSPECTIVE

T he UJA Women's Division was founded by men, not by women. It was never expected to become the powerful force it has proved to be in terms of its impact on the overall campaign and on the development and growth of its own leaders as major players in the UJA, the federations, and the greater community. Nor was the Women's Division expected to raise the enormous sums it has raised and still continues to raise.

At its birth in 1939, when women were not yet a presence in the business world or leaders of industry, men controlled the bulk of Jewish wealth. The Women's Division was seen as a support system for the men's campaign—the principal fund-raising effort of both UJA and the Federation. This was neither the first nor the last time that male leadership misjudged the potential role and impact of women's efforts.

Faced with the European persecutions, Henry Montor, then UJA's executive vice chairman, together with UJA's lay chairman, Henry Morgenthau, Jr., persuaded William Rosenwald [who was to succeed Morgenthau as chairman] to prevail on Rosenwald's sister, Adele Rosenwald Levy, to accept the chairmanship of the nascent UJA Women's Division.

Adele Levy, like her brother Bill, represented one of America's leading patrician German Jewish families. She would bring dignity and honor to the newly formed programs. To her credit, she, like the other Rosenwald siblings, followed in her parents' tradition of community service, including Jewish communal affairs. [Her brother Julius, unlike her brother Bill and her sisters Edith Stern and Marion Ascoli, became one of America's most vocal opponents of a Jewish State.]

At the same time, Montor convinced Edward Warburg to persuade his mother, Mrs. Felix M. Warburg, the doyenne of the German Jewish aristocracy, to serve as honorary chair of the Women's Division, which she did beginning in 1939.

Montor's strategy was successful. By accepting these positions, Mrs. Warburg and Adele Levy brought in their patrician friends and also women of Eastern European background who welcomed the opportunity to meet socially in a common cause with those beyond their own circles. Despite the accomplishments of their husbands in industry and commerce, it was Jewish rescue, Jewish statehood, Jewish community, and Jewish freedom that began to bring down the social barriers between the groups.

Women involved in the Division's earlier years were either born in Europe or were the children of immigrant parents who arrived in the United States at the turn of the twentieth century. They became partners with their husbands, accompanying them to UJA / Federation events and participating on their own with token gifts to the Women's Division. The pattern rapidly changed when the next generation, their daughters, took over those same responsibilities. These young American-born, college-educated women were raised in an atmosphere of gender equality. They made inroads in the workplace, and at the UJA demanded, earned, and won greater roles in leadership, program planning, and the development of the Women's Division. These daughters were the wives of real estate developers, manufacturers, insurance brokers, doctors, film industry executives, and legislators. They reflected the varied and growing wealth of American Jewish leadership and their entrée into professional organizations and trades previously closed to them.

One of the major differences in the election of male and female chairs is that women are more often chosen for their ability than for their wealth. With men, those who lead are often chosen for their ability to make pace-setting gifts, a *sine qua non* for leadership of the overall campaign.

Henry Montor's successors deserve credit for recognizing the importance of the Women's Division. They encouraged and did not hinder the development and involvement of women as leaders or the expansion of the women's fund-raising goals. The Women's Division has been raising 20 percent of the annual campaign [over $140 million]. The annual Washington Conference raises more than $10 million annually. Because of individualized and collective growth, the Women's Division leaders are capable of playing greater roles in federations and other Jewish national organizations.

Women's giving is fiscal evidence of the influence women exert as full partners in decision-making in the family and the community. Where does this power come from? More than 50 percent of Jewish women work. The percentage rises to 70 percent for those women under forty-five. Today in the United States, women run 60 percent of family foundations. In 1991, it was estimated that more than two million women of all faiths had personal incomes in excess of $500,000.

So it should not seem surprising that many of the women who served as chairs of the Women's Division moved on to other organizations. Their two years of leadership gave them the opportunity to reach out, meet and impress their fellow Jews on local and national levels.

Elaine Winik, who was head of the Women's Division from 1972 to 1974, went on to become president of the New York City UJA/Federation, the largest community federation in the world; and Sylvia Hassenfeld was elected president of the JDC and then chairman of its board.

At the end of 1967, as a sign of the changing times, UJA Executive Vice Chairman Herbert Friedman sent Women's Division Chairman Jennie Jones of Detroit to Israel with UJA General Chairman Edward Ginsberg of Cleveland, Young Leadership Chairman Leonard Bell of Lewiston, Maine, and me, then UJA's Associate Executive Vice Chairman.

We were charged with studying the impact of the war on our funded programs and on Israel in general. We were one of the first groups to arrive in Israel just as the Six-Day War ended, and we were warmly welcomed and briefed by the country's political and military leadership. We witnessed firsthand the material and human costs of the war.

When we returned, we reported to our constituents via a telephone hook-up. We spoke to all of America's federations and independent communities. Those who attended reflected the makeup of our delegation—campaign chairs and leadership in the Women's and Young Leadership divisions, as well as campaign professionals.

Factually and emotionally, we made clear that the government of Israel had emptied its treasury to meet the costs of war and that it was now our obligation to fund the Jewish Agency and JDC programs in Israel. The message was effective, and the campaign was energized. This was only one example of how UJA's individual divisions worked separately and together for the overall benefit of the campaign.

The Women's Division has always been adept at developing imaginative and creative programming. During Sylvia Hassenfeld's term of office, in addition to arranging the Washington Conference, the division arranged a meeting on the Annenberg estate in Palm Springs for those in the national Women's Division who gave $5,000 or more.

Ambassador Walter Annenberg had become involved in the campaign in his hometown of Philadelphia after he returned from London and hosted the annual Big Gifts meeting. Chuck Hoffberger spoke at the first event, and I spoke at the event held the following year.

The Annenbergs had often hosted U.S. Presidents, visiting royalty, and dignitaries at their prestigious Palm Springs estate, but never a UJA meeting. Realizing that a Women's Division meeting held at the estate would be very successful, Sylvia Hassenfeld prevailed upon William Rosenwald to join her, and together they drove to Philadelphia to visit Ambassador Annenberg and his wife, Lee. They were graciously received by the Annenbergs, who agreed to host the Palm Springs meeting.

It was a coup for the UJA in view of the prominence and distinction of their hosts and the unique location. Therefore, the Women's Division was able to attract attendees from all over the United States, and the Annenberg meeting set new standards of giving.

Following the meeting, Lee Annenberg agreed to help the Women's Division hold their next yearly meeting at the Sinatra estate in Palm Springs. Her efforts and those of former First Lady Betty Ford were productive, and the Sinatra home was opened to the Women's Division.

Although at the last moment Sinatra himself was called away for a performance, his wife, Barbara Marx, hosted the meeting in his stead. Sinatra had left a special tape for the women, and Barbara Marx spoke to the group about the role of the UJA. In gratitude, the Women's Division established a forest in Israel in memory of Sinatra's mother, who had lost her life the year before in a plane crash in Palm Springs. This Women's Division memorial for and tribute to his mother deeply moved the Sinatras.

One of the UJA Women's Division's most successful programs was the Ketubbot Emunah Mission. In 1978, at the Women's Division's first international conference in Jerusalem, co-chairs Marilyn Brown of South Bend and Peggy Steine of Nashville presented *ketubbot* to Prime Minister Menachem Begin and Yigael Yadin, whose ministry was responsible for Project Renewal.

Modeled on the traditional marriage contract, the *ketubbot* represented the Women's Division's commitment to raise $50 million for Project Renewal. The *ketubbot,* the Women's Division "covenants of faith," were presented to women who donated a minimum of $1,000. In this way, they surprised everyone and surpassed the fundraising goals they themselves had set for the program.

And this commitment was passed from generation to generation. In 1996, Sylvia Hassenfeld's daughter, Ellie Block of Chicago, chaired an Emerald Zehava event in Los Angeles for women who give between $25,000 to $50,000 each year.

In 1990, as chairman of JDC's Communication Committee, I urged Sylvia Hassenfeld, then the JDC chair, that to celebrate JDC's seventy-fifth anniversary we attempt to hold a meeting with President George Bush for JDC's leadership. Sylvia agreed, and I called Max Fisher, who arranged it. Sylvia briefed the President on JDC's new initiative in Eastern Europe and the Soviet Union and talked about JDC's nonsectarian projects in Armenia and Ethiopia. President Bush congratulated JDC on its seventy-fifth anniversary, calling its years of service an example of American volunteerism at its best.

Besides Sylvia and Merrill Hassenfeld, who served as national chairs at the same time, it is interesting that other wives and sisters rose to the same kind of prominence as their husbands and brothers because of their activities in the national UJA's Women's Division. Notable examples are Adele Levy, sister of Bill Rosenwald; Fannie Schoenen, sister of Jake Feldman; Harriet Sloane and her husband,Stanley; and Bernice Waldman and her husband, Bernard.

***

Teddy Kollek was twenty-four when he arrived in Palestine from Vienna in 1935. As a young immigrant to Israel, he helped found Kibbutz Ein Gev on Lake Kinneret and lived there with his wife, Tamar, for many years.

Through the years, his combination of Viennese charm and Israeli directness made him one of the most popular figures in Israel and in the world among people of all faiths. In his love of all things Jewish and Israeli, and in his devotion to the city of Jerusalem, he has become one of Israel's popular unofficial ambassadors and a superb fund-raiser. In Jerusalem, even taxi drivers and tourist guides bring their Jewish and non-Jewish passengers to meet with him and share his enthusiasm for Jerusalem—whether or not they make contributions to UJA or the Jerusalem Foundation.

In Israel, Kollek generally played the role of host for UJA missions. Teddy effectively spells out Israel's, and particularly Jerusalem's, needs to those who come to him. He personifies Jerusalem and is one of the few Israeli leaders who were on board when UJA was born. He was David Ben-Gurion's right-hand man when Ben-Gurion was the chairman of the Jewish Agency—then the *Yishuv's* governing body—and was Ben-Gurion's contact to the outside world.

When Ben-Gurion was prime minister in 1954, Teddy continued his close association with him as director general of the Prime Minister's Office. What isn't generally known about Teddy is that in 1938 he met with the notorious Adolf Eichmann in Europe and persuaded him to release three thousand Jewish youngsters from concentration camps. Eichmann permitted their emigration from Germany, Austria, and Czechoslovakia to England, after which a majority of them left for Palestine.

Teddy also directed the Jewish Agency office in England in 1941, under the direct supervision of Ben-Gurion. They dedicated themselves to further the illegal immigration from Europe and to organize Jewish resistance to the Germans. He worked in coordination with the U.S. Office of Strategic Services (OSS) and British military intelligence. Teddy's responsibility was to contact Jewish underground groups in Nazi-occupied territory, help Jewish resistance, and further the efforts of *Aliyah Bet*, the illegal immigration into Palestine.

In the ensuing years, Teddy had many opportunities to be a

member of the Knesset, the cabinet, and the establishment that governs Israel. In the minds of many, he would have made an excellent prime minister. But since 1965, when Ben-Gurion persuaded him to become the mayor, his love affair with Jerusalem blossomed into full passion and Teddy has refused to be unfaithful. For decades he has nurtured his beloved city with his knowledge and appreciation of culture, art, and music. Teddy founded the Israel Museum and the Jerusalem Foundation to add stature to Jerusalem and to develop the city.

Teddy's *affaire de coeur* is visible in the nooks and crannies of one of the oldest, most beautiful, and most cosmopolitan cities in the world. When Sylvia Hassenfeld came to Teddy to seek a memorial for her husband, she and her children—Steve, Alan, and Elie—chose Jerusalem because of its spiritual connection to their family and its uniqueness in history. Sylvia and Merrill had spent their honeymoon there in 1952, and the Hassenfeld family was one of Jerusalem's first investors. They were as much in love with the city as Teddy.

It was no wonder then, that when Teddy took the Hassenfeld family in search of a fitting tribute to a great father and husband, they chose the Sultan's Pool in Jerusalem and turned it into a magnificent memorial for Merrill Hassenfeld. Together they created a world-class modern concert facility, which attracts the Zubin Mehtas, the Itzhak Perlmans, and the Isaac Sterns of the world. Teddy's unique creative efforts on behalf of Jerusalem have earned him honorary doctorates from many universities, including Harvard, Notre Dame, and the Jewish Theological Seminary.

15

YOUNG LEADERSHIP:
IRWIN S. FIELD

I rwin S. Field served as president of the Jewish Federation Council of Greater Los Angeles and was the national chairman of UJA from 1978 to 1980 [induced to take the position by his dying wife, Joanna].

Field's Jewish communal involvement includes service as the national chairman of UIA and as a member of the boards of the JDC, the Jerusalem Institute of Management, and the Jewish Telegraphic News Agency. Additionally, he serves on the Jewish Agency Board of Governors and is the founding trustee of the Center for Foreign Policy Options.

Prior to becoming president of the Federation, Field was a member of its board of directors and chaired the 1974 and 1975 United Jewish Fund campaigns and the Finance Committee. He also served on the Planning and Allocations Committee, the Los Angeles Hillel Council Board of Directors, and the Brandeis-Bardin Institute Board of Directors. He has been a trustee of the Jerusalem Foundation's advisory board since 1971.

Field has also served with the United Way of Los Angeles [notably as chairman of the board], the Los Angeles Chamber of Commerce Board of Directors, and the Occidental College Board of Trustees. His work has been recognized with the Federation's Robert Greenberg Leadership Award; the Jewish Community Relations Committee's Gunther Israel-Diaspora Award; the National Conference of Christian and Jewish Brotherhood Award; and an Intra-Science Research Foundation Humanitarian Award.

He is president of the Liberty Vegetable Oil Company and a former board member of the National Institute of Oilseed Products. A native of Detroit, he earned both a Bachelor's Degree and a Master's of business administration from UCLA.

He and his second wife, Helgard, live in Los Angeles.

Interview by Irving Bernstein
following Edward Ginsberg's funeral in Cleveland, Ohio
January, 1997.

Q: Irwin, you came from Los Angeles, Mel Dubinsky from St. Louis, Lenny Bell from Florida, and Judy, I and Ralph Goldman from New York. We are here because Eddie was a treasured friend as well as a chairman who made a unique contribution to Israel-American relations and the development of UJA.

What were your thoughts as you flew in today to be with Eddie and his family?

A: I have come into contact, over these turbulent years, with many different people and many of them have become lifelong friends.

For a long period of my leadership life, Max Fisher was a mentor, an advisor who made an enormous impression on me in terms of leadership, vision, philosophy and outlook.

In addition, there were others of my generation who influenced my life: Trevor Chin of London with whom I worked closely on international reunions and Mendel Kaplan of Johannesburg, who brought an essential depth and breadth of Judaism and Jewishness to the role of leadership.

But the reason I am here in Cleveland is twofold. First, like Max Fisher, Eddie was also a mentor of mine, available whenever I needed him. I remember his first visit to Los Angeles on behalf of UJA and leaving behind a dynamic impression of greatness, the sense that what we were involved with was far more important than our individual selves. He exuded the optimism that we could make a difference if we were willing to become so totally involved as he was then and throughout his years of leadership.

During the 1967 war, I was deeply influenced by Eddie's performance, and then again during the 1973 war. To me he became the role model for dynamic Jewish leadership. I never before saw and felt the kind of total commitment Eddie was willing to give to Jewish rescue, Jewish unity, and to the survival of the Jewish State. It was a privilege to be part of his team.

His passing is not only a great loss to those who knew, loved and respected him, but to our whole people.

Q: How did you become UJA national chairman when there were so many Jewish leaders in America who were older and had more experience?

A: I think it was because I had already been one of the youngest chairmen on the campaign in Los Angeles—one of our major campaigns. Prior to that, I was active in Young Leadership campaign activities, traveling across the United States. I had a great deal of experience in fund-raising, and I understood the way the UJA worked.

I also think it was a condition of the time and moment. There were external factors that can thrust a person into leadership. At the time, UJA needed a certain kind of personality; it was thought I could fill that role. They didn't want a dogmatic leader, they needed someone to bring people together and create a sense of unity. Parts of the community were in disarray.

Q: Do you think you were representative of your generation? Did you share the same values and the goals as your colleagues in Young Leadership?

A: I was part of a core group involved in the formation of the Young Leadership cabinet. We were members for seven or eight years. The group really did share a common sense of values, a common philosophy, a common view of Israel. We agreed on the importance of Israel in the Jewish world, on what role the UJA plays, and on the programs we wanted to do.

There were others who came and went, but the strength was in this core group—and many of us have remained in contact with each other. We still share a common view.

Q: Is that group still involved in the community and in UJA? Or have they become distant from it?

A: Most of them have become involved in other organizations, and many of them have gone through all the chairmanships in their community. Others attained national leadership.

Q: You apparently had an unusual childhood in Detroit. Your father was a poet, a writer, and a teacher. Did he have an impact on your leadership years?

A: I had a variety of stimuli in my life. I grew up in a Zionist home, with Israel as the center of its focus.

I was bar mitzvahed on May 15, 1948. Now that was a momentous occasion in my home, because it was tied to an enormously important event—the founding of the State of Israel. My mother was very active in Hadassah, and my father was always very active in Zionist organizations.

I grew up knowing that Israel was important and that Jewish peoplehood was vital—that Jewish people have a legacy to transmit. There is the concept of heritage, of the people who made great contributions to civilization. Those are the kinds of things we talked about at home.

After I was married and living in Los Angeles, on my own I started getting involved in leadership activities. My parents encouraged me, and it gave them a great sense of pride.

I wasn't doing it for them, but still you could sense that this was something that was important to them and they felt very good about it.

Q: Was there anything special about Detroit? So many others from there have become national leaders. Or was it coincidence?

A: I think, in my case, it was coincidental. What's special about Detroit is that its Jewish community has remained an intact and cohesive community, even though it has moved physically four or five times.

I left Detroit in my junior year of university. I was too young to have had any real involvement. But I cared because of my background at home. My wife, Joanna Sinaiko, was also interested in Israel and the Jewish community. Her parents were Zionists and very much involved in the Los Angeles community. In Los Angeles I didn't have to be put into a "leadership progression ladder," which would have happened in Detroit. In Los Angeles I wasn't somebody who was the son of "somebody."

Q: I recall you could have been elected chairman of the Young Leadership cabinet, a post you earned, and I believe you wanted it. You gave it up to be chairman of the Los Angeles United Jewish Welfare Fund Campaign. I remember walking the streets with you for an hour, as you debated with yourself and finally decided on L.A. Why did you give up the national position?

A: I realized that the strength of a national leader stems from that person's standing and status in his local community. I can't speak for other organizations—although I've had experience in United Way, it's not quite the same. In the national Jewish community and in the UJA at that time, that's how it worked. It was pointed out to me, and I understood it. I had a very memorable lunch with Bram Goldsmith [longtime Los Angeles leader], who mentored me with great knowledge and understanding about Jewish life in Los Angeles.

He impressed upon me that I could go and do something that I wanted to do on a national basis, and I still wouldn't have any status in my own community—he didn't say that in a demeaning sense; he said it in a realistic sense. On the other hand, I could take a position of importance in my own community. That would have a greater deal of significance because the community needed a leader at that time, and it would enhance my status if I wanted to do anything else nationally.

I debated with him, but he was right. I came to realize what I should do, and I did it.

Q: Not too many years later, you had an opportunity to be chairman of the Board of Governors of the Jewish Agency, one of the most prestigious positions in organized Jewish life; or to be the president of the Los Angeles Federation at a time they needed you to lead.

Again we walked the streets, and I tried to convince you to take the position at the Jewish Agency. In the end, you chose to be president of the Los Angeles Federation, a position with less international impact. Why?

A: My memory serves me differently. The opportunity to stand for nomination as the chairman of the Jewish Agency came four or five years before I became president of the Los Angeles Jewish Federation.

I turned that down because I felt—and I still do feel —that to become chairman of the board of the Jewish Agency, you must have the economic underpinning in business to be able to spend huge amounts of time away from home.

At the time, I did not have the freedom to do that. I believed the chair of the board of governors would spend several months a year in Israel and many weeks traveling to other places in the United States and abroad.

I didn't want to undertake a job that I didn't think I could do well. I felt there was another candidate who would be better. I think history has proved me correct. Mendel Kaplan [from South Africa] served with great distinction.

Q: You mentioned Joanna. In the chapter on Golda Meir, I refer to Joanna coming to a UJA meeting in Southbury, Connecticut. I know you remember—I spoke to Golda about Joanna's combating advanced breast cancer and asked her to stop and say hello. And Golda did, and then invited Joanna to her house.

What was it like with you and Golda in Israel?

A: In a certain way, it was a typical Golda meeting. Golda was in retirement. I was the national chairman of the UJA. Joanna and I had let her know that we were going to be in Israel. She arranged an afternoon coffee.

We came to her home, which you know was a rather simple, nicely kept home. In her sitting room there was a corner arrangement with an easy chair and a couch sitting at right angles to each other. As she ushered us in, she motioned to Joanna to sit on the couch next to the easy chair. And she told me to sit on the other side of Joanna.

When she sat down, she said to me, "Your wife and I have things to talk about; I'll get to you later." And she proceeded to talk to Joanna for almost an hour. And then, when that was over, she turned to me, we talked about fifteen or twenty minutes about the UJA, about various things. And that was the end of the visit.

Golda had the unique ability to focus in on a single individual. We didn't know—very few people knew—that Golda had leukemia at the time. She had this unusual ability to talk about inner feelings and sensitivities with Joanna in a way other people could not.

Q: What was Joanna's reaction?

A: She was very much touched by it, and it was very stimulating to her. She didn't talk about it a lot, but Joanna had always admired and loved Golda.

Q: As national chairman of UJA, did you have any serious problems in UJA—or in Israel—because of your relative youth?

A: No, in fact, I think I had an advantage because I think there were many older people who deferred to me because of my age—when they may not have been as open with someone their own age. I remember on a number of occasions going to solicit or to speak in places where people felt good about seeing somebody younger at the helm.

Q: Are there experiences during that period that you particularly recall?

A: I think the ones I particularly recall were when we sold—and I use the word in the nicest sense of the word—Project Renewal to the country. I remember how many communities were not in favor of it, how especially the then serving chief professional officers in the communities didn't want another campaign, didn't want another effort intruding in their community.

I remember a number of meetings where we had to really convince them of the value of Project Renewal, convince them of what it was going to mean for the communities. I remember speaking about it at a CJF quarterly held in Denver. And I think that was one of the points at which we turned the professionals around and got them to support Project Renewal.

I always felt, and I still feel very strongly, that Project Renewal changed the dynamic between the federations and Israel and the Jewish Agency. It provided opportunities for federations to have direct contact with Israeli communities. Afterwards, Project Renewal relationships with the Agency began to change. And that's what the Agency is struggling with today. It has never been able to come to grips with, or reconcile itself to, those changes.

The fact is, the communities need and want more direct contact. Those communities that participated in Project Renewal gained a great deal because of the relationships, because of the activities, because of what they did, and the contacts they made. When Project Renewal ended, there was a void, now being picked up by a program called Partnership 2000, which attempts to replicate it with fewer problems.

[Partnership 2000 began in 1994. It is designed as a "living bridge" built by Keren Hayesod and the UJA in cooperation with the Jewish Agency's Rural and Urban Development Department. Modeled on Project Renewal, it links American know-how and business acumen with the resourceful Israeli spirit in twinned communities.]

Q: Were there any personal experiences you recall fondly during that period?

A: There are a number of lay leaders with whom I shared great experiences. There were wonderful experiences with a whole variety of people from different parts of the country that I sometimes reflect on. I particularly remember my meeting with Bob Russell [Miami chairman, Project Renewal], when we worked to get the project moving in the right direction.

I recall the caucuses we had in the Knesset on Prime Minister's Missions. They were moving, emotional and very inspirational. It was the timing, it was the moment, it was the atmosphere. It was electric because of all that was going on at the time.

Q: You came in after there was a schism and some leaders left the organization. Did you have trouble solving the problems they left behind? Or were you able to go in and move forward?

A: The past was not easily forgotten. In the beginning, there were problems with UJA staff. Some felt that there were people who were ahead of me in the line for the chair. I think those feelings dissipated rather quickly, but they were there in the beginning.

There were a number of lay leaders who were sympathetic, friendly, collegial with those who left, who wanted to see some kind of an amalgamation with the group that had left.

But I think time overcame people's personal feelings. Project Renewal, fund-raising—we had to make decisions. I tried to create a leadership group of officers who would make those decisions. I don't think my predecessors operated in exactly the same way. I think most of the decisions made, before I took office, were made by the national chairman and the chief professional of the UJA.

I wanted people to take responsibility. We had some very long meetings and contentious debates about the policies and programs we were going to put forward in the campaign.

By doing that, we solved some of the problems. I made overtures at the time to those who were disaffected, but was unable to convince them that the cause was greater than personal feelings.

Q: If you had to do it all over again, would you have made the same choices—L.A. over national Young Leadership?

A: Yes. I would have made the same decisions, and I think that if I look back, the decisions I made were fortuitous. Because of the events that followed them, I believed that had I taken the chairmanship of the Young Leadership cabinet, I would not have become the national chairman of the UJA.

I want to be clear about the cabinet. A lot of very committed, very decent individuals have been national chairmen of the UJA Young Leadership cabinet. To my knowledge, I don't think any single one who was chairman of the Young Leadership cabinet has ever gone on to become chairman of the UJA. I was the first member of the Young Leadership cabinet to become a national chairman. Other cabinet members followed.

When I became president of the Los Angeles Federation, and in the two years I was president, I always felt I had an advantage over all of my predecessors in Los Angeles. That was because I was able to bring to the presidency of Los Angeles my national and international experience. It allowed me to make decisions by using a "data" base my predecessors didn't have. I knew what was going on nationally and internationally, and I didn't need the primer most other federation presidents have to have. You know: who is active, who is leadership, which organization does what and how they do it and how they interact. Any decisions made locally are based on what's going on nationally and internationally.

Q: Would you have done anything different if you could do it over again?

A: No, I don't think I would have done anything differently. I think I had the unique opportunity, in each position, to be able to bring something to each organization, and create something for each organization that wasn't there before. Some of it was due to external circumstances, and some of it had to do with views I felt the organization should reflect.

Q: You have observed some of your colleagues who preceded you or followed you drop out of leadership activity after doing their stint. What would you say to them if you could reach out to them?

A: I would say that our organizations are poorer because they did not stay around to provide a leveling force, a historic memory, a sense of continuity. I think that in Jewish organizational life, it is very important to provide a sense of continuity and role models for younger people coming up in the system.

A younger person has to see that being involved at the top is important for the organization, but more importantly, to the individual. There is the opportunity to develop relationships—social, business, and political—that can come out of it. Relationships don't develop when leadership is going through a revolving door. And it seems to me that organizations have suffered because of this lack of continuity. So I think it's important to stay involved and express your opinion on subjects.

Q: I recall you chaired two events that required special skills. One was a UJA national conference with a dinner with Max Fisher and Henry Ford, in which Ford was presented with a special award. And the other was a Prime Minister's Mission in Moshe Dayan's garden. What went through your mind? The Moshe Dayan meeting was your first as chairman. You had been in the garden before, but that was the first time you had to introduce every individual to him as they posed for photographs. Did you have any difficulty coping with it?

A: The meeting with Henry Ford was my first brush with "royalty." I don't mean royalty in the classic sense of the word, but if ever there was royalty in this country, Henry Ford exuded it. Henry Ford came to a meeting with his handlers. He always traveled with vice presidents. People preceded him to make sure every step along the way was planned for him.

And yet, when you met him, he was a very gregarious person, very open, very down to earth. I remember there were two things going on that night in the same hotel—our event and a sales meeting of Ford regional dealers. He first greeted those people. That was his business side. You could see how he went from group to group and shook hands and talked to each person.

Then he came into our meeting. I remember introducing him to people, getting a little mixed up because of all the tumult that was going on around me while everyone talked with him as we walked around the room. He was very open, a very easy person to talk to. And yet he had all this action going on around him, which gave him a different sense of reality.

It was an exciting and memorable evening; it was something very special at that stage of my life.

Also, there were other things going on with Joanna. I was living two lives—UJA was one life, and coping with Joanna's illness was another life. In a way, UJA was my salvation. It gave me the chance to do things that were incredible, like visiting Moshe Dayan's garden.

It was fascinating. Here was a man completely different from Henry Ford, who couldn't care less about the trappings, who didn't know if he had a suit or work shirt on. He couldn't care less about things the average person thinks about.

He cared about ideas and big issues. And, you know, the evening we had in his garden—I think it was an evening that he would rather not have done. But once he started doing it, he became more comfortable and enjoyed it. I think he was the kind of person who was put off by these kinds of evenings. He didn't like the large groups that he had to deal with. He did it for the UJA. He did it for . you, Irving; he did it because he believed in the UJA.

Once he began to meet the enthusiastic members of our group, it began to change the way Dayan felt about the people as he went around and talked with them and took pictures with everyone— another thing he normally didn't like doing. But as he kept doing it, he kept getting friendlier and warmed up for the evening.

You could see it as he spoke—he became very personal about his comments and feelings that evening. It wasn't just, "Well, I've got to make a speech tonight, so I'll make it." He changed. The group changed him. You could see that. You could sense that in him.

Q: You and Yael Dayan are included in this section, since both of you are in the same generation. But there are critical differences. You reflect American society, and she Israel's. How would you evaluate her and her values and attitudes and goals as compared to your own?

A: Well, that's very difficult, Irving, because, frankly, I've never spent a great deal of time talking with Yael privately. So I can't say that I can understand her real values. I spent more time talking with her father privately than I did with her.

She's certainly a very independent thinker. She has definite ideas that she has put forth in a very independent way in her books and in her talks, and yet she hasn't gained a great following. She's been an individual, very much an individual.

Q: What do you think the priorities should be for American and Israeli leadership today?

A: One is that they ought to study successful organizations, even successful organizations not in the same field. There are great examples of successful organizations in business, in academia, in institutional life, in philanthropic life.

The only organizations I know doing "business" the way they did it twenty years ago are national Jewish organizations and federations. Most others have changed. Medicine has changed, law has changed, business has changed, manufacturing has changed, communication has changed, and the way the government does business has changed. Everything has changed, except Jewish organizations.

I believe that those organizations need to be led by professionals who are willing to open themselves up and be bold and courageous enough to change.

Q: If you were asked to define UJA's primary role, and the role of its leadership, how would you do it?

A: UJA's primary role is to raise money for overseas needs, to raise money for activities undertaken by the JDC and the Jewish Agency. I'm not sure that the UJA is going to confine itself to what the Jewish Agency is doing, unless the Jewish Agency reorganizes itself in a way that allows it to do things that communities see as relevant. After all, the communities raise the funds. And the UJA is a different instrument today because the world is different, because circumstances are different.

When I was national chairman and until four or five years ago, external circumstances framed the agenda of the UJA. And the UJA took those external circumstances and molded them into a national campaign. The communities could readily understand that we were dealing with serious issues, and you didn't have to explain. Everyone understood what was going on.

Q: That changed with the ending of Operation Exodus [immigration from the Soviet Union]. It doesn't mean people aren't still immigrating to Israel. But the external circumstances are not as critical as they were then. At a JDC meeting I attended, the new chairman of the JDC said that there were more elderly Jews wandering around Eastern Europe than there were in the DP camps after the war. Could it be that the UJA isn't telling its story right?

A: Well, that's possible. It's also very possible that that story is no longer stimulating people to give money in the same way it did before.

There are probably 50,000 elderly Jews wandering around Los Angeles in need of help. And if the numbers would be determined the way JDC identifies people in Eastern Europe, the number may be even greater in America, if you include New York, Chicago, Los Angeles, and Miami. It will be even worse if welfare and food stamp rules are changed.

The story today is different. I don't know if that is going to move people to a sense of responsibility as it did in the past. It certainly is a story that needs to be told, and needs to be told properly.

Q: You have worked with a variety of professionals. How does that experience guide you in advising professionals on how to work with their lay people?

A: That's a complex question.

Q: I know it is.

A: There are a couple of things I would emphasize. A professional needs to be someone who can lead an organization following a lay person without appearing to do so. What do I mean by that? A lay person who is the head of the organization may have a direction, philosophy, or vision. If leadership agrees with that vision, then the professional has to be, to a certain extent, a follower. In that respect he must guide and lead the staff while remaining a follower.

It is a very challenging position. The professional has to build a leader, to help that lay person think through issues and processes by debating, on a friendly basis, their agency vision, philosophy and concepts.

I don't think professionals today do that. I think that's one of the things that has changed in Jewish community life.

When I say professionals are not helping, that doesn't apply to all of them, because there are a variety of styles. Some do help and try to guide and encourage their people to grow. But the vast majority of them are not doing what their predecessors tried to do. Some of their predecessors gained great pride and satisfaction when one of their leaders became the leader of a national organization. That gave them a sense of their own accomplishment.

I also think that most professionals are technologically deficient for the world we live in. They are not guiding their organizations in dynamic creative ways. Therefore, they are unable to be as creative, effective, and efficient as they can be.

Q: Are there any other communal posts in which you believe you can contribute to the greater good of our communities, ourselves, and the people of Israel? Or do you feel, now that you are a "senior citizen," that you have had it?

A: Well, in a certain way I am a senior citizen, and I should be. When I was president, I said that the community belongs to the next generation, we should give it to them and let them run it. On the other hand, I think there are still a number of things I can do to help the Los Angeles community without being at the top of the table. There are other organizations with which I am involved, where I think I can have an impact on their future development.

Q: That's a tribute to you. What do your sons and Helgard's children think of your continued involvement in national community leadership? Do you believe they will follow in your footsteps? What advice would give your children and others?

A: My sons think my involvement is my way of life, and they have accepted it because they were very young when I started.

I think they have gained from it. They certainly grew up with a wider perspective on world events than most of their schoolmates. I think as a family we have gained from it. I think they and I went through some terrible moments in our lives, during the years of Joanna's battle with cancer and her death. A number of things held us together, and certainly my communal activity was very important.

I believe it brought a sense of fulfillment to the family, because I always tried to involve them in my activities. Even when they were very young, they met with people and knew about events as they happened.

My stepchildren, Helgard's children, come from a small town in

Switzerland where the nature of involvement is different. In Europe people don't get involved in the same way people do in this country. There is no federation system—there is neither the intensity nor the number of meetings and activities that we have here.

It took them a number of years to understand what it was all about and why it made sense. Now they have accepted what I do, and I think they've also gained as we have brought things into their lives that they wouldn't otherwise have experienced or known about.

Q: Helgard has become involved, hasn't she? Didn't she speak at a recent meeting?

A: Helgard has a very strong feeling for the Jewish people and for Israel. After her husband died, she took her children to Israel twice a year, during the spring and fall holidays. She is very supportive and has been very helpful. But she feels that I'm the leader and the one who is more directly involved. She doesn't want to be a co-leader or co-involved person.

My sons are involved in activities in community life—not the same ones I've been in—and I think that is a good thing. They have a hard time being involved in the same activities. I think it is difficult for a son to follow a father who has been a leader, unless he has a very strong personality or something that pushes him in the same direction. Maybe after a period of time they will be able to do so.

I've said the same things to my sons that I've said to many young leaders in Los Angeles—that they should spend as much time as is required to secure their economic position. I've seen too many potential leaders fall by the wayside—not because they were not good leaders, but because they did not have the economic security that would allow them the time to be a leader. I'm not trying to hold them back, but I think that if you are going to be a leader of the future, you are going to have to be able to afford it.

Q: When Ephraim Katzir was Israel's president, he met with one of our large *Koach* young missions. There were a thousand people on the mission. He told them the same thing because in the course of one generation, they had moved from being engaged in *hatzalah* [rescue], in saving the lives of Jews abroad, to uplifting their own Jewish lives.

Do you believe from your own breadth of experience that we, as well as young leadership, are moving in the direction of uplifting our Jewish lives and building spiritual bridges to Israel? Should we work in that direction?

A: Ideally, we should move to a deepening of *ruach* [spirit], but I don't know if we can do it quickly enough to make it matter. It may take a long time, and it is going to require some big changes in organization and outlook on all sides.

Q: Why is it so difficult to recruit others to become so involved if there is so much benefit to be derived from this kind of involvement and this kind of leadership?

A: The circumstances have changed, the conditions have changed. Eddie Ginsberg, one of my predecessors in national leadership and a mentor, came along at a time when the cause was bigger than Eddie, bigger than anybody. That was to build a state, a state with growing pains, a state with security concerns and internal turmoil. It lifted people up and gave them a great cause to believe in. Through it, people like Eddie came in contact with dynamic personalities, because they, too, were involved.

This is what I meant when I said external circumstances guided and challenged us. We wanted to rise to the challenge. The same external stimuli are no longer here today, so we are trying to create a different modality in which leadership can function, grow, and gain something.

We need a different kind of chief professional officer. Without them, we are not going to have leaders that can create a following. We will have leaders that will come and go. You'll find successful people that will give you a certain amount of time, and they'll give you leadership, but you won't have the commitment you have had before.

Q: Why isn't the message getting out there? Why isn't the involvement there?

A: For a multiplicity of reasons. One of them is that our relationship with Israel has changed. Today, it is on the way to becoming one of the great economies of the world. It is not a debtor nation struggling to remain alive. As long as there is peace, it is financially secure. Another is the polarization of life in Israel between religious and secular Jews, which is now reflected in our communities in America. As I indicated before, the passion brought about by external circumstances has not been replaced with something that motivates beyond one's "obligation" to one's community.

Q: My last question. Your father is ninety-five. I'm sure he takes great pride in what you've achieved in Jewish life. What do you think he would like to see you do with the rest of your life?

A: I don't think he has any thoughts about it. He believes I should spend more time studying history and gain knowledge and respect for individuals who are Jewish or of Jewish origin who have made important contributions to civilization. And he thinks I should get others involved in that kind of study and appreciation of what Jewish life is all about.

We have talked a good deal about creating a greater sense of understanding among younger people of what Judaism is all about and what Jewish life has meant to the world. Younger people are not going to remain part of the Jewish people just because they have a post-Holocaust mentality.

He believes people who carry on traditions and who are educated will ensure Jewish continuity, and those who don't, won't. I think that the majority will remain Jewish because they believe they come from a people who have made important contributions and have given important things to the world. They'll have a sense of pride. If you don't have a sense of pride, why bother?

I think that that's one of things that I'd like to work on, and my father and I have talked about it. I think it ties into why young people would be involved and what we're all about. Is Federation going to be the Jewish United Way? Or is the Federation going to be an organization that can represent more than being a collector and dispenser of community dollars? Will it meet the challenges of continuity and Israel-Diaspora relations? Will it keep the community whole? That remains to be seen.

16

YOUNG LEADERSHIP: YAEL DAYAN

Yael Dayan was born in 1939 in Moshav Nahalal, a cooperative village in Israel. Her parents were Ruth and Moshe Dayan, both well-known Sabras. Her father was an outstanding soldier, military hero, and cabinet member in both Labor and Likud governments. Her mother was head of Maskit, the marketing arm of the Israeli handicrafts industry. Yael, who has two brothers, studied political science at the Hebrew University in Jerusalem and biology at the Open University in Tel Aviv. One brother, Assaf, is an actor; and the other, Ehud, is a farmer on the Moshav Nahalal, the settlement where they were all born.

Dayan was elected as Labor Party member of Knesset in June 1992 [a four-year term] and was a member of the Foreign Affairs and Defense Committee; the Constitution, Law, and Justice Committee; the Gay and Lesbian Rights Committee; and the Violence Against Women Committee on domestic violence. She also chaired the Women's Rights Committee and the subcommittee on the administration of the occupied territories.

During her first term, Dayan also advanced and secured gay and lesbian rights and initiated the legislation that made the Women's Rights Committee a permanent statutory Knesset committee.

In 1996, Dayan was reelected to a second term, and she will continue to chair the Women's Rights Committee. She also continues to be a member of the Constitution, Law, and Justice Committee.

As chairperson of the Women's Rights Committee, Dayan has promoted equality and women's rights, equal pay, and the right of women to choose abortion. Dayan also chaired the Knesset committee on domestic violence.

Outside her Knesset duties, Dayan's political activities include Peace Now, the Women's Network for Peace, and the International Center for Peace in the Middle East. In 1991, Dayan's work with those groups was recognized when she was awarded the Bruno

Kreisky Human Rights Award. In Tunis, in January 1992, Dayan was the first Jewish member of the Knesset to meet with Chairman Yasser Arafat.

Dayan has authored eight books—six of them novels—including *New Face in the Mirror, Death Has Two Sons, Sinai Diary-67*, and the nonfiction biography, *My Father, His Daughter*. She has been a journalist for thirty years, writing political commentary for the Hebrew and foreign press.

Dayan lives in Tel Aviv with her husband, General [Reserves] Dov Sion. They have two children, Dan, twenty-nine, and Racheli, twenty-seven.

**Interview by Irving Bernstein in her Knesset office
June 1996**

Q: I've been rereading *My Father, His Daughter* and found it more moving than the first time. I couldn't help wondering, knowing you and your family, how you could write so dispassionately and objectively only four years after your father's death and the settlement of his estate—which did not favor you, your mother, and your brothers.

A: Four years is not immediate in Israeli terms—immediate is usually yesterday. It wasn't something that I had to get out of my system, but it was an important story to tell. As a writer, I find the best way to express anything is through writing. I had no difficulty in divorcing myself from the emotions involved. Where the emotions were strong, they were present in the writing. It was obvious to me that one day, and in this case it took four years, I would sum up our relationship in writing.

I don't say that the Dayans represent Israel, but what we went through in three, now four, generations is a reflection of what happened in Israel. Today I am the only third-generation member of the Knesset. My grandfather was in the first and second Knesset, my father was a member until his death in 1981, and I have now begun my second term.

Q: I can't believe your children are now twenty-seven and twenty-nine. I can still remember when Racheli was born in Tel Hashomer Hospital. Your mother and I came to see you and had to climb through the window of your room because it was after visiting hours. You were sleeping, so we kissed you and left a note.

After the publication of your first book, *New Face in the Mirror* [which was well-received in the Western world], you became the first member of your family to be invited to UJA in the States. As one of UJA's first Sabra speakers, what was your initial reaction to the visit and the relationship you found between American Jews and Israel?

A: At that time, 1961, I was probably the youngest visitor from Israel to speak to an American audience. In the beginning, I wasn't comfortable—the age difference between the audience and me was like the one between my grandparents and me. Only later were there young women, young couples, and young leadership.

Q: Yossi Beilin said that Israel didn't need philanthropic funds. We felt his statement was counterproductive and lacked credibility. I believe no country in the world, even America, can resolve social problems with government funding only. How did his statement go over in Israel?

A: No one took it seriously here.

Q: Some people in America use it as an excuse not to give or to lower their giving. We are having difficulty in explaining his remarks.

A: UJA is a wide organization, which includes all the federations. It reaches more Jewish homes than any other Jewish organization. We wondered if UJA could be useful in other ways—not just fund-raising. We're not degrading or lowering the importance of the funding aspect, but I would like to encourage the use of this wonderful, huge, pluralistic machine for other goals. That is something I'm concerned with—greater understanding of Israel and its society, as well as its social problems.

You have so many meetings and functions that I think they should be more like missions to Israel. Many of them are not, and they should be. Going on a mission means much more than fund-raising; it's more important than that. Someone may not raise the amount of their gift even if they are moved by a visit to an air force base, but something else is going on—they see what Israel is about and come back again.

To me, UJA is the largest tourist agency bringing Jews to Israel, Jews who are predisposed to caring and identifying with what they see. I suggest we find additional uses for a UJA that is reaching into so many different communities.

Q: What should those goals and uses be?

A: I think they have to do with peace, because we're far from the Western world and we are on the defensive. We are in "the new Middle East," and Jews should have a relationship with an Israel based on the future, with an advanced Israel, a democratic Israel. They should be concerned with our democratic values, our human rights; they should share the responsibility in a world of haves and have-nots.

The United States willingly plays a role like that (sometimes less willingly). America is the only super-nation left today and must take responsibility for the rest of the world—sometimes through financing, sometimes through guidance, sometimes through policy. Israel is trying to do similar things, without patronizing others in the Middle East.

Such a project would be a wonderful chance for Jews in the States, however strong they are, to share in the extraordinary experience of peace, of building a new Middle East, of building Israeli democracy and turning Israel toward implementing its potential. This means education, this means activities in different communities, and this means more people must come here.

I would like to see a whole system of summer camps for American Jewish children in Israel. I would like to see many more university exchange students than we have now. I would like to see investment in business, in industries in the Middle East and Israel. I would renew Project Renewal in those communities where poverty is still a problem. There are major development towns that are not yet complete, where Project Renewal can be very helpful.

We still have absorption problems with the Russians, Moroccans, and Ethiopians. We have a problem now with religious bigotry among ourselves, and I would like to see pressure and support from the American Jewish community to help us develop cooperation and understanding in terms of religious pluralism. If Jews are excluded from Israel as Jews, we must reexamine our entire existence.

Q: Is Israel a state like all other states, incidentally founded by Jews, or is Israel a Jewish state? How do you balance religious pluralism and still have a spiritual center coming out of Israel?

A: They are two different things. Israel will always be a Jewish state. It will be a Jewish state by the fact that the majority of the people here are Jews and that the language is Hebrew. The language is a source of terrific creativity and culture. A whole civilization builds itself up and progresses around it.

We will remain a Jewish state, even if our society is 90 percent non-religious, secular Jews. I don't think Israel will lose its Jewishness. But if there is pressure to preserve Orthodoxy as a monopoly, we are going to lose our democracy. Frankly, between the two, I think democracy is more Jewish than *halakhah* [Jewish law]. It's a question of values, and I think pure Jewish values have to do with pluralism, with democracy and equality with respect to minorities and human and civil rights. We are struggling for this in Israel now. That's the difference between the last government and this government.

I'm probably a terrible Jew in the eyes of the rabbis who sit in this Knesset. But they can't prevent me from having my say, since I was democratically elected, as they were. On the other hand, I can't allow political pressure to give them control of my body, to diminish my rights as a woman before the law [divorce, domestic violence, sexual harassment]. I cannot give them control over the rights of minorities if they make decisions any rational person, and I, would find undemocratic.

Until now, the Supreme Court has always chosen democracy over *halakhah*. Now, because Likud has grown smaller and dependent on the Orthodox parties, they will try to legislate laws that will bypass the Supreme Court and take away its power and authority. The Supreme Court has religious and secular judges, who have decided that there is no clash between civil law and *halakhah*, because Judaism in its universal sense is a democratic, not restrictive, religion. Now, with these attempts to strip the Supreme Court of its authority, we may be in trouble—trouble that can affect American Jewry, too. When we go back to the barricades, we hope you will join us.

Q: As a successful writer more at home in arts and letters than anywhere else, why did you decide to enter the political arena and run for the Knesset?

A: For two reasons, really. First: the possibility, feasibility, of an immediate peace. I was more comfortable being part of Peace Now and protest movements, standing on street corners carrying signs. Then I felt that I could do more if I became part of the decision-making process. I felt the Israeli public was ready for it, and I was right. I hope we don't regress now. Second: because human and civil rights have to coincide with peace. If we have peace, we won't be able to use "security" as an alibi for the prevention of rights—whether it's the rights of Palestinians or women or anybody.

I believe we must go in the direction of building an Israel the way my grandparents envisioned it. We must let our Jewishness flow and adjust to changes in time. But we must make sure we don't lose democracy and peace in the process.

There is danger. Until now, security was an alibi for everything. This is going to disappear. Then the extreme religious right will show up and use religion to deprive us of our rights. History clearly points out the dangers of extreme religions and what happens when religious fervor drives national extremists.

I must tell you that the murder of Rabin was precise proof of what happens when these two things are bound together. There is no question that it was anti-peace and anti-democracy. It was done to stop peace. It was an attempt to speak in the name of God and not in the voice of the people. I'm in the Knesset to guard against these things. My fear that these would happen drove me into the Knesset.

Q: When Irwin Field came in as the youngest chairman of UJA, he had to deal with an older group and gain their respect. Aren't you also dealing with people twenty, thirty years older than you are?

A: Not anymore. There are many younger than I am. We have an amazingly young average, and I'm almost in between. There are some older than I am. Yossi Beilin is ten years my junior, more or less. Like so many others, including Chaim Ramon.

Q: Rabin's death will probably go down in history as one of the most traumatic events in Jewish life, because the thought of a Jew killing a Jew was inconceivable to Jews and non-Jews alike. At the UJA, we sat *shivah* [in mourning], and the tears flowed. Everyone was in shock, from the Right and the Left.

In view of all that happened, how do your fellow parliamentarians react to you in view of the strong statements you made? You're younger, you're a woman, and you are very strong-minded. You're less "political" than many of your colleagues, in and out of your party. With all of those strikes against you, have you been able to play a meaningful role? Have you been an effective Knesset member?

A: I operate very well. I do it on my own, because of all the things you mentioned. Sometimes I find partners. I don't have friends here, and I don't look for party advancement in any way. I don't think about political maneuvering. In the last four years, I was a member of the Foreign Affairs and Defense Committee, which is a sought-after position. I was the first woman they put there. I chaired the committee on women's rights and gay rights and made a difference.

No one can take these accomplishments away from me, even if they don't want to give me any credit for them. And I was reelected. I'm quite alone here and I don't mind, because I had a life before I got here, and I will have a life after my time in the Knesset is over. I'm very disappointed in the results of the last election, but I would like to see the peace process completed. I would like to see our electoral system take final shape. I want to see democracy strengthened in Israel, and I would like to see us break away from religious coercion. I want an Israel where we can really live and let live, be and let be.

Q: Do you think that's the direction the country will be going?

A: Yes, yes. And it's evident in the Likud, too. It's even evident among the religious and Orthodox. Only their generation does not represent anything new, because they are followers of the elders. We come here to innovate and experience new things and have new ideas and have creativity, but in many Orthodox quarters you are measured by the fact that you are a follower, not by the fact that you are a revolutionary.

Q: Your mother, Ruth, and then your father, Moshe, followed you to the United States as speakers for UJA. She was widely praised and recognized for training Bedouin women to do creative handwork—which she then marketed through Maskit [handicrafts, arts, and crafts marketing]. Your father is a legend because of his military heroism and skills, especially during the Six-Day War.

In all my forty years at UJA, he was the most sought-after speaker in the Jewish and non-Jewish worlds. And I don't know of any other Israeli or American family where a father, mother, and daughter were all speaking to Jewish communities on behalf of UJA. In view of this collective experience, do you recall any discussions at home of experiences, good and bad, that you shared, of moments you found moving, humorous? Did you discuss disappointments? Did the three of you share the same sense of role and value for the UJA and American Jews?

A: We did. Because we were together on many of the trips, we developed close relationships with American leadership—like with you, Sy Lesser [director of the UJA speakers' bureau], Bess Simon [associate director]. We became friends for life. And I mean friends. It was not duty. It was a feeling for knowing each other. Like any organization, the UJA can't remain abstract. It is people. It is really family.

My family cannot think of the UJA in the abstract, because when we had no one close to us, we would come to you and fulfill ourselves by doing something that needed to be done. We felt very strongly that in the UJA there were people who believed in us and who thought that although we are a crazy family, they could benefit from our originality. We are always forgiven for being Dayans because we, including my mother, were never able to fit a given pattern.

Q: You also developed personal relationships outside the UJA that you maintain, probably to this very day. For example, the one you have with Ray and Betty Epstein of Chicago.

A: It's not because they were president or chairman of the community. I don't think there is one community where I haven't been. I like them because they could be humorous about things, could debate openly and would not put me in a corner because I said something that is not in consensus. I'm very proud that I have friends in the States from the literary community who don't connect at all to the UJA, they don't want to hear of it. For them it's institutional Judaism—people like Philip Roth, Lillian Hellman when she was around, Peter Edelman, and many of my friends in Hollywood who you know won't come to meetings. But in recent years, we've connected some of them because of the peace. I also think I brought them closer to the UJA because I lived in both worlds. I'm very grateful for those who have come to Israel often and cared in the deeper sense, not like people who have to have honors and meet the prime minister. But we are getting older. The real question is how will our children communicate.

Q: Your father had no patience for fools, even less for small talk, and was often uncomfortable at social receptions. Strangely enough, he agreed to host UJA missions of one hundred to two hundred people in his unique garden. It should have been kept as a state park, an Israeli landmark—not keeping it was a great loss. At those receptions he agreed, always with a smile, to stand for photographs with each couple or individual. Why did he do that for UJA?

A: He liked you and he did it for you, because you presented it on a personal level. You can also call it ego, but I think he really liked the fact that American Jews saw him as a hero, whatever his position was—whether he was in government or out of it. He was really a symbol and he liked it. He saw the pleasure people got from meeting him. And I think it was not a weakness. He had paid his dues to get where he was. He earned his reward, which was fame and enjoying the pleasure he could give others. He was comfortable with it.

He was very proud of our house and garden, and there he could be himself. For these missions, he didn't have to put on a tie or a suit. To him, these were dues that were not a burden to pay.

Q: He was in a documentary that Peter Freistadt produced. I was the chairman of Peter's committee. We were making a film to show children so that they wouldn't think Sharett was a housing development, Ben-Gurion was an airport, and Dayan just a legend. It was well reviewed and shown in all the schools. How do you and Ruth feel about it?

A: To do my father justice, you need a big screen, you need a colossal feature with the greatest director and an excellent actor. There were several projects suggested, and nothing came of them. As you well know, he was very complex and had elements of tragedy and heroism and humor and loneliness and aloneness. It's unfortunate that history, including documentaries, makes him some kind of postcard, a two-dimensional figure. He was very difficult to grasp. I tried to do it a little in my book, to capture his complexity of character. And while I don't remember your film in detail, it was an effort by good people to remember a unique personality. All of you deserve a *kol ha-kavod* [literally the term means "all my respect"; colloquially, it means "hats off!"] for trying to take him off the page of a book and bring him to life.

Q: He and I walked into the Four Seasons Restaurant in New York City. Everyone eating dinner stood up and applauded. As happened with Golda, the curtain in the theater would not go up until everyone stopped applauding. There was something about him that you cannot describe, you cannot paint, you cannot touch. It seems to me that he and Golda were the most charismatic of all Israelis I have known.

I recall many memorable gatherings at your parents' home, one forever etched in my memory. Your grandparents, Zvi and Rachel Schwartz, were there with your father and Ezer and Reuma Weizman. I think it was for a holiday. Ezer and your father were both away at funerals for two different soldiers. When they came back, it wasn't an evening of humor—it was a serious evening of the family coming together. And I also remember many gatherings where Ezer was the life of the party and there was just a lot of laughter. He had a great sense of humor those days and he called me a "united Jew with lots of appeal."

My question relates to your following your father to Vietnam, he in a military capacity, you as a reporter. I remember how the American press reported that they were awed at his courage for going to the front lines after they told him not to. Your experience came after his, and I believe the two of you came away with similar impressions. Would you do it again? Were there any negatives due to your being a woman and an Israeli? Did you meet any Jewish military personnel when you went to Vietnam?

A: If I were as young now as I was then, I would do it again. I was free to come and go and I was reporting. That was my job. Later, after I had children, I wouldn't do it even with the IDF. In '67 I was a frontline war reporter. But I think what we had in common was the courage to complete our "missions," whatever they were—reporting or learning something or fighting for something you believe in. You don't think in terms of price.

We talked about the futility of the Vietnam War quite a lot. I didn't meet anybody Jewish; I had no problems being a woman. The U.S. Army and the press did everything possible to be helpful. They gave me credentials, they flew me everywhere, and I could participate in any mission I wanted. That's when you know there is real freedom of speech—and you had the freedom to die in preserving it or getting it. That was in our more adventurous days, and it was somebody else's war, so while you cared to a certain extent, you didn't get so emotionally involved.

Q: Do you think you were closer to your father than your two brothers because you were more like him than they were?

A: I think I chose to be closer to him. I'm his firstborn, so that has some meaning. My brothers chose to be further away from him. They were not interested in the same things he cared about, so we each had the space that we wanted to occupy. This was not because they loved him more or less than I did, but because they were much less interested in the contents of his life than I was.

Q: You visited and spoke for us in countries besides the United States. Did you find any major differences in the process, the people, the feeling, the mood, in other countries?

A: Not entirely. I spoke everywhere, but I spoke in Europe and in South America quite a lot for the Keren Hayesod. South American communities are different—except for Mexico.

Q: In what way?

A: They're more liberal. They are less confined to set ways. You don't have to be 100 percent representative of what they think the Israeli government should be, not even what it is. Britain and France are much less liberal. I mean, again it's a set performance with set rules and you have to go along with it; it's less exciting than in the States. In the States it depends on the groups. The younger groups and women's groups still turn me on in the nicest ways because we communicate. There's lots of sincerity and caring.

Women are not politicized. They are completely open to what you have to offer and they absorb it. They listen. They listen more than men do. Young people listen much better than older ones, and even when they debate me, it's—a result of listening, disagreeing, and then debating.

The older generation debates on principle; before they even hear the end of what you say, they already disagree. So there are places where it's fun, and there are some communities that are conservative and lacking in liberal thought. I'm saying this with great caution—whenever a rift exists between Israel and American Jewry, in many cases it is caused by ignorance made stronger and deeper by disinformation. This is something that I really cannot forgive. Disinformation deprives people of truth. That's one thing. Disinformation added to ignorance creates a community that is confused, doesn't know where it should be, what its health or its mind should be. Disinformation is like censorship.

Q: If you come to the States now, you will find relatively little disinformation in our UJA community. You will see that there is transition to young leadership and to women—more than in Israel, for obvious reasons. Our Women's Division today raises more than

20 percent of the campaign.

A: They are fantastic, they really are.

Q: I have two questions about Shimon Peres. Shimon wrote that he and your father were both selected in 1946 to go to the Zionist Congress in Basel because they were the two best young leaders. He also writes how, throughout his career, he always admired your father and recommended him to Levi Eshkol.

A: They were quite close. My father was not close to anyone in a chummy way—like going out after work or going on trips—but they were close. Shimon was younger than my father was.

Q: Your father was six years older than I, and I think he was eight years older than Shimon. Shimon is what, seventy-three, right?

A: Yes. My father was born in 1915. My father was not a friendly person, he did not have close friendships—but they were close. And I have great respect and admiration for Peres, because during the years when my father was boycotted by Labor and labeled a traitor, and then when he left Begin because he felt Begin was messing up the peace process, he was left all alone. Shimon was the only person who made a real effort to convince Labor to bring my father back in, and he failed.

But Shimon kept in touch with him, informed him about important developments, consulted with him. I think it has to do with Ben-Gurion—because it really has to do with sharing a mentor and a line of thought and vision. They were both Ben-Gurion's boys much more than Eban, who was also part of the young Turks. I think Ben-Gurion was really the strong adhesive between them.

Q: Shimon writes that your father developed the art of regional warfare. Would you say this concept is really a commentary on the way your father did a lot of things?

A: Yes, it's nonconformist. Everyone walks down the path of life and they think they have only two options. So they take one road instead of another, and then there is an obstacle or a blockade. My father had the brain, initiative, and creativity to find a third way, a less troubled path. He had this originality; you could call it using his imagination, because he would reread the map according to new circumstances, as Shimon does today. They would blame him for changing his mind. You could come to Dayan every few years and say, "But you said something totally different in the past!" And he would say that only an ass doesn't change its mind.

Q: It's fifteen years since your father died.

A: Yes, he died in 1981.

Q: I never came to Israel without seeing him, never came without having dinner with him. When he died, although I can't compare my void to the void of your family, it was difficult for me to come to Israel and not see him. To this day, it isn't the same. Memories cannot make the difference.

A: He is missed, in a national sense, even by young people.

Q: You've succeeded in everything you attempted so far in your life. What are your personal goals now?

A: I want to go back to writing. After we achieve our political aims, civil and human rights, and peace the way I see them (which means an independence day for the Palestinians, equality with all nations, and the democratization of the regimes around us), I would have left my little mark after eight years. Then I could go back to fiction writing.

As a writer, my message is not measured so much in terms of this year or next year—it's more in terms of human relationships, in a kind of abstract, "forever" way. My message as a speaker is much more immediate, much more precise. It stems from the same motivation and the same beliefs: I can't preach one thing in my writing and another in my speaking. The difference is that in my speaking, the message has to be more concise and relevant to the moment. It's got to be put in this time and this place, whereas in writing it's forever and always.

17

IRWIN FIELD/
YAEL DAYAN:
RETROSPECTIVE

I rwin Field and Yael Dayan, born just a few years apart, are representatives of the best of their generation. Both were raised in relatively successful families, but they chose to serve their communities instead of resting on their families' laurels. Despite their independent and outgoing personalities, both Dayan and Field are modest to a fault.

Both, at relatively young ages, achieved prominence in Israel and America. Field is a successful manufacturer in his own right. Instead of choosing a country club life, as so many of his generation did, he chose instead, at sacrifice to family and business, to become involved with the Jewish community in Los Angeles. Gaining the recognition and respect of his peers, Field was elected by his elders as the youngest national chairman of the UJA.

It was my personal and UJA's good fortune that I met both Irwin Field and Yael Dayan when they were on the eve of their creative careers. My colleague and friend Julius Ratner, then the Los Angeles campaign director, believed, as I later did, that Field had unlimited potential for leadership. Field was then married to Joanna Sinaiko, whose family I had known when they lived in the Midwest when I had represented UJA in their small community.

Even in those early years, Field was perceptive. He has a probing mind and excellent interpersonal skills. He also has a deep sense of Jewish commitment. It was natural that Ratner and I would do all we could to direct him to a leadership role.

The Field family first lived in Detroit. Theirs was an observant household, where Shabbat meant that the family would be together, where no appointments would be made, where Jewish tradition played an important role. Field's father, Walter, a lifelong Zionist, was a paint manufacturer and teacher—who also authored stories for Jewish children.

The Fields were active members of Congregation Shaarey Zedek and close to Rabbi Morris Adler, who was murdered during a service by a brilliant but crazed young member of his congregation. Rabbi Adler's death was a great loss to *Klal Yisrael*. He was a former national UJA rabbinical chairman.

As a youngster in Detroit, Field remembers helping his father set up chairs for Zionist meetings held in their home. The strident, antisemitic comments made by Father Charles Coughlin over the radio reverberated throughout the national Jewish community, and Field recalls the heated debates, discussions, and decisions about issues of common concern that took place at his parents' table.

Irwin Field's membership in the national UJA Young Leadership cabinet had a deep impact on his life. He was part of a group of young Jewish business and professional leaders from all over the country. Together, they talked about their visions for the future, the ferment in Israel, the Six-Day and Yom Kippur Wars. The experience taught Field how to raise funds, how to debate issues among peers in leadership, and how to deal with strong minds and strong views without creating enemies.

Every year Field conducts the family Passover seder for his family, his first wife's family, and his parents. During the service, he always points out that all of us are immigrants in America, not unlike those we help in Israel today.

When Field first moved to Los Angeles, it was natural for him to become a block captain with the UJA Federation campaign in Encino, where he lived. He worked his way up the leadership ladder one rung at a time, from community to national leadership. It was part of his upbringing, consistent with his lifestyle. And he has had the unswerving support of his family: his first wife, Joanna, who died of cancer at an early age; and his second wife, Helgard, who was born in Europe and knew the effects of prejudice.

Field is a natural teacher. As his father before him taught, as he teaches at the Passover seder, so did he teach while in his leadership positions at the UJA. He strongly believes that leadership of a Jewish entity is a Jewish act—that it must be carried out in a Jewish way—that there must be a link to the heritage and traditions of Judaism. He also believes that he is not alone in his thinking, that most of the young men who came out of UJA's Young Leadership cabinet and programs have that same sense of heritage, history, and religiosity in their lives.

Field feels deeply that UJA has been a continuous catalyst for change in the American Jewish community and in Jewish and human development, producing leadership that has been beneficial to the international Jewish community.

Field minimizes the problems he faced as the incoming chairman of national UJA, replacing a predecessor who resigned over differences about the professional direction the UJA was taking.

Despite his relative youth, when he assumed the national UJA chairmanship, Field was blessed with a deep insight into interpersonal relations that he had gained through his experience in campaigning. He was not affected by ego and was well received both by individuals and communities who were energized by his enthusiasm, knowledge, and his willingness to share both his time and experience. To his credit and UJA's advantage, he was respected in Israel by both the government and the Jewish Agency.

Field was also a large contributor and effective solicitor because of his deep commitment to physical and spiritual Jerusalem. His challenge, therefore, was to keep the UJA united, to communicate with all individuals, to recruit leadership for the forthcoming campaign and to be responsible for constructive lay-professional relations. And this he did, earning the respect of his elders and the UJA staff, as he led campaigns that increased over previous years.

***

I first met Yael Dayan in Israel, at a time when it was obvious that she was trying to express her own identity in a family with a world-famous, charismatic father and a creative, involved mother. Yael eventually found her way through writing, reporting, and political activism. In her early years she was independent, something of a rebel. With the courage of her convictions, she never hesitated to express herself publicly.

My predecessor, Herb Friedman, first brought her to UJA; and even though she might at times have shocked her audiences, she was always respected for her intelligence and courage.

Thus, Yael succeeded in gaining recognition in her own right. In the United States and in Europe, stars of the film and theater, as well as nationally recognized authors, were drawn to her. Like Field, she respected honest criticism, open discussion, and differing opinions as long as she had the opportunity to reply.

Yael's determination and strength of character did not lessen as she grew older. In 1996, during difficult negotiations between Prime Minister Netanyahu and Yasser Arafat, Yael Dayan, a member of the Knesset, visited Hebron, a hotbed of ultrareligious right-wing activity. She had already offended members of the ultrareligious groups by taking a stand against their position denying women the right to pray as a group at the Western Wall. They were also at loggerheads on women's rights.

During that Hebron visit, a man in a *kippah* asked her if she would like a cup of tea. When she said yes, he threw the hot tea at her, scalding her face and chest. The police later apprehended him.

Knowing Yael as I do, I reminded her that anything could happen because of prejudice and hatred. I urged her to use caution in these troubled times.

Yael's comment about Hollywood in the interview, about film stars and writers not doing all they could for UJA, must be taken into context. It was, and is, true to a degree. But at the same time, her statement does not do justice to the many who volunteered their services.

When I was West Coast UJA director, before coming to New York first as associate vice chairman and then as national vice chairman, I recall many stars volunteering their time. Those experiences helped me later to deal with many successful achievers in both the United States and Israel. The stars, like any well-known personalities, treasured their privacy and needed to be sure that those requesting their public appearances were not amateurs but tried and true professionals who would not detract from their public personas.

Yael's father, Moshe Dayan, was such a star, no less than the elite of Hollywood and Broadway—his distinctive, handsome face, the sparkle in his eye, the dramatic black patch made people want to reach out, and shake his hand, and touch him. Dayan disliked and tried to avoid these displays. He dealt in issues, not in small talk. He was an analyst, not a reporter. He never spoke for effect but for substance; his speeches were not for applause but for understanding.

Yael may not know which stars were on the UJA roster, perhaps because her path did not intersect with theirs. I remember calling

Jack Benny and asking him to help us raise cash and pledges at a major regional meeting in Dallas. In a packed ballroom, someone handed him a signed check for $100,000, good at any bank east of the Pecos and west of the Brazos. The UJA cashed it at a Dallas bank.

Harpo Marx helped us with California campaigns. His pantomimes had everyone in hysterics for the first twenty minutes, and then he startled his audience with an emotional ten-minute address on Israel and the UJA.

Carol Channing, who is not Jewish, was the star of a show for UJA's thirty-fifth anniversary in 1974 produced by the versatile Issachar Miron at the Mark Hellinger Theatre on Broadway. She asked if she could sing "Diamonds Are a Girl's Best Friend," the hit of one of her recent productions. Everyone was silent, and she realized something was wrong. I explained that we were trying to rescue men, women, and children trapped in Eastern Europe, and that the song might be out of sync with the tone of the evening. She then suggested "Romania, Romania," which she had learned, in Yiddish, as a young performer in the Catskills. She stopped the show, drawing tears and laughter from her audience.

Edward G. Robinson surprised me when I called for his participation in an important meeting by asking me to write his speech. I did, and with my heart in my mouth, I drove to his home in Beverly Hills. We met in his study, surrounded by his world-famous art collection. I gave him what I had written and sat waiting for his reaction on pins and needles. While smoking his favorite cigar, he turned to me and said "Good speech. Good speech." As I finally released my breath he added, "Now read it to me."

I stuttered for a moment and he said, "Look, kid, I know what you want me to say, but now tell me how you want me to say it." I read it back to him—and at the appointed time he delivered the speech in his inimitable voice and with a dramatic flair that made it his speech, not mine.

In 1973, during the Yom Kippur War, Danny Kaye, General Aharon ["Areleh"] Yariv [Israel's chief of intelligence during the Six-Day War], and I spoke to packed houses in Los Angeles.

Kirk Douglas accepted many invitations to speak at UJA meetings. He has been, without a doubt, the best and most effective UJA speaker due to his personal experience in Israel and the knowledge he gained playing the role of Mickey Marcus [the West Point graduate who lost his life fighting for Israel]. When I left the West Coast for New York, Douglas sent me an autographed photo wishing me success, which he signed in Hebrew.

Because of my relationship with Yael's father, Moshe Dayan, Howard Squadron, then president of the Conference of Presidents of Major American Jewish Organizations, and Yehuda Hellman, its executive director, asked me to share my impressions of Dayan at a meeting of the conference shortly after Dayan's death in October 1981. I did so at the Presidents' Conference tribute to Moshe Dayan in November 1981, and I reprint it here.

> Dayan's death was not unexpected. Three weeks earlier, Judy and I had been to dinner with him at his favorite restaurant, the Casbah in Tel Aviv. When we were given our table, it was evident that he was having problems, as he bumped into a wall before finding his chair. Knowing him as we did, we couldn't believe that this proud independent man could ever live with cancer and blindness.
>
> We had met for the first time in 1956, on his first visit to the United States after the drama and heroism of the Sinai Campaign. And by accident of planning, after New York, he came directly to me in Los Angeles, when I was still regional director.
>
> I was thirty-five, he was six years older. I was a first-generation American. He was a first-generation Israeli. I was a teacher and social worker, process-oriented, brought up on American merchandising and marketing. He was a farmer and a soldier, convinced that the only way between two points was a direct, straight line. He was never able to flatter or exaggerate, even when it was expected or demanded of him. I was from a small town in upstate New York, full of fears and doubts stemming from antisemitism directed at an immigrant family. He was from Nahalal, a small *moshav* [settlement] in northern Israel, self assured, confident, with all the pride and even arrogance of the Sabra.
>
> As we traveled together and continued to meet through the years, I learned that his celebrated rudeness was due more to his lack of hearing than to any insensitivity. In his mind the lesser embarrassment was to be apart from others if he could not be part of them, and so, on many occasions, he chose to be alone.

Although he fully accepted our American informality, which was not unlike his own, his emotions always ran deep under the surface, and were rarely expressed in any form except the written word. It was in his books that he felt free to write openly and intimately of his emotions as a friend, a father, a husband, and member of a Jewish family.

It wasn't until after he contracted cancer and I had my heart attack, which occurred one year to the day before his death, that I felt a change in him. He came to see me at Beth Israel Hospital in New York, directly from JFK, and again a week later on his way back to the airport. Although he did not fear death as others did, he sensed and knew that I needed some of his strength, confidence, and vision.

As we deal with life, we use our senses to grasp reality. Dayan used the senses of the farmer, of a man brought up on the soil. He sensed things by touching them, and if you once looked at his hands you would know why, for they were stubby and gnarled and rough. They were the hands of a soldier and a farmer, not a poet and a statesman.

We sometimes argued about programs he didn't like and didn't want to do. If I succeeded in changing his mind, he would accept the initially rejected program with full enthusiasm. The past was forgotten and was never referred to with a grudge. Nor was he able to harbor resentment for changing his own predetermined positions.

He was not a gossip, did not tell stories or care about the foibles of others. Jokes were beyond him, although he had a delightful sense of humor and a wonderful, beautiful smile. He loved to deal with issues, analyzing serious concerns— geopolitics, military matters, and affairs of the world—and he welcomed guests to his lovely home and garden as long as they had more serious thoughts than the idea of just being with him. Throughout the years, whether he was up or down, in or out of Israel's political arena, he remained faithful and loyal to those who saw him for what he was. He could not tolerate sycophants. But he understood the importance of the links between world Jewry and spent the last decade of his life working on issues of Jewish continuity and bridge building between the Jews of Israel and America.

Moshe Dayan left the bulk of his estate and the house and garden in Zahala, on the edge of Tel Aviv, to his second wife

Rachel. He believed Ruth, Yael, and his two sons [Assi and Udi] would be able to make it on their own much more easily than she would. It was not only a deep blow to the family but, to a lesser degree, also to UJA and me. Rachel sold the house to a lawyer who destroyed Dayan's garden, and so there was an additional spiritual break in the UJA's relationship to Dayan. Our annual meetings in his famous garden, which I had hoped to continue as a tribute to his memory and his dedication to UJA, could no longer be held there.

And so, with the death of Moshe Dayan, a special chapter in the history of Israel came to an end.

The most effective way to sum up my personal impressions of Moshe Dayan is in his own words from his last book, *Breakthrough*. This was not his celebrated dream of death as reported in the media. This was his statement about life, about his sense of purpose, about the depth of his commitment. After the signing of the Camp David accords, he wrote:

> I was tired. The hour was late. I longed to be home. Had I been there, I would have celebrated in the way I like best, eating a snack in the kitchen with Rachel, and afterwards reading to her the poems of Alterman. That night it would have been the noble one which deals with the chronicles of the House of Israel, songs about the long and weary road, paved with hardship, trekked by the Jewish nation, my nation, my people, dispersed, denigrated, oppressed, massacred, a people who had hung on desperately to life almost with their fingernails, in order to survive.
>
> The Jews have always faced a dual challenge—having to fight their oppressors and to fight for the preservation of their singular identity. How poignantly was this expressed in Alterman's "A Battle for Grenada," a poem which portrays the remarkable Shmuel Hanagid. He was a Hebrew poet, scholar, statesman, solider, who 900 years ago was leader of Spanish Jewry and, at the same time, was chief minister of state for the Berber King of Grenada and commander of his army.
>
> Alterman sets a battlefield scene where Shmuel, the Jewish general, is addressed by a Spanish commander. The Spaniard tells him in this rough translation of Alterman's exquisite Hebrew—far apart from the military campaigns of Grenada—

you have another war, a war of your own, an unending war. It is the war of your language whose host you command. It is the war of your children whose teacher you are, to teach them the meaning of our antiquity.

This was the man I knew and will always remember.

18

ELIE WIESEL

Holocaust survivor, Nobel Laureate, and Boston University professor Elie Wiesel has taken on battles for oppressed people for most of his adult life. His efforts have earned him the Presidential Medal of Freedom, the U.S. Congressional Gold Medal, the Medal of Liberty Award, the rank of grand officer in the French Legion of Honor, and the 1986 Nobel Peace Prize. He has received more than seventy-five honorary degrees from institutions of higher learning.

In 1978, President Jimmy Carter appointed Wiesel chairman of the President's Commission on the Holocaust, which later became the U.S. Holocaust Memorial Council [of which he is founding chairman]. Wiesel is also the founding president of the Paris-based Universal Academy of Cultures.

His more than thirty-five books have won numerous awards, including the Prix Medicis for *A Beggar in Jerusalem*, the Prix Livre-Inter for *The Testament*, and the Grand Prize for Literature from the City of Paris for *The Fifth Son*. Wiesel's most recent books published in the United States are *A Passover Haggadah, Sages and Dreamers*, and *The Forgotten*. The first volume of his memoirs, *Tous les fleuves vont à la mer* [*All Rivers Run to the Sea*], was published in Paris in 1994, and in English by Knopf in 1996.

A native of Sighet, Transylvania [Romania], Wiesel and his family were deported by the Nazis to Auschwitz when he was fifteen years old. His mother and younger sister perished there, his two older sisters survived. Wiesel and his father were later transported to Buchenwald.

After the war, Wiesel studied in Paris and later became a journalist in that city, yet he remained silent about what he had endured as an inmate in the death camps. During an interview with the French writer François Mauriac, Wiesel was persuaded to end that silence. He subsequently wrote *La Nuit* [*Night*], which has been translated into twenty-five languages since its publication in 1958.

A devoted supporter of Israel, Wiesel has defended the causes of Soviet Jews, Nicaragua's Miskito Indians, Argentina's *desaparecidos* [those who mysteriously disappeared at the hands of the military dictatorship], Cambodian refugees, the Kurds, South African apartheid victims, famine victims in Africa, and the recent victims and prisoners in the former Yugoslavia.

Three months after he received the Nobel Peace Prize, with his wife Marion, Elie Wiesel established the Elie Wiesel Foundation for Humanity. Its mission is to advance the cause of human rights and peace throughout the world by creating a new forum for the discussion of urgent ethical issues confronting humanity.

The first major project undertaken by the foundation was an international conference of Nobel laureates convened jointly by Wiesel and French President François Mitterrand. Seventy-nine laureates from five continents met in Paris in January 1988 to explore issues and questions related to the conference theme, "Facing the Twenty-first Century: Threats and Promises."

This was followed by other conferences: "The Anatomy of Hate," first in Boston, co-sponsored by Boston University [1989]; then in Haifa, co-sponsored by Haifa University [1990]; in Oslo, co-sponsored by the Norwegian Nobel Committee [1990]; and finally in Moscow, co-sponsored by *Ogonyok* magazine [1991].

In November 1992, after the Crown Heights riots, a conference was held at New York University on "The Anatomy of Hate: Saving our Children," co-sponsored by Mario Cuomo, governor of New York.

Wiesel has been distinguished professor of Judaic Studies at the City University of New York [1972–1976] and the first Henry Luce Visiting Scholar in the Humanities and Social Thought at Yale University [1982–1983]. Since 1976, he has been the Andrew W. Mellon Professor in the Humanities at Boston University, where he also holds the title of university professor. He is a member of the faculty in the Department of Religion as well as in the Department of Philosophy.

An American citizen since 1963, Elie Wiesel lives in New York with Marion and his son, Shlomo Elisha.

Interview by Irving Bernstein in New York
January, 1997

Q: You say that you are a seeker, not a leader, that the only role you have sought is that of writer, witness, and teacher. But isn't it true that through your words you've become an activist? That you are, in spite of yourself, a leader? You took the lead when you wrote one of the first books on the Holocaust. Your leadership was critical in helping the American people build a museum in Washington to preserve the memory of the Holocaust. You have spoken out whenever you perceived the violation of human rights—in the Former Soviet Union (FSU), in Bosnia, in Africa, in the United States. You censured a President of the United States publicly, when you felt his actions would result in giving Nazis a stamp of approval. You speak and write words which motivate our national community—whether under the auspices of the UJA or other organizations.

A: Irving, my friend, we've known each other almost fifty years. It's a lot of time. So you know that what I say, I mean.

I never wanted to be a leader. I am not a leader. I do not see myself as such. If people want to give me that title, I refuse it. It's my privilege to bear witness, which means to do something, which means to take sides, which means to say this is how it happened—even if the whole world may say no. If you are a witness you can say the three words, "I was there." And your words carry a certain weight.

It doesn't mean much, because it doesn't mean that everyone will accept those words. If the words come from a minority, a minority of one, and they are heard, they may be taken into consideration by those who are activists, by those who want to listen.

Q: That may be true, but I think you are being modest. You have set standards for others to follow. I know that you're not trying to be a leader. But to several generations now, you're someone that people look to, respect, and follow.

A: That's because I am not a leader. I really do refuse conventional leadership. I'm just a good student, and I think I am a good teacher; and when I teach, I write. When I write, I teach. The main thing is, I don't play games. I'm a Jew. I say it openly, without any embarrassment. Whatever I do, I do as a Jew. Even when I work for other people, I work for them as a Jew.

At my age, I don't say words to cater to people. I've never catered to anyone. I say what I say because I believe in what I am saying. So people have attitudes and opinions about me, negative and positive. There is a word in French: *incontournable*. It means you cannot bypass certain things. There are certain issues a person such as myself cannot bypass. There are certain themes at given times, certain topics: Soviet Jewry, for example.

You and I worked so well together, in such harmony as a team for UJA, for what the UJA stood for—should stand for. We could not be ignored because we were ready to undertake any project, any endeavor, as crazy as it may have sounded—even full-page ads in *The New York Times*.

We did many creative things. It's true. Therefore, I worked with you, and very few people realized really how close we were. I worked from the outside and you from the inside.

Q: In the magazine section of *The New York Times*, December 22, 1996, there was an article by William van der Heuvel. He wrote that the Holocaust was no secret, that Churchill and world leaders knew about it, that there was nothing they could do except win the war. He wrote that even if the railway lines to Auschwitz had been bombed (an issue we've heard about so many times before), it wouldn't have made any difference. Did you ever reply to that article?

A: I did not. I did not, because I think I was among the very first to raise these questions about President Roosevelt and the bombing of the railways leading to Birkenau.

Look, what van der Heuvel says about winning the war, of course, is true. But the fact is that parallel to that war, there was another war against the Jews going on, and in that one, Roosevelt did not fare too well. You know that, Irving. You were here.

I told you the story. When I visited President Carter for the first time [1978], he offered me the appointment as chairman of the President's Commission on the Holocaust. Several months later, he had a present for me, he said, and showed me unusual pictures that American planes took when they flew over Auschwitz. No one had seen them before. But Carter had asked the CIA to find out something about the places where I'd been.

I asked President Carter if President Roosevelt had seen them. Though the photos had been taken by military aerial reconnaisance at that time, they had never been developed until 1978 when a photo interpreter working for the CIA, Dino Brugioni, found and developed them.

Had Roosevelt seen them, who knows what might have happened? In any event, ten thousand people were killed in Birkenau every day—every night. Even if the Germans had to repair their railways, it would have taken them more time. Furthermore, the Germans—Hitler, Himmler, and the others—interpreted in their own way the inactivity or the inaction of Roosevelt and Churchill.

It seems the Allies didn't care. If they had bombed the railways, the signal would have been different, because then Hitler would have known the world was outraged. If the Allies had done something, Hitler would have known that the world did care about Jewish lives. So I don't accept van der Heuvel's premise. The only thing that was very disturbing in what he said was that the Jewish leaders had actually advised the Pentagon or the White House not to bomb Auschwitz.

That is serious. That Jews themselves, Jewish leaders themselves, were against it. It's not just a question of the railways. That was so silly, because I remember when the planes went over Auschwitz, we were praying for them to bomb our camp and the barracks.

Q: You knew they were American planes?

A: We saw the planes. We wanted them to bomb Auschwitz. We wanted to die under the bombs rather than being gassed. But the Jewish leaders said it would cause too many casualties. That's what van der Heuvel said, and he apparently has documents that give names. That is disturbing. It doesn't answer the question about the railways. There is no answer. I call it indifference. It was total indifference to the Jewish tragedy.

Q: There are those of us who say that there was a time when you literally became the voice and conscience of UJA in the seventies and eighties. Since those days, you have had a variety of experiences with many Jewish organizations because people see you as a spokesman for the Jewish community. It seems to me that you've seen leadership, and especially Jewish leadership, in all its forms. What role do you believe a Jewish leader, a layman or professional, should take today?

A: To be a leader means to me to be a teacher. And teachers are guides. Therefore, they should serve by example. That's what being a leader means.

I don't believe I was the conscience of the UJA. You can't be someone else's conscience. Everybody has his own.

How many crises did we deal with? The moment a crisis occurred, you and I would meet and do something. Right or wrong, we at least did something, and it was usually something dramatic, something spectacular.

True, Jewish leaders must be especially sensitive to what is happening in the world around them—always sensitive to Jewish fears and concerns, and they must see everything in terms of Jewish history. They must take a long-term view. They must not judge the present as if the present existed in a vacuum. The context is much wider. Jews must always remember that we are a people four thousand years old.

Otherwise, what are we doing here? Are we here just to be? Who needs that? Who can live in such suffering and struggle unless we know that the struggle is not a new one? Our missions are old and our dreams are eternal. Our leaders must know that and teach it to our people without alienating them.

When you possess such knowledge, and you put it to use, as we did, things begin to happen. But in the beginning, I think the UJA was like all other Jewish organizations—just a professional organization. The first time I came to Kansas City, to address the CJF General Assembly in 1969 or 1970, I was shocked. I arrived at the council for Shabbat and had the feeling that I came to a meeting of labor unions. There was nothing Jewish there. All the talk was how to raise funds, from whom, for what purpose. It was professional, but it lacked inspiration. There was simply no soul. Then slowly things changed. And thank God, today, it's totally different. The Federation General Assembly is Jewish, but I believe our communal leaders should know a bit more about our tradition, about our culture, about our civilization.

I remember years and years ago, I was at a meeting of a major Jewish organization and suggested that any Jew elected to a leadership position should attend a four- to six-week seminar to learn what it means to be Jewish. They laughed at me and I was attacked by everybody. I still feel that should be done today. Look, you meet young people in UJA. They are better because they know that they don't know. The older leaders thought they knew everything. So I would say today, why don't you learn more? Study Jewish history, Jewish culture. Leaders should read books, discuss ideas. They should know more about the Bible, something about the Talmud. Then at least, he or she would know what they are talking about when they speak about Jewish education, which is and must be their priority.

Q: Isn't there some irony in your life in more ways than one?

A: When I came to America, I was very, very poor. Early, in New York, until '63 or so, there were days I had nothing to eat. I was hungry. I had to steal soap from the UN men's room. I did not have money to buy soap. I was destitute.

And nobody knew, because I'm proud and nobody should know it. But when I came to America, Yediot Aharanot sent me. They said, "We'll give you the same salary you had in Paris. A hundred and sixty dollars a month." I asked if one could live on that. The editor said, "No, you'll do what everybody else is doing." I said,

"What's that?" They said, "You'll do speeches." "Speeches? What kind of speeches?" "For UJA." In the plane from Paris, I met a UJA professional. He worked for the New York office. I asked him about lectures. I said, "You think I could get to do lectures?" He said, "You will."

So I came to the UJA office the first or second day. I met the secretary. I sat down and she said, "I hear you want to make speeches. I hear that you wrote a book." (By then I had written one book in Yiddish on the Holocaust.) "You want to speak on the Holocaust?"

I said, "Oh no, I don't speak on the Holocaust."

"What do you want to speak about?"

"I don't know. I don't know what people speak about." We spent a very nice hour. At the end she said, "It was very nice meeting you. But we cannot employ you." I called my airplane acquaintance and I said, "Tell me, suppose I had been accepted. What would I have made?" He said, "Fifty dollars a lecture." For me fifty dollars was a lot of money.

I couldn't get it, so when you came to see me about Munich, and your discourse was, "Look, many, many of the UJA groups ask for you. You always say no." I began lecturing around '65, '66, through the Speakers' Federation, then through Lily Edelman from the B'nai Brith, and that brought me the huge sum of $500 for a lecture. You said, "For some reason you refuse the UJA. They are ready to pay you the same thing. Furthermore, for this special lecture, Munich, it's a national conference, they'll give you whatever the price is."

All of a sudden, I remembered. When I wanted to speak for the UJA, I couldn't get $50. And now you say ten times as much. I smiled and accepted your invitation, but I never took money from national UJA, particularly since you and I had a creative time together doing programs that interested me and were meaningful for the Jewish community.

In all the years of our relationship, I never took a fee, although I know you would have given me anything I would have requested. But I couldn't help smiling every once in a while, thinking back to those early days when I wasn't considered good enough to speak for UJA.

Q: I think our first experience together took place in 1973, I remember coming to you in almost a panic to ask you to speak at the national conference—this was after the Yom Kippur War.

A: No, Irving. No.

Q: Wasn't that the first time?

A: No. The first time you came to see me was after the Munich massacre of the Israeli athletes at the Olympics, in 1972. And you said I should come and speak. I said I don't speak to the UJA.

Q: You have a better memory than I do.

A: After the Munich massacre, I came on a Shabbat after you and I spoke about the meaning of *oneg Shabbat* [celebrating the Sabbath]. That's when it began. The second time was after the '73 war. I came to speak against despair. After that you showed the film version of my play *Zalman, or The Madness of God* at Carnegie Hall. Subsequently, we had many good and creative meetings.

Q: Did you believe when you made the speech "Against Despair" [which was distributed throughout the country] that it would have the impact it had?

A: No, I did not. I simply said what I felt. It's not that important to me to know if a book is doing well or not. It's better not to think about it. Whatever I do, I try to do the best I can.

And I do have weaknesses. Sometimes I am pained if in an audience of two thousand people, someone in the far corner yawns. I feel it. [Laughter.]

But in this case, I knew "Against Despair" was the proper title. We chose that title together. I knew that was the problem, the difficulty we had to overcome—despair was everywhere in the Jewish community. Israel almost lost the war, which means Israel was almost destroyed. And what would it have done to the Jewish people, the Jewish community, Jewish awareness, Jewish pride, and Jewish hope?

I came with notes, as you remember. I wrote it out, and I worked on it for many, many days, as I always do. I always take speeches very seriously. I worked it out in me what I would want to say about the Yom Kippur War, about attitudes toward despair, Jewish attitudes toward despair. Later on, you told me about its impact. I had no idea. I knew people in the audience were moved. But even then, I didn't fully appreciate what happened because, as you remember, I ran out quickly. I didn't want an ovation—I ran out, as I always do after lectures.

Q: I still get calls about the booklet that we made up with that memorable speech. Others call to ask if I saw your book, *A Jew Today*, which includes "Against Despair."

It was an address that changed attitudes. Then came *The Madness of God*. You put a lot of confidence in UJA when you permitted us to show *The Madness of God* at Carnegie Hall.

A: Yes, I did.

Q: It was with Lee J. Cobb, Theodore Bikel, Herschel Bernardi, and our Issachar Miron as the director. Although we had done many kinds of musical performances, we had never done a play before.

A: It was a play with Joseph Wiseman, not Lee J. Cobb. It was a play performed on Broadway, and also in Washington. Then PBS filmed it, and we decided, because at that time [1974] our community went through various difficulties, we decided that we were going to have the premiere of this film at Carnegie Hall on a Friday afternoon.

Q: The question is, why did you have such confidence in the UJA? After all, we're a fund-raising organization.

A: Come on. I didn't have confidence in UJA. I had confidence in you. You know me, organizations don't mean anything to me as such. It's always a personal question. I must confess I never participated in fund-raising and I appreciate you never asked me to—because you knew I wouldn't do it.

Q: But I want to ask you something about *The Madness of God*, which I've always wondered about. Did you model Zalman after yourself?

A: Naturally. Zalman always *noodges* [irritates] the rabbi to get mad. There is a madman in every one of my books. I love madmen and they love me—too much. The idea was to urge the rabbi to speak up, to burst out, and become free. Naturally, I was screaming in that play.

Q: President Carter appointed you as chairman of the Holocaust Memorial Museum Committee?

A: President Carter wanted me to become chairman of the President's Commission—to advise him on how to memorialize the victims of the Holocaust. His was a very long title. But I had good ears for titles. I said it was too long, and I changed it to the President's Commission on the Holocaust.

Q: At the same time, he appointed a number of board members. Senator Frank Lautenberg and I were appointed. There were many survivors, many experienced people. Yet, you chose me to be the chairman of the Museum Committee, even though I was one of the younger members and not a survivor. Why did you choose me for that position?

A: As a rule, I wanted survivors to be chairmen of committees because they suffered so much, not only during, but after the war as well. They were always second-ranked Jewish citizens in their Jewish communities. Even in UJA, show me one survivor who was a national chairman or anything of that sort. They were humiliated. I felt this was my chance to glorify the survivors—to give them the power they deserved.

But I chose you for that vital position because I knew you were practical and a doer, which I am not. You are a superb organizer. You were a member of the Museum Council, and you did all kinds of things. That came later.

As chairman, I insisted on two activities. The first was to have a national ceremony, a remembrance ceremony for the Holocaust, either in the White House or in Congress. It takes place every year. If I ever did something that I'm proud of, it is that remembrance ceremony—because it has impact.

The second condition was that we travel to Russia, Denmark, Poland, and Israel. It was clear we had to go—I wanted to meet with the refuseniks. The Soviet ambassador didn't understand why I wanted to go to Russia after '66 because of my position on Soviet Jewry—the Russians had refused to give me a visa. The only way to go back was as chairman of a President's commission.

I had to go back, I had promised Russian Jews that I would return again and again.

Q: I didn't realize that.

A: It was Dobrynin, the Russian ambassador. He was very clear. He said, "Why do you want to go to Moscow? It has nothing to with the goal of your commission. I understand you want to go to Poland, even to Kiev. But why Moscow? What do you want to do in Moscow?"

"Fact finding," I said, "I want to see all kinds of people."

Q: I remember one dramatic incident in Moscow, besides the synagogue being full when you chanted the *Haftorah* [the scriptural passage that corresponds with the week's Bible chapter.] Frank Lautenberg and I had *aliyot* [were called to make a blessing over the reading of the Torah] just before you, and so we were standing at the *bimah* [altar] with you. We could look out and see that unbelievable mob. You took us to meet the dissidents. I remember we walked out of the back of the hotel. We took a subway, then a bus, and then we walked, and we got to the building. The KGB was there. They told us it was on the third floor, and we went upstairs.

Alexander Lerner and all of them were there. They were singing Hebrew songs, even though they knew the room was bugged, and we were with them. I'll never forget that moment, as long as I live.

A: Of course not.

Q: Just an unbelievable, unbelievable moment. Did you really believe the Holocaust Museum would be built? Is it living up to your expectations?

A: I knew it would be built because we got the Mall, where most Washington museums are located. We knew something would happen there. I wanted something smaller. You remember the first project they showed us? It said a building with bricks?

Q: Yes.

A: I liked the idea of a small, modest memorial. Now one member of our council refused. He said the building would collapse, something like that. But I didn't think in my wildest dreams that we would be so successful. I'm grateful that it is. Is it what I wanted it to be? I would have wanted it somewhat different. I may have been wrong. In truth, I told you a year earlier that I wanted to resign.

Q: I remember.

A: I'll tell you why. I said it was because I was afraid that it wouldn't be what I wanted it to be. For me the Jewish emphasis is too important, Jewish centrality is too important, and the entire project was going to be difficult and complicated. We had to make compromises. And I also realized there were too many quarrels among the members, among the Jews themselves.

I cannot stand quarrels. There were jealousies. There was pettiness over who got this chairmanship and that chairmanship, this committee and that one.

I could not stand it. I didn't want to be involved in it. I cannot say "no" to someone who wants anything from me. How can I cause pain to others? So I said to you, Irving, I want to resign. You urged me not to, so I stayed a couple of years more as a result of your urging.

Q: Yes, a smaller memorial would have affected fewer people, but your vision and experience were critical. Another important contribution was to include audiovisual materials and computerization.

A: That's what I'm grateful for—the fact that you and I were together at the beginning of the endeavor. I was there for eight years. And it's good that those who continue afterwards have had the ability to raise funds. The truth is, I must confess that I tried to help raise funds when I was there. I didn't succeed very well on that, either. But you were there. We didn't do too well in fund-raising. It was only when those who could give, did, so that we were able to convince others to give.

Q: After that, you made a very courageous statement to President Reagan about speaking "truth to power," when he was going to visit Bitburg. [In 1985, President Reagan made a commitment to the German chancellor to visit a Waffen SS cemetery—a cemetery for elite storm troopers in Bitburg, Germany.]

It created a great deal of unrest among the White House staff. The President was scheduled to speak to a capacity crowd about the museum at Abe Pollin's Capitol Center on the Maryland/Washington border. I remember calling Max Fisher, who set up an appointment for me with Reagan's staff. I told them they were making a mistake. That Elie Wiesel was not political. If they didn't want you to say something they didn't like, they shouldn't have somebody say or do something immoral. If they were going to say something immoral, you would have no alternative but to reply to them. We then had that meeting at the basketball stadium, which went very well.

I wondered whether you had spoken to Reagan after he went to Bitburg.

A: In truth, the Jewish leadership didn't help me. Many tried to prevail upon me not to make the speech I made in the White House, remember?

Q: Yes.

A: But I had to say it, after all. Now everybody speaks "truth to power."

Q: It was one of the most dramatic moments I've seen on television.

A: It was the only time Reagan was down in the polls. They asked where the Great Communicator was.

Most Jewish leaders, actually, tried to say to me, "Look, after all, you need to have a larger agenda. We have to look to the future. Don't antagonize the President." Only afterwards when it became such a "success," they all said they were with me.

Now, what they didn't know is that out of respect and out of affection for Reagan, and because we always got along very well, I sent him a copy of my speech beforehand.

Q: You did?!

A: Of course. The day before. I did it out of respect for the office and the man.

Q: I didn't know that.

A: Naturally, I sent him my speech. Mr. President, this is the speech I'm going to make tomorrow. And then the next day, I saw him before the ceremony and I asked him, "Did you read it?" And he said, "Yes, I did."

I was respectful and it was, after all, live television. Those in the White House were grateful to me, so much so, that Reagan asked me to go with him to Europe on Air Force One. Reagan, his chief of staff, said that only the President and I would speak in Germany. Then he sent two senators to see me.

They quoted Reagan. "Elie Wiesel is my hero. You know how I like him. How I admire him. Let him come with me. Why doesn't he want to come with me?"

I was respectful. But the Jewish leaders were not. They were frightened and they had no courage. None at all.

Q: You acted with integrity if you sent him the speech ahead of time, so it shouldn't have been a shock.

A: It wasn't a shock. The shock came later. In the beginning, the ceremony for giving me the Congressional Gold Medal was supposed to take place in the East Room. I had 150 seats, and the

White House also had 150 seats. Then they realized two weeks before the event that it was going to be something unpleasant. So they moved it to the smallest room in the White House. I had four tickets.

And they then thought they could get away with it quickly. They didn't realize it was going to be on live television. That was shocking, not the speech. They knew the speech.

Q: I didn't realize that, and I think that most people weren't aware that the President knew what you were going to say.

A: They knew the speech. I said to Reagan beforehand, "Mr. President, I have an idea for you. You give me the medal, and then I will speak. Afterwards, just imagine, you come back to the lectern and you simply say, "All right, I am not going [to Bitburg]," I said, "You would be the hero of the world."

Q: You're so right!

A: I said, "This is the scenario I set for you, Mr. President. Do it." And he said, "I can't. I spoke with Kohl. Chancellor Kohl doesn't let me off the hook. I promised, and he doesn't want me to retreat from my promise. And then my advisers tell me I must go."
I felt sorry for him, because he didn't want to go. He really didn't.

Q: "Truth to power" is not simply within the Jewish community. "Truth to power" is in the general community now.

A: Everybody says it now. I said, "I belong to a tradition that commands me to speak truth to power."

Q: It was one of those rare moments on television that will always be remembered.

A: It is because you think afterwards, "Look, who am I?"

Q: Frank Lautenberg and I always talk about and will always regret that other commitments prevented us from going to Oslo when you were awarded the Nobel Prize. I understand from others that afterward, children, non-Jewish children, sang Hebrew songs under your hotel balcony. What were your thoughts on that momentous occasion? You brought so much pride to the whole Jewish community, world over, when you were awarded the Nobel.

A: People were very special there. There was a torch parade below us. I was on the balcony. Everybody participated. The entire Norwegian nation was represented. Everybody. Even the PLO had a delegation there. Everybody! They were singing Hebrew songs. It was very, very moving.

What I felt? You will read my memoirs. I felt something special? What I didn't know was that during the morning ceremony when they gave me the prize, there was a demonstration outside, those who denied the Holocaust.

There was a demonstration against us, the deniers had come from all over Europe. Somebody gave them money to organize it. They were there. I found out later only because my security was so tight that a journalist asked at the press conference, how come your security is tighter than our king's is? The director general of the Foreign Ministry had a marvelous response. He told the journalist that the king of Norway has four million citizens to protect him.

Q: [Laughs.] Here I rely on your memory. In your home, one day, at the other apartment on Central Park West, we invited Shimon Peres, Yitzhak Rabin, or Moshe Dayan to meet with writers.

A: Once we had Peres, once it was Dayan. And once it was Rabin.

Q: And I believe it was with writers.

A: Yes, and Golda, also.

Q: I remember they stood at the fireplace. The writers were sitting on the floor and on chairs. For Dayan and for Peres, it was most unusual—they remembered and often talked about it. The question is, did you think it was worthwhile?

A: You know I have a hang-up about Israel. I've always tried to help Israel, to the best of my abilities. Modestly, as I can. And whoever is the prime minister, I am ready to help. I am not involved in Israeli politics. I'm closer to certain people, but the prime minister is after all the prime minister. He speaks on behalf of all Israel, and therefore if he or she needs anything from me, I must say yes.

So I arranged several receptions, which created problems with my neighbors. The prime minister's security blocked the elevators; the New York police closed the street. But I think it was good for the prime minister to meet Jewish intellectuals. There is always a chasm between the politicians and the intellectuals. In my house, there wasn't. It was good.

Q: True. Now when it comes to our meeting in Israel, I know you'll recall when I convinced the Jewish Agency Board of Governors to invite you to address the Jewish Agency Assembly. It was 1974, the first time they ever had an outside speaker. And again, you spoke "truth to power." As you look back now, how would you evaluate that experience? And what would you say if you were speaking to them today—in a divided Israel that is swinging to the right?

A: Remember the sequence of events. You came to see me with a few of your colleagues. Maybe Max was with you. At that time, there was something in the press about Israel every day—affairs, scandals, recriminations. And you said, "You must come to talk to them."

And I said I had to ask. First I asked Shaul Lieberman, my teacher and friend. He said, "Look, you are not an Israeli. They're going to attack you for speaking the truth. That is the price you pay for not living there."

Golda said, "Absolutely. Come speak, yes." She had a hard time back in Israel. There too, you remember, I prepared, just as in the White House, I prepared every word. And I came and I showed it to you. I stayed in Israel for less than eighteen hours.

Q: That's right.

A: Okay? I didn't want to do it. You insisted, and because it was you, I felt I had to do it, so I came. The idea was gently, gently, to tell certain things to our Israeli brothers and sisters. I began by saying *mea culpa*, we Diaspora Jews, what is wrong with us? I remember everybody was so happy when I said how terrible we were.

And then I said: now, what about you? And I realized all of a sudden that a wind from Siberia was blowing in the hall.

Q: On both of us.

A: It was Siberia. "Who is he to come and tell us what we have to do?" and I was so kind. I was so tactful. So much so, that I didn't finish the speech. I improvised another ending.

I published it in *A Jew Today*. They were not ready for my frankness in Israel. I cannot criticize Israel. It's true. Who am I? The only time I did it then, I did not finish the speech. I felt the hostility that was there. I came back immediately, and already found a message from you.

If I had remained, there would have been a lynching. "Who is he to comment? He lives in New York and tells us what to do?"

Of all the people that I knew, who after all were friends of mine, who were members of the Jewish Agency, not one said a good word on my behalf. Not one.

But then the most beautiful thing happened a year later. Pinhas Sapir [former finance minister and chairman of the Jewish Agency] called me from Israel. He said "I'll be in New York; I would like to come and see you." I said, " I'll come and see you in the hotel." He said "No, I and my wife want to come and see you at home."

I didn't understand why. He came, and twenty others accompanied him. "You want to know why I wanted to be here? I'll tell you why," he said. "I wasn't there when you spoke. But I was there when they attacked you. Since I didn't hear your speech, I have nothing to say. But now I know how right you were. I came to say, please forgive us. And I want those with me to hear it. That's why I came." At which point, for the next few days, or weeks, all those who had kept quiet came to see me.

Q: He was a doer; I truly loved Sapir. He was a real *mensch* [a person of good quality].

A: Today, the worst things in Israel are fanaticism and hatred. There is too much hatred in Israel. Not toward the Arabs, but of Jews toward each other. I have never, never felt such hatred there before.

Now there is the religious against the secular, and vice versa. Leaders against leaders. Settlers against left-wingers. Religious people against each other. Young against poor. Jerusalem against Tel Aviv. I have never sensed so much hatred accumulated in one place. They must find a way to fight hatred. It cannot go on like that.

Q: How would you deal with religious pluralism?

A: By teaching. By teaching the effects of *sinat hinam*, of baseless hatred. We cannot live as fanatics. It's not Jewish. The Yemenite from Yemen and the tailor from Moscow—they have something in common even when they are so different. There are people who don't even know their languages.

And yet, they are Jews. And therefore, I would say, every Jew is vital to our survival. We must bring the Jewish people together to inspire not some tolerance—I'm not talking about tolerance—but respect. They must respect one another, whoever somebody is and whatever his opinion is, irrespective of religious belief or political affiliation.

Q: How would you assess our strengths and our weaknesses as a community?

A: I'll tell you, it's stronger than before. I mean, American Jews have become more Jewish than before. During the Bitburg affair, I was the only one to speak up. That is not the case now. During the Second World War many American leaders were timorous. If Jewish leaders had spoken up then the way some of them do now, the situation would have changed. But when they came to see the president or to advise anyone, they were so small, so prudent.

Today they are not. Today that's strength. The weakness is our lack of education. We are not emphasizing education enough. That should be the number one priority. For every community, that should become the one priority today. To make Jews better Jews.

I believe the Jewish teacher is the most important civil servant in the Jewish community. They need higher wages, and places of honor, to attract the best. But for the moment, we don't.

Q: So true. You've answered this question many times before. What does it mean to you to be a Jew?

A: To me, to be a Jew is to accept the destiny of my people. I want to believe in Jews. Whatever happens to my people must affect me. I also believe in constant interrogation. What am I doing here? What is my place? Why am I here? Why are you? A Jew is somebody who questions himself or herself, all the time, and lives through the question. There is a quest in question.

How I deal with the quest, the constant quest for something, is personal. But again, Jews should know that there is something about us that to others seems secret and mysterious, so much so it provokes hatred from others. So what? Nothing should destroy our solidarity.

Q: You have written almost forty books.

A: Right, and forty books have been written about me. Now the question is, who is going to outdo the other?

Q: I'm struggling with one book. Forty books are more than one lifetime of accomplishment, and you're only at the beginning of your life.

A: Accomplishment, I don't know. But anyway, it's my work.

Q: The question is, why do you continue to write?

A: I haven't even begun. Irving, I'm serious. I'm not just saying it. Believe me. My feeling is, I've written so many books but I haven't even begun. One day I'll begin. What I wanted to say, I haven't yet said. I love to teach. But I learn, I learn. I learn every day, and I teach. To me, my passion for studies is what governs my life.

Q: The last question, it's almost a repeat in a sense. During the seventies and eighties, there were quite a few years when we practically lived together, you made a very unique and unforgettable contribution to UJA with your speaking and writing. People of all ages still talk about it. It becomes the substance of not only their lives, but the way they deal with a lot of Jewish issues and their families.

Why were you so ready and willing to do it for the UJA when so many others, authors and writers, were not?

A: I don't know about others, but I believe the Jew must always be linked to his community. It's personal, really, it's based on our friendship. You and I quickly became very close. We worked well. There was nothing personal to gain from it. No gain for me or for you. I never took anything from UJA. I think that those were good hours. Churchill would say "the finest hours." Whatever crazy idea you had, you'd get a response. Whatever idea I had, you responded. We did things there that nobody has ever done before or since.

19

EPILOGUE

T
he success of any philanthropic endeavor depends to a great
degree on the ability of the fund-raising professional to earn
the respect and loyalty of the volunteer. When that happens,
both the volunteer and the professional grow in confidence in their
respective roles, and their relationship benefits the cause they
represent.

The responsibility for this symbiotic relationship rests primarily
on the professionals, because volunteers, by their very nature, have
multiple interests. The professional's primary concern, however, is
the agenda of the organization he or she works for, but the success
of the endeavor depends on the quality and the degree of
involvement of the layperson.

Although many philanthropic and volunteer-oriented agencies
know that this kind of relationship is significant, they do not train
either their professionals or their volunteers. As a result, both learn
through the test of experience—by stumbling over one block after
another before they begin to achieve productive and successful
partnerships. However, in this unplanned manner, many
professionals and volunteers burn out and leave, wasting money,
manpower, and time. Then, all too often, interested and capable
volunteers refuse to accept leadership positions.

Max Fisher, a veteran leader in the political, secular, and Jewish
worlds, realized and understood this dilemma. In a lifetime of
communal leadership, he followed the philosophy of the legendary
David Ben-Gurion, who believed that leaders have to make decisions
in spite of risks to themselves and those around them. For Ben-
Gurion there were never any hopeless battles, only leaders who lost
hope and failed to confront problems—allowing their silence to lead
to failure.

In January 1997, to come to grips with this perennial professional/
volunteer problem, Fisher, in consultation with Jehuda Reinharz,

the creative and innovative president of Brandeis University, established the Max M. Fisher/Irving Bernstein Institute for Jewish Leadership at the university. He believed that in an academic setting provided by a nurturing institution of higher learning, this issue and other serious concerns confronting Jewish leadership and the Jewish people could be resolved. Through his own experience he realized that those responsible for the stewardship of Jewish organizations, volunteers and professionals, must together develop constructive working guidelines.

I am not aware of any other program named for both a volunteer and a professional. By twinning my name with his, Fisher has made a statement about the significance of the professional/volunteer relationship for future communal growth. He believes that the close working relationship we had for almost forty years can serve as a model to help our community realize its funding goals, and also resolve other fundamental issues that may determine the future of the American Jewish community and the community of Israel.

In establishing the institute, Fisher and Reinharz hope to develop leadership with vision unlimited by the physical horizons of their respective organizations. The American Jewish community is no longer an immigrant community. We are primarily the children and grandchildren of immigrants, who today have the capacity and strength to change the Jewish future of American Jewry and influence the destiny of the people of Israel and Jews around the world.

Leaders trained at the institute will not be limited by artificial horizons. They will have access to cyberspace, in real time, and can be anywhere inside of twenty-four hours; telecommunications may even allow them to stay where they are and accomplish more than they would by globe trotting.

By establishing the institute, Fisher also raises the stature of all professionals and challenges them to act as leaders in the Ben-Gurion mold.

The key to success is to determine if the programs we have today answer the questions that desperately need to be answered regarding how volunteer and professional leaders can work together to find mutually acceptable solutions.

The institute might explore some of the following issues:

1. Guidelines for symbiotic relationships between lay and professional leadership.

2. Leadership training programs for professionals and volunteers on all levels.

3. Changing methods of fund development to meet growing needs in the United States and overseas.

4.Resolving questions of religious pluralism and inter-denominational strife.

5. Creating viable and realistic Jewish education programs that teach joyful and lasting Judaism.

6. Examining and developing the role of women in organizational and communal endeavors.

7. Examining the relationship of the Diaspora to Israel and the role of Israel in the twenty-first century.

The vexing problem of Jewish continuity—continuity of leadership, continuity of involvement, continuity of identity—must be the number one priority on the agendas of every religious and secular entity in the Jewish establishment.

Rabbi Henry Sobel of Brazil wrote, "We are so concerned with the idea that we may some day be denied the right to be Jews, that we neglect our duty to remain Jews."

The loss of our young men and women, including many of our best and brightest, adds up exponentially. And as heretical as it may be to say so, saving American Jews is no less critical than rescuing Russian Jewry.

Continuity is the main challenge facing our community and its leadership. Any attempts to limit debate over whether it is more effective to assure continuity through Israel or through domestic programs are specious, counterproductive, and self-defeating.

By so narrowing the focus, the few leaders who care enough to deal with the issues willingly are forced to expend their energies on the minutiae that divide us instead of concentrating on the core values that bring us together. Although there are always casualties whenever we are confronted by crisis, the center of the Jewish people has held firm, and I believe the center will continue to hold firm.

Miracles are biblical fantasy, and our overall community cannot hope for them to occur spontaneously. In the final analysis, as Rabbi

Lamm said [quoting Bernstein when he was awarded his honorary doctorate], "we must learn and teach that philanthropy has to be supported by education, giving by learning, compassion by commitment, feeling by understanding."

Therefore, leadership must come together to act. Although the problems confronting us at home and abroad may seem overwhelming, we have unlimited potential that can be tapped to solve them. We know our constituents: individual Jews and Jewish communities who have shown their willingness to follow leadership they respect into the trenches and unto the heights. We know, because our experiences with UJA proved that anything is possible.

The late, revered Rabbi Abraham Joshua Heschel summed up our individual and collective challenge:

> What is at stake in our lives is more than the faith of one generation. From this moment, we, the living, are Israel. The past begun by the Patriarchs and the Prophets carried out by countless Jews of the past is now entrusted to us. We are the only channel of Jewish tradition to the future. It is we who are responsible for the entire past of generations to come. It is we who will either forfeit or enrich our legacy of the ages.

20

APPENDIX

Appendix A

Tel-Aviv, February 19, 1968

Dear Irving,

I really do not know how to apologize for the postponement of my visit to the United States.

I want you not only to believe but also to understand that I could not have acted otherwise. The situation we are facing now with our neighbours is a most complicated one. It is not only the military conflict which might blow up any time, but mainly the political implication that will follow (Security Council, pressure from the State Department, etc.). In addition to that, we have the million Palestinian Arabs that we are trying to keep under our control and out of the other Arabs' active hostility. These objectives are, in my opinion, of the utmost importance, and I am trying personally to direct them.

I have gone into all these details, endeavouring to explain that it is not so much the immediate clash that prevented me from leaving, but I thought it unjustified to be absent from Israel for two weeks under the present circumstances.

There is no need to tell you how much I appreciate your work and the tremendous efforts made by you, which have really led to unbelievable results. No other nation but ours, and no other people but you could have achieved them.

I am sure that each one of us in Israel has a feeling of deep obligation to you, and, whoever is called up must respond and join you in your work. And that, of course, includes me.

Please convey to Herb and to all the other people involved in the matter my apologies and promises to try and repair some other time what I have damaged now.

With my warmest regards,

Yours sincerely,

Moshe Dayan
Minister of Defence

Mr. Irving Bernstein
UJA, New York

Appendix B

"We Are One":
The Challenge Facing the Jewish Community

In my thirty years of Jewish communal service I have witnessed not only the achievements of rabbinic leadership but also their unfulfilled potential to the community. I will not discuss taxes, deficits or budgets. Instead, I will review challenges and alternatives facing Jewish leadership. Those of you who have met me know me as an eternal optimist and therefore I do not question nor even raise the thought of survival. *K'lal yisrael* will survive despite us and change to meet changing times.

What is at stake, as you very well know, is the kind of Jewish community we will all live in, the degree of its commitment to mercy, compassion and justice and the depth of its knowledge and awareness about itself, its past, present and future. I firmly believe that each of us in this room will play a determining role in the Jewish strength of that community, both by what we do today and by what we do not do tomorrow.

You and I, rabbi and fund raiser, synagogue and UJA campaign have much in common despite elemental and basic differences. Together we have succeeded in reaching more Jews than any other community has ever done, and yet we have also failed to reach more Jews than ever before in history, at a time when we have had not only the opportunity but the right and encouragement of government and society to do so. Even though this 1977 UJA campaign will raise more money than any other year except during the Yom Kippur War, we still will receive contributions from only

From an address by Irving Bernstein to the Rabbinical Assembly Convention, May, 1977.

one million of the two million Jewish families in this country. It is strange that all our synagogues and temples also reach about the same number; we both leave the other million families to themselves, to television and to the American melting pot.

Our purpose is the same, to reach out to this other million, to bring them into the fold, to touch their Jewish nerve and to make them one in purpose, one in mind, one in spirit. This is why we created a National Newspaper Supplement, an educational supplement with a central message by Elie Wiesel stressing that a Jew cannot be a Jew alone but only as a member of a Jewish community, and delivered it to one million three hundred thousand homes. This was the reason we planned a National Shabbat in March, our effort to bring Jewish families and Jewish leaders into the synagogue to gain understanding that the concepts of giving and belonging are holy and not secular. Reaching that missing million is the reason for UJA's National Walk-A-Thon, a program aimed at getting Jewish families in every community to walk together for Jewish unity and solidarity on the very same day, to walk with the sponsorship of Jewish communal institutions and to walk for understanding of the significance of these institutions to Jewish continuity.

It is true that the wars of 1967 and 1973 may have had more to do with our achievements and the success of the campaign than our organizational ability, but there was something else happening at the same time. The melting pot with its secular pressures was changing before us; cultural pluralism emerged and with it an affirmative ethnicity. UJA, through its broad-based appeal and through the drama of war, rescue and survival, created an awareness and stimulated a new generation's search for the meaning of Jewish identity. But awareness is not enough, and these young men and women are seeking Jewish content and Jewish values, particularly as our emphasis shifts from the rescue of individual Jews to the future of the Jewish people. That is the reason for UJA's outreach for an active Rabbinical Advisory Council, its strong and potent role in UJA, the participation of its leaders in our Executive Committee and therefore my outreach to you for closer and deeper cooperative and supportive relationships.

How do we resolve all of our problems? I confess I do not have all the answers. But after three decades of communal experience I believe that by giving our people confidence, knowledge, strength, and faith and by bringing them together in unity, perhaps we can begin to grope with the problems. But that awareness, knowledge and security can only come from leadership.

I have been stressing leadership all over the free world, for when we as leaders fail our community pays a terrible price. When we fail, the human cost is immeasurable. Not too long ago there was an international leadership meeting in Milan, Italy. At the end of the meeting a young man, a rich, sophisticated, well-educated Milanese, rose and said, "Ladies and gentlemen, this has been one of the most moving meetings of my life, but my friends, you have come too late. My generation is lost." The question that we must ask ourselves as leaders is: Will we come too late, too late to our own community, too late to Moscow, too late to Jerusalem?

Argentina contains the largest Jewish community in South America. It comprises only two percent of the general population but twenty percent of the leftist movement. Many of the young boys and girls being lost every day are the sons and daughters of upper and middle class Jewish families. This, again, is because concerned Jewish leaders failed to act, failed to teach, failed to unite, failed to lead. These are the failures within our community. For when we fail within, we also fall victim to our enemies outside.

The Wall Street Journal carried a two-page spread by a 2.5 billion dollar Texas-based conglomerate, Dresser Industries, threatening Jews with antisemitism for supporting legislation against the Arab boycott. Jews are warned that if they continue their efforts America will lose 500,000 jobs and billions of dollars. Americans are told that the boycott is a matter of business and not morality. The question is: Will Americans remain silent? Will we?

As Washington speaks of moderation, we recall that Washington and the rest of the world were silent for nineteen years while the moderate Kingdom of Jordan controlled the Old City of Jerusalem, silent while they desecrated the Western Wall, silent while they destroyed its ancient synagogues and used the gravestones of Mount of Olives for urinals. And now the United Nations, led by the Soviet Union, intensifies the attacks on a united Jerusalem, a Jerusalem open to all for ten years. Will the world remain silent again? Will we?

This was the reason for our program, "This Year in Jerusalem" in which Stanley Rabinowitz, President of the Rabbinical Assembly, played such a vital role. We marched through the streets of Jerusalem to the Western Wall, three thousand strong from fifty states. We wanted then, as we will continue in the future, to tell the world that we are one, that Jerusalem is united and will always remain united. This is why our mission program is now called, "This Year in Jerusalem-Every Year in Jerusalem."

If there is any issue that has special meaning to all concerned Jews, and especially to Jewish leaders, it is the quality of life in America and in Israel for that is the sum and substance of the UJA campaign. While roughly two thirds of the national result is spent overseas through the Joint Distribution Committee and the United Israel Appeal, one third remains at home for education, health, welfare and community services in each community throughout the country. What is our responsibility as leaders of the strongest and largest Jewish community in history? I believe as we move into 1978 that this Rabbinical Assembly, individually and collectively, can lead us in reaching two million families, can strengthen our community at home and overseas and can bring us clarity and purpose.

If ever there was a time for thunder from the pulpit, challenge from the pulpit, it is now. We must send thunder at our enemies within and without and provide challenge to leadership in the synagogues, in the community, in national organizations and in Israel as well. Thunder and challenge are needed to alert six million American Jews to the major issues: that *aliyah* must be an open and chosen priority, for the fate of *Yerushalayim* will eventually depend more on this factor than any other; that Soviet Jewry is every Jew's responsibility and the struggle to reach Vienna deserves as much of our energy and public debate as the fate of Russian Jews after they leave Vienna; that the Holocaust not become another paragraph in a history book or just a physical memorial, that it remain as vivid to all generations as it does to those remaining few who chanted *ani ma'amin;* that raising funds for our Jewish community here and overseas is honorable, dignified and a vital part of Jewish life and that we have the moral and historic mandate to ask every Jew to be one with the people of Israel; that a Jewish community professional be Jewish as well as professional; that both rabbi and social worker recognize that campaigning is an educational process and without it there are no funds and no programs; and, above all, that the Jewish community be seen as a community of Jews and not just of institutions, organizations and campaigns.

Since the cities in which we live are not limited by their physical horizons, leadership for the greater community is as much the obligation of the rabbis as the fund raisers. Our General Chairman, Frank Lautenberg, is one of the ablest men I have ever met. I didn't find him; a rabbi did. A young rabbi guided him to work beyond the synagogue and inspired him to community work. There are many more men and women in the congregations of America who have the same potential for national leadership!

Because leadership is seeking Jewish content and Jewish values, there is today a greater need for rabbinic leadership in the community. But it cannot come by right or demand. It is a fact of today's life that one of the direct ways to communal leadership and community direction is through the fund-raising process, through the power of funding. Through personal participation in our annual campaigns every rabbi can and should be a strong voice on Federation boards, on campaign committees and in budgeting meetings to serve Jewish needs at home and overseas for a stronger Israel and for a stronger America.

There must also be a readiness on the part of leadership to look at strengths as well as faults, to see the totality of life. The Jewish Agency is the butt of black humor, but despite our frustration with this remarkable human experiment, it has settled one and a half million immigrants, created 717 settlements, six new ones this year, built 520 kindergarten centers, nurseries and schools and it has the courage to undergo a study by a task force from the Harvard Business School. Furthermore, this agency has included non-Zionists as well as Zionists on its board, a feat the so-called giants of yesteryear failed to achieve.

Those of us who are quick to criticize Israel tend to forget that it is also a land with 3,200 books published a year and twenty-seven newspapers appearing daily. Last week, in a society with a total population of less than half of New York City, one could choose between twenty-nine theatrical performances, five special shows for children, six ballets and concerts, theatre performances of

Shakespeare, Pinter, Miller, Ibsen and Chekhov, as well as ten original Hebrew plays including one dealing with the problems of an Arab student living in Tel Aviv. This is truly an act of inner strength and courage for a land with immigrants from 102 countries speaking eighty-one languages!

It is fitting that I conclude with a recent experience in Israel where I witnessed the ultimate meaning of alternatives for leadership and life as I stood at Yad Vashem with a group of leaders from all over the world. As we gathered outside that memorial for our six million, Moshe Rivlin, then of the Jewish Agency, spoke to us and said, "Anatevka is buried here, Anatevka, Sholom Aleichem's *shtetl*. There is no more Menachem Mendel. There is no more Sheine Sheindle and Stephanu. Stephanu no longer plays his fiddle for there is no one for him to play for, and Tevye is weary of looking to the skies for his endless dialogue with God."

But on the other side of that hill in the military cemetery was buried the hero of Entebbe, Colonel Yonathan Natanyahu, Yoni, who also looked to the skies but for a different dialogue, a dialogue to save Jews. And that is the difference. Tevye was of our grandfather's generation. Tevye said to God, "Perhaps it is time you chose another people." Yoni knew what he had been chosen for. That is also our choice as leaders: to save lives and to build life at home and in Israel.

As Jewish leaders we often find ourselves alone, alone all by ourselves, alone within a group, alone at the head of a crowd, even alone on the pulpit. But out of the loneliness of our individual commitment comes collective will and out of the loneliness of our individual decisions comes collective strength. Out of that will and strength, together we will make "We are one" more than a slogan, more than words. We will make "We are one" a Jewish way of life. That is the chosen alternative of Jewish leadership.

Appendix C

The citation by Dr. Norman Lamm, president of Yeshiva University, when Irving Bernstein was awarded his honorary doctorate at Yeshiva University in 1987.

Your acknowledged expertise in American Jewish communal affairs has grown steadily over the decades and your concern for the quality of Jewish life throughout the world has been the guiding principle of your leadership in the international Jewish community. You have said that it is not enough to merely affirm a Jewish identity, but that it is necessary to suffuse that identity with content, with the knowledge of our history, our Torah, our people. A prime mover in the historic institutionalized philanthropy of American Jewry, you learned and taught that charity must be supported by education, giving by learning, compassion by commitment and feeling by understanding.

You recognized that a different Jewish generation is coming of age, a generation that was not present at the creation of the State of Israel. And you have understood that these younger Jews, not moved by the emotions that shaped and defined their parents, require a higher level of Jewish education to bind them to their people.

Appendix D

Edward Ginsberg
"In Memoriam"
(Eulogy delivered by Irving Bernstein in Cleveland, Ohio January 7, 1997)

It is difficult, nigh impossible, to pay proper tribute to Eddie Ginsberg—an incomparable man with an infinite capacity for sharing his life with family, friends and fellow Jews all over the world.

It is forty years since we first met. I, at the bottom of the ladder, he at the top, as a national and international leader. But in the time we spent together, he became more than a colleague. Eddie was both a teacher and friend, and I joined him as a partner in some of the most dramatic events in current Jewish history. He played the critical role with his daring planning, creative imagination and unbelievable lack of ego. His personality enabled him to get the most out of those who joined him in his historic venture into Jewish unity and Jewish rescue.

Eddie, leadership in the Cleveland Federation, National UJA, the Jewish Agency, the Joint Distribution Committee and the United Israel Appeal brings to mind the lyrics of a song I heard long ago.

No one can take away
No one can wash away
No wind can blow away
No tide can turn away
No fire can burn away
And Time cannot wear away

...the memories of Eddie Ginsberg, especially those of Rosalie, Billy, Inger, Bobby, Jan, their families and all of us who were privileged to shake his hand, share a drink, who worked and planned together with him to help those in need.

Eddie, you loved being with people. It made no difference if they were taxi drivers or multi-millionaires. When you entered an office to solicit a six or seven-figure gift, one could see and feel the tension drain from the prospect as he felt the respect, affection and dedication in your face and presence. More often than not, you succeeded, Eddie, and the two of you became lifelong friends.

Eddie and Rosalie's beautiful home in Caesaria, on the sea in Israel, was symbolic of their openness and warmth with people. For a snack, lunch or dinner, anyone could show up—Moshe Dayan, Ezer Weizman, a chief of staff, Chaim Vinitzky, director of the UJA Israel office, Eliezer Shavit, director of the Israel Education Fund, one or two visiting Americans, or Englishmen, a guide, gardener, a neighbor or two. Eddie, you and Rosalie treated them all alike—as members of your extended family.

At times, Eddie, you thought your house was the Hilton Ballroom, but Rosalie was always there when you needed her, to keep life in proper perspective. The two of you were more than partners—you were never apart. It was clear to all that you had never fallen out of love.

Eddie, so many of your close friends are here with us today, among them one of your oldest friends, Mel Dubinsky from St. Louis. Do you remember when the three of us went fishing in a small boat in Canada for northern pike? At times like that, your capacity and love for food was more than evident, and frankly, a matter of concern.

[Also present:]

Irwin Field of Los Angeles, who soon followed you as head of UJA—the two of you bringing a new dimension of leadership to this great American Jewish community.

And Ralph Goldman, JDC-Israel's executive, when you were the chairman. Together, the two of you developed some of the most creative programs in Israel and Eastern Europe, programs that were designed for the elderly, who thought they had been forgotten.

And Lenny Bell of Maine and Florida is here. He was the Young Leadership chairman who joined you, your son, Billy, and me as the first Americans to visit Israel just before the end of the Six-Day War.

If you were ever at your best, Eddie, it was then—with tears of joy for the victors and tears of sorrow for the young lives lost. When we visited active units still on alert in the Sinai, you put them all at ease with the warmth of your boundless embraces.

These are moments that will live forever for those who knew you and loved you, Eddie. These are moments we will dream about all our lives. These are moments, which will always be remembered by the many who crossed your path, and joined you in the historic Jewish and human drama of rescue and state building, which you led with passion, devotion and achievement.

From Jerusalem to Cleveland, from New York to Los Angeles, wherever Jewish leadership will gather, they will tell your story, Eddie.

And although you have well-earned your place among the immortals above, as you were in life, Eddie, you will so be in our hearts and minds.

Appendix E

NATIONAL UJA CHAIRMEN*

1939–1943	Rabbi Abba Hillel Silver	Cleveland, OH
	Rabbi Jonah B. Wise	New York City, NY
1944–1947	Rabbi James G. Heller	Cincinnati, OH
	William Rosenwald	New York City, NY
	Rabbi Jonah B. Wise	New York City, NY
1947–1950	Henry Morgenthau, Jr.	Washington, DC
1951–1954	Edward M. M. Warburg	New York City, NY
1955–1957	William Rosenwald	New York City, NY
1958–1960	Morris W. Berenstein	Syracuse, NY
1961	**Philip M. Klutznick	Chicago, IL
1961–1964	Joseph Meyerhoff	Baltimore, MD
1965–1967	Max M. Fisher	Detroit, MI
1968–1971	Edward Ginsberg	Cleveland, OH
1971–1974	Paul Zuckerman	Detroit, MI
1975–1977	Hon. Frank R. Lautenberg	Montclair, NJ
1977–1978	Leonard R. Strelitz	Norfolk, VA
1978–1980	Irwin S. Field	Los Angeles, CA
1980–1982	Herschel W. Blumberg	Chevy Chase, MD
1982–1984	Robert E. Loup	Denver, CO
1984–1986	Alexander Grass	Harrisburg, PA
1986–1988	Martin F. Stein	Milwaukee, WI
1988–1990	Morton A. Kornreich	New York City, NY
1990–1992	Marvin Lender	New Haven, CT
1992–1994	Joel D. Tauber	Detroit, MI
1994–1996	***Richard L. Pearlstone	Baltimore, MD
1996–	Richard L. Wexler	Chicago, IL

*From 1939 to 1984 the title of the leading officer was "general chairman," and the lay leaders serving under him were referred to as "national chairmen." In 1984 the title of "chief officer" was changed to "national chairman," and the titles of those serving under him changed to "national vice chairs."

**Resigned to accept ambassadorial appointment from President John Kennedy.

***"Generation to generation": Pearlstone is the grandson of Joseph Meyerhoff, who served as national chairman, 1961–64.

EXECUTIVE VICE CHAIRMEN*

1939–1950	Henry Montor	New York City, NY
1951–1954	Dr. Joseph J. Schwartz	New York City, NY
1954–1971	Rabbi Herbert A. Friedman	Denver, CO
1971–1983	Irving Bernstein	New York City, NY
1983–1991	Stanley B. Horowitz	Cleveland, OH
1991–1996	Rabbi Brian L. Lurie	San Francisco, CA
1996–	Bernard Moscovitz	Montreal, Canada

*As of 1996, the title Executive Vice Chairman has been changed to Executive, Vice President.

NATIONAL WOMEN'S DIVISION* CHAIRS

1939–1956	**Mrs. Felix M. Warburg	New York City, NY
1946–1947	Mrs. David M. Levy	New York City, NY
1950–1952	Mrs. S. Alexander Brailove	Elizabeth, NJ
1953–1954	Mrs. Albert Pilavin	Providence, RI
1954–1955	Mrs. Hal Horne	New York City, NY
1955–1956	Mrs. Henry Newman	Kansas City, KS
1957–1960	Mrs. Jack Goodman	Indianapolis, IN
1961–1963	Mrs. Israel D. Fink	Minneapolis, MN
1964–1966	Mrs. Jack Karp	Los Angeles, CA
1967–1968	Mrs. Harry L. Jones	Detroit, MI
1969–1972	Mrs. Bernard Schaenen	Dallas, TX
1972–1974	***Elaine K. Winik	New York City, NY
1975–1977	Sylvia Hassenfeld	Providence, RI
1977–1979	Peggy Steine	Nashville, TN
1977–1979	Marilyn Brown	South Bend, IN
1979–1981	Bernice Waldman	West Hartford, CT
1981–1983	Harriet Sloane	New York City, NY
1983–1988	Harriet Zimmerman	Atlanta, GA
1985–1988	Judith A. Levy	Boston, MA
1988–1990	Bobi Klotz	New York City, NY
1990–1994	Roberta Holland	Providence, RI
1992–1993	Yona Goldberg	Washington, DC
1993–1995	Carole E. Solomon	New York City, NY
1995–1997	Betty Kane	Cherry Hill, NJ
1997–	Rebecca Newman	San Diego, CA

*In 1993, the name was changed to Women's Council
**Honorary chair
***Beginning in 1972, women began asserting their own identity.

YOUNG LEADERSHIP CHAIRS

1962–1963	Alan Sagner	Metropolitan New Jersey
1963–1965	Joseph H. Kanter	Miami, FL
1965–1967	Leonard D. Bell	Lewiston, ME
1967–1968	Herbert J. Garon	New Orleans, LA
1968–1969	Gordon Zacks	Columbus, OH
1969–1970	James H. Nobil	Akron, OH
1970–1971	Robert M. Schrayer	Chicago, IL
1971–1972	Don Benjamin	Metropolitan New Jersey
1972–1973	Michael Pilavin	Flint, MI
1973–1974	Dr. Allen Pollack	New York City, NY
1974–1975	Don Gould	Albany, NY
1975–1976	Alan Rudy	Houston, TX
1976–1977	Joel Abramson	Portland, ME
1977–1978	Neil Cooper	Boston, MA
1978–1979	Ralph J. Stern	Morris-Sussex, NJ
	*Jane Sherman	Detroit, MI
1979–1980	Stanley D. Frankel	Detroit, MI
	**Bobi Klotz	NewYork City, NY
1980–1981	Lawrence Jacker	Detroit, MI
	Barbara K. Wiener	Ft. Lauderdale, FL
1981–1982	Edward B. Robin	Los Angeles, CA
	Vicki Agron	New York City, NY
1982–1983	David S. Gre	Washington, DC
	Nita Levy	Kansas City, MO
1983–1984	Stephen M. Greenberg	Metro/West, NJ
	Mickey Baron	Louisville, KY
1984–1985	Carl H. Kaplan	Washington, DC
	Betsy R. Gordon	Philadelphia, PA
1985–1986	Michael M. Adler	Miami, FL
	Ann Louise Kleper	Chicago, IL
1986–1987	Daniel Rubin	Bergen County, NJ
	Sandy Neuman	St. Paul, MN
1987–1988	Theodore A. Young	Philadelphia, PA
	Anita Gray	Cleveland, OH

1988–1989	Frank S. Hagelberg	Rochester, NY
	Amy N. Dean	Miami, FL
1989–1990	Eric J. Zahler	New York City, NY
	Margery Stone	Delaware
1990–1991	Thomas A. Falik	Houston, TX
	Heidi Dansky	Birmingham, AL
1991–1992	Stuart T. Rossman	Boston, MA
	Susan K. Stern	New York City, NY
1992–1993	***Jerry Benjamin	Milwaukee, WI
1993–1994	***Max R. Schrayer	Chicago, IL
	Emily F. Zimern	Charlotte, NC
1994–1995	Joel S. Beren	Toledo, OH
	Debra F. Pell	San Francisco, CA
1995–1996	Robert W. Fisher	Cincinnati, OH
	Diane Fox Prystowsky	Charleston, SC
1996–1997	Jeffrey Snyder	Washington, DC
	Karen Marcus	San Diego, CA
1997–1998	Joel Alperson	Omaha, NE
	Jody Schwartz	New York, NY

*Beginning in 1978, Young Men's and Women's leadership conducted joint programs.

**Served both as Young Leadership chairs and then as chairs of the national Women's Division.

***"Generation to generation"; as the sons were elected to the same leadership positions held by their fathers.

RABBINIC CHAIRS

Rabbi Morris Adler z"l	Detroit, MI
Rabbi Haskell M. Bernat	New York, NY
Rabbi Joseph H. Ehrenkranz	Stamford, CT
Rabbi Gary A. Glickstein	Miami Beach, FL
Rabbi David Golovensky z"l	New York, NY
Rabbi Robert I. Kahn	Houston, TX
Rabbi Stanley M. Kessler	West Hartford, CT
Rabbi Doniel Z. Kramer	New York, NY
Rabbi Vernon H. Kurtz	Highland Park, IL
Rabbi Irving Lehrman	Miami Beach, FL
Rabbi Haskel Lookstein	New York, NY
Rabbi Joseph H. Lookstein z"l	New York, NY
Rabbi Alvin M. Marcus	West Orange, NJ
Rabbi Norman R. Patz	Cedar Grove, NJ
Rabbi Stanley S. Rabinowitz	Washington, DC
Rabbi Jacob S. Rubenstein	Scarsdale, NY
Rabbi Hillel E. Silverman	Greenwich, CT
Rabbi Matthew H. Simon	Rockville, MD
Rabbi Dudley Weinberg z"l	Milwaukee, WI
Rabbi Michael R. Zedek	Kansas City, MO

*The Rabbinic Cabinet originally was formed in January 1939.
It is the oldest constituent organization within the UJA.*

INDEX

21 Club 14

A

"A Battle for Grenada" 253–254
Abramson, Joel 302
Abramson, Samuel H. 4, 8, 17
Adelman, Albert 62
Adenauer, Konrad 142
Adler, Michael M. 302
Adler, Rabbi Morris 246–247, 304
Agron, Vicki 302
A History of the UJA 1939–1982 xvii
Al Hamishmar 73
Aleichem, Sholom 293
aliyah 36, 47, 90, 194
Aliyah Bet 207
Allon, Yigal 54, 55, 56, 67, 68, 100, 175
Almogi, Yosef 149
Alperson, Joel 303
Alterman 144, 253
American Council for Judaism 2
American Financial Development Corporation
        for Israel xvii, 103
American Friends of the Hebrew University xiv, 63
American Jewis Committee xiii
American Jewish Joint Distribution Committee (JDC) 3
American Society for Technion-Israel Institute
        of Technology xiv, 63
Annenberg, Lee 205
Annenberg, Walter 205
Antek 189
Arafat, Yasser 231, 249
Argov, Shlomo 99, 161, 162
Ariel, Ya'akov 24
Ascoli, Marion 202
Auschwitz xiv, 178, 260
Avner, Yehuda 38
Avraham Harman Institute of Contemporary Jewry xvi, xviii–xix

B

Baerwald, Paul 83
Barenboim, Daniel 176
Barnett, Fanny 103
Barnett, Ruby 103
Baron, Mickey 302
Battling for Peace 131
Bauer, Yehuda 71
Begin, Menachem 27, 38, 40, 41, 42, 44, 46, 48, 124, 140, 206
Beilin, Yossi 233, 237
Bell, Leonard D. 204, 211, 297, 302
Ben-Gurion, David 4, 17, 18, 79, 84, 87, 103-104, 124, 130, 136, 139, 140, 157, 158, 186, 191–192, 194, 196–197, 199, 207–208, 240, 243, 280-281
Benjamin, Don 302
Benjamin, Jerry 303
Benny, Jack 250
Bensley, Charles 196
Beren, Joel S. 303
Berenstein, Morris W. 4, 298
Berle, Milton ix
Bernardi, Herschel 70, 265
Bernat, Rabbi Haskell M. 304
Bernstein, Bob xii, 156
Bernstein, Irving vi–vii, viii–xv, xvi, xvii, xviii, xix, 39, 102, 110, 168, 172, 188, 221, 258, 286, 288, 294, 300
Bernstein, Joe xiii
Bernstein, Judy xii, 66, 211, 251
Beyer family 198
Beyer Home for the Aged 198
Bikel, Theodore 70, 265
Bitburg 269, 271, 275
Block, Ellie 206
Bloom, Melvyn H. xiv
Blumberg, Herschel W. 298
Board of Governors of the Jewish Agency 5, 120, 123, 214
Borscht Belt ix
Boschwitz, Rudy 116
Boxenbaum, Joe 155

Boyar, Louis 4
Brailove, Mathilda 4, 5, 6, 8, 9, 177
Brailove, Mrs. S. Alexander (Mathilda) 301
Brandeis University vii, xv, 109, 139, 152, 153, 281
Bronfman, Charles 135, 137, 163
Bronfman, Edgar 135
Bronfman, Sam 135
Brown, Marilyn 206, 301
Brugioni, Dino 260
Burg, Avrum 127
Burg, Yosef 127, 141
Burns, Arthur 114–115
Burns, George ix
Bush, President George 108, 115, 116, 142, 153, 206
Butzel, Fred 122

C

Caesar, Sid ix
Cantor, Eddie ix
Cardin, Shoshana 5, 152
Carlos 162
Carter, President Jimmy xiv, 50, 63, 68, 71, 256, 260, 266
Casals, Pablo 192
Channing, Carol 250
Chin, Trevor 211
Chinitz, Rabbi Zelig 127
Churchill, Winston 259, 277
Clinton, Hillary 182
Clinton, President Bill 142
Cobb, Lee J. 265
Cochini Jews 174
Cohen, George 18, 20
Conference of Presidents of Major American
        Jewish Organizations 116, 118, 161
Consul's Program 31
Coons, Isador 4
Cooper, Neil 302
Coughlin, Father Charles 247

Council of Jewish Federations (CJF) v, 4
Council of Jewish Federations and Welfare Funds 4

D

Daman, Jeanne 5, 8, 10
Dansky, Heidi 303
Dash [Democratic Party for Change] 24
Davis, Moshe iii, xix, 8, 52, 69, 71
Dayan, Assaf 230, 253
Dayan, Ehud 230, 253
Dayan, Moshe iii, 68, 69, 99, 100, 139, 140, 144, 158, 175, 220,
    220, 221, 230, 238, 240, 249, 251–254, 272, 287
        works by: *Breakthrough* 253-254
Dayan, Rachel 253
Dayan, Ruth 230, 238, 240, 253
Dayan, Yael iii, 221, 230–243, 246, 248–249, 251
        works by: *Death Has Two Sons* 231
        My Father, His Daughter 231, 232
        New Face in the Mirror 231, 232
        Sinai Diary-67 231
Dayan, Zorik 139
De Gaulle, Charles 142
Dead Sea Scrolls 24
Dean, Amy N. 303
Denmark School 197
Department of Rural and Urban Development 48
Detroit Free Press 117, 154
Diaspora 143
Dinitz, Simcha 99, 175
Dinsteins 175
Dobrynin, Anatoly 267
Dole, Bob 153
Douglas, Kirk 250–251
Dor le-Dor 72
Dresser Industries 290
Dubinsky, Melvin 4, 85, 110, 211, 296
Dulzin, Leon 29, 31, 41, 44, 45, 68, 127

E

Eban, Abba 6, 19, 98, 123, 175
Edelman, Lily 263
Edelman, Peter 239
Ehrenkranz, Rabbi Joseph H. 304
Ehrlichman, John 115
Eichmann, Adolf 207
Einstein, Albert 12, 197
Eisenhower, President Dwight D. 113, 115, 123, 153, 158
Eisner, Shulamit 137
Ellis Island viii
Ellis Island to Ebbets Field ix
El Al 72, 119, 149, 173
Epstein, Betty 239
Epstein, Ray 239
Eshel Program 198
Eshkol, Levi 77, 124, 130, 243

F

Falik, Thomas A. 303
Federation of Jewish Philanthropies vi
Feinberg, Abe 190
Feldman, Jake 198, 206
Field, Helgard 210, 224, 225, 247
Field, Irwin S. iv, 97, 98, 178, 210–228, 236, 246–248, 296, 298
Field, Joanna Sinaiko 97, 98, 214–216, 224, 246–247
Fink, Mrs. Israel D. 301
Fisher-Bernstein Institute for Jewish Leadership 289
Fisher, Julie 163
Fisher, Margie 163
Fisher, Marjorie 109, 117, 155
Fisher, Mary 163
Fisher, Max M. iv, vi, vii, 38, 39, 40, 41, 46, 48, 91, 92, 108–
    128, 135, 137, 148, 191, 211, 220, 269, 273, 280, 281, 298
        "court Jew" 161, 162
Fisher, Philip 163
Fisher, Robert W. 303

Ford, Ann 117
Ford, Betty 205
Ford, Cristina 155
Ford, Henry 108, 115–117, 153–156, 158, 164, 220
Ford, Henry, Sr. 117
Ford, President Gerald 66, 113
Forman, Fred 4
Fortress Husan 144
Frankel, Stanley D. 302
Freistadt, Peter 240
Friedman, Joel S. xiv
Friedman, Rabbi Herbert A. xii, 25, 62, 69, 111, 150, 177, 204, 300

G

Garon, Herbert J. 302
Gibson, Harvey 18, 19
Ginsberg, Billy 296
Ginsberg, Edward 91, 92, 149, 151, 161, 162, 204, 211–212, 226,
    295–297, 298
Ginsberg, Rosalie 296
Glickstein, Rabbi Gary A. 304
Goldberg, Yona 301
Golden, Peter 152, 163
Goldenberg, Edward 37
Goldenberg, Harold 80, 83, 89, 100, 101
Goldman, Harold 4
Goldman, Ralph 179, 188, 191, 197, 198, 211, 296
Goldsmith, Bram 214
Goldstein, Dov 187
Golovensky, Rabbi David 304
Goodman, Mrs. Jack 301
Goodman, Sarah 177
Gordon, Betsy R. 302
Gould, Don 302
Grass, Alexander 39, 298
Gray, Anita 302
Gre, David S. 302
Greenberg, Stephen M. 302

Grueskin, Zeke 4

H

Haber, Sam viii
Hadassah 25, 26, 151, 194, 213
Haganah 12, 14, 79, 84, 130, 186
Hagelberg, Frank S. 303
Halpern, Rose 151
Hammer, Gottlieb 8, 16, 18-19, 20, 21
Hanagid, Shmuel 253
Harman, Abe 118
Hassenfeld, Alan 176
Hassenfeld, Merrill 168, 171, 175, 176, 182, 195, 206, 208
Hassenfeld, Steven 176
Hassenfeld, Sylvia iv, vi, 5, 116, 166–184, 195, 196, 204, 205, 206, 208, 301
Hayes, Walter 154, 156, 157
Hebrew University of Jerusalem xvi, 24, 109
Heller, James G. 298
Hellman, Lillian 239
Hellman, Yehuda 118, 251
Herzl, Theodor 143
Herzog, Chaim 69
Heschel, Rabbi Abraham Joshua 283
Histadrut 76, 78
Hitler, Adolf 260
Hoffberger, Jerrold "Chuck" 46, 110, 127, 205
Holland, Roberta 301
Holocaust 2, 3, 25, 133, 143, 189, 192, 259, 263, 267, 272
Holocaust Memorial Museum Committee 266
Holocaust Museum 268
Horne, Lea 5, 8, 12
Horne, Mrs. Hal 301
Horowitz, Stanley B. 300
Hotel Fourteen 103

I

Ibn Zahav, Ari 74

Indyk, Martin 176, 177
Institute of Contemporary Jewry xvi, xvii
Israel America Petroleum Corporation 103
Israel Bonds iv, 58, 88, 100, 101, 109, 197
Israel Education Fund xiii, 194, 196, 197, 296
Israel Museum 208

J

Jacker, Lawrence 302
Jackson, Henry 66
Jackson-Vanik Amendment 65, 67
Jacobson, Charlotte 151
Jerusalem Foundation 199, 207, 208
Jessel, George ix
Jewish Agency 14, 17, 29, 30, 34, 36, 38, 44, 82, 118,
    158, 162, 204, 222, 274
Jewish Brigade 14
Johnson, President Lyndon 113, 123
Joint Distribution Committee (JDC) viii, xiii, 9, 11, 188, 198, 291
Jones, Jennie 204
Jones, Mrs. Harry L. 301
Jordan, Charles 93

K

Kahn, Rabbi Robert I. 304
Kane, Betty 301
Kanter, Joseph H. 302
Kaplan, Carl H. 302
Kaplan, Eliezer 17, 18, 78
Kaplan, Mendel 211, 215
Karp, Abraham J. xvii
Karp, Mrs. Jack 301
Katz, Israel 27
Katzav, Moshe 37
Katzir, Ephraim 175, 225
Katzki, Herbert 8, 11
Kaufman, Menahem xvii, 8, 25, 52
Kaye, Danny ix, 250

Kennedy, President John F. 62, 113, 142, 153, 299
Keren Hayesod 3, 6, 34, 36, 37, 41, 42, 47, 59, 70, 136, 151, 217, 242
Kessler, Irving 178
Kessler, Rabbi Stanley M. 304
Ketubbot Emunah Mission 206
Kibbutz Ein Gev 186, 207
King Abdullah 76
Kirshblum, Rabbi Mordechai 127
Kirya 105, 157
Kiryat Malachi 37
Kiryat Menahem 28, 30
Kissinger, Henry 53, 54, 55, 65, 66, 67, 99, 100, 116, 158
Kleper, Ann Louise 302
Klotz, Bobi 301, 302
Klutznick, Philip M. 62, 153, 298
Koach missions xiii, 72, 225
Kohl, Helmut 271
Kollek, Amos 187
Kollek, Tamar 207
Kollek, Teddy iii, 104, 175, 176, 186–200, 206–208
    works by: *For Jerusalem: A Life* 187
    Jerusalem, City of Mankind 187
    Jerusalem, Policy Papers 187
    My Jerusalem 187
    Teddy's Jerusalem 187
Kolno viii, xv
Kornreich, Morton A. 298
Kramer, Rabbi Doniel Z. 304
Krueger, Harvey 137, 163
Kurtz, Rabbi Vernon H. 304

L

Labor Party 131, 230
Lamm, Rabbi Norman 283, 294
Laskov, Chaim 68
Lautenberg, Frank R. iv, vi, xiv, xviii, 39, 50–60, 62–74, 97, 120, 173, 266, 267, 292, 298

Lavon, Pinchas 140
Leavitt, Moses 83, 93
Lehrman, Rabbi Irving 304
Leidesdorf, Sam 20
Leiwant, Sidney E. 8, 21
Lender, Marvin 298
Lerner, Alexander 267
Lesser, Sy 238
LeVette, Henry xi
Levi-Strauss family 152
Levine, Harry 84
Levine, Peter ix
Levy, Adele 203, 206
Levy, David 141
Levy, Judith A. 301
Levy, Mrs. David M. 301
Levy, Nita 302
Lewis, Jerry ix
Lieberman, Shaul 273
Lion of Judah 168, 169, 174
Lion of Judah Endowment Program (LOJE) 169
"Living Bridge" 6, 217
Lookstein, Rabbi Haskel 304
Lookstein, Rabbi Joseph H. 304
Loup, Robert E. 298
Lubriani, Uri 116
Luckman, Sol 5
Lurie, Rabbi Brian L. 46, 70, 300

M

Ma'abarot 173
Machon le-Tipul be-Ochlosiot Nechshalot 86
Magic Carpet 62
Malben 86, 102, 103
Mandel, Morton 40, 127, 137, 163
Mapai [Labor] Party 104, 130
Marcus, Karen 303
Marcus, David "Mickey" 197

Marcus, Rabbi Alvin M. 304
Margin for Peace 138
Marks, Simon 188
Marx, Barbara 205
Marx, Harpo 250
Maskit 230
Materials for Israel 12
Mauriac, François 256
Max M. Fisher/Irving Bernstein Institute 281
Mazer, Joseph 4, 5, 8, 15, 16
Mazer, William 5
McCracken, Paul 114, 115
Mehta, Zubin 173, 195, 208
Meir, Golda iii, xviii, 4, 8, 15, 16, 17, 20, 76-93, 96–105, 124, 159, 183, 215, 216, 240, 272, 273
Meirowitz, Fannie x
Mendès-France, Pierre 142
Meyerhoff, Joseph J. 5, 62, 196, 197, 298, 299
Michel, Ernest xiv, 193
Minhalot Program 198
Miron, Issachar xvii, 70, 71
Mitchell, John 113, 116
Mitterrand, François 142, 257
Moda'i, Yitzhak 141
Mo'etzet ha-Poalot 78
Montor, Henry x, xvii, 4, 14, 15, 16, 17, 78, 80, 82, 83, 84, 85, 100, 101, 103, 135, 150, 168, 188, 190, 191, 202, 203, 300
Morgenthau, Jr., Henry iv, 2, 18–19, 83, 102, 202, 298
Moskovitz, Bernard 300
Myerson, Morris 76

N

Netanyahu, Benjamin 249
Netanyahu, Yonathan 293
National Refugee Service (NRS) 3
Neuman, Sandy 302
Newman, Mrs. Henry 301
Newman, Rebecca 301

Nixon, President Richard 66, 99, 100, 105, 108, 113, 114, 115, 116,
       118, 124, 153, 158
Nobel Prize 140, 256, 271
Nobil, James H. 302

O

Operation Exodus 63, 222
Operation Ezra 116
Operation Independence 125, 137, 159, 163
Operation Moses 63
Operation Solomon 63
OSE (Organization for the Rescue of Children) 11

P

Palestine xi, 2, 9, 12
Patz, Rabbi Norman R. 304
Paul Baerwald School for Social Service Work 103
Pearlman, Moshe 187
Pearlman, Robert A. xiv
Pearlstone, Richard L. 298, 299
Peled, Israel 37, 38
Pell, Debra F. 303
Peres, Shimon iii, 67, 125, 130–145, 163, 243, 272
       works by: *David's Sling* 131, 138
       Entebbe Diary 131
       The New Middle East 131
       The Next Step 131
Peres, Sonya 131, 138
Perle, Richard 66
Perlman, Itzhak 192, 208
Peron, Eva 179
Persian Gulf War 173
Pilavin, Michael 302
Pilavin, Mrs. Albert 301
Pincus, Louis 104, 119, 148, 149, 160, 196
Pollack, Dr. Allen 302
Pomerenze, Shalom J. xvii
Postal, Bernard 17

Precious Legacy Exhibit 66
President's Commission on the Holocaust 256, 260, 266
Presidents' Conference 162
Project Ezra 62
Project Renewal xiii, xviii, 6, 24, 26, 27, 36–48, 137, 193, 206,
  216, 217, 218, 234
Proskauer, Joseph 90, 91
Protocols of the Elders of Zion 117, 154
Prystowsky, Diane Fox 303

R

Rabin, Yitzhak 54, 55, 57, 67, 98, 99, 100, 123, 131, 136, 140,
  141, 162, 163, 175, 237, 272
Rabinowitz, Rabbi Stanley S. 291, 304
Rafi (Reshimat Po'alei Yisrael-the Israel Workers List) 104, 130,
  139
Ramon, Chaim 237
Raphael, Marc Lee xvii
Ratner, Julius 246
Reagan, President Ronald xiv, 66, 108, 109, 115, 153, 269–
  270, 271
Reinharz, Jehuda 280, 281
Reisman, Bernard 153
Republican Party 113, 153, 162, 164
Rivlin, Moshe 293
Robin, Edward B. 302
Robinson, Edward G. 250
Rockefeller, Nelson 113
Romney, George 113
Roosevelt, President Franklin Delano 2, 102, 103, 112, 259, 260
Rosen, Moshe 178
Rosenwald, Adele Levy 202
Rosenwald, Julius 2, 202
Rosenwald, Lessing 2, 3
Rosenwald, William 2, 4, 5, 13, 80, 82, 83, 84, 88, 120, 135,
  151, 177, 190, 202, 205, 206, 298
Rossman, Stuart T. 303
Roth, Philip 239

Rothberg, Sam iv, 5, 16, 82, 85, 89, 91, 100, 101, 190, 196
Rothschild family 150
Rubenstein, Arthur 192
Rubenstein, Rabbi Jacob S. 304
Rubin, Daniel 302
Rudy, Alan 302
Ruppin, Arthur 175
Rural and Urban Development Department 217
Russell, Bob 217
Russell, Madeleine 152

S

Sachar, Howard M. vii
Sacher, Michael 120
Sagner, Alan 302
Samuel, Lord Herbert Louis 90
Sapir, Pinhas 64, 68, 117, 155, 156, 196, 274
Schaenen, Mrs. Bernard 301
Schneider, Michael 116
Schoenen, Fannie 206
Schrayer, Max R. 303
Schrayer, Robert M. 302
Schwartz, Dr. Joseph J. vi, 15, 122, 189, 190, 300
Schwartz, Jody 303
Schwartz, Rachel 240
Schwartz, Tamar 186
Schwartz, Zvi 240
Scranton, Gov. William 113
Sharansky, Natan 66
Sharett, Moshe 116, 240
Shavit, Eliezer 296
Shazar, 93
Shazar, Zalman 73
Sherman, Jane 48, 302
Shertok, Moshe 19, 20
Shimshoni, Dan 31, 45
Shitrit, Meir 37
Shorr, Milton xiv

Shulman, Avis 4, 5, 8, 13
Shulman, Charles 13
Shultz, George 125
Sieff, Israel 188
Silver, Rabbi Abba Hillel 4, 298
Silverman, Rabbi Hillel E. 304
Simon, Bess 238
Simon, Rabbi Matthew H. 304
Sinai Campaign 91, 140, 251
Sinatra, Frank 205
Sion, Dan 231
Sion, Dov 231
Sion, Racheli 231, 232
Six-Day War iv, 3, 89, 91, 142, 204, 238, 297
Slater, Irving 103
Slavin, Haim 84
Sloane, Harriet 206, 301
Sloane, Stanley 206
Snyder, Jeffrey 303
Sobel, Rabbi Henry 282
Solomon, Carole E. 182, 301
Sonneborn Group 103
Sonneborn, Rudolph 12, 83, 84, 103, 190
Soviet Jewry 53
Squadron, Howard 251
Stein, Martin F. 298
Steine, Peggy 206, 301
Stern, Edith 202
Stern, Isaac 173, 192, 195, 208
Stern, Ralph J. 302
Stern, Susan K. 303
Stone, Dewey D. 5, 84, 102, 151
Stone, Margery 303
Strelitz, Leonard R. 39, 40, 298
Suez Campaign 144
Suez Canal 156
Sukenik, Eliezer 24

Sultan's Pool 175, 195, 196, 208

T

Tabatchnick, Marc 149
Talisman, Mark 66
Tasca, Henry J. 159
Taub, Henry 50, 63, 65, 103, 178
Taub, Joe 50
Tauber, Joel D. 298
Taubman, Al 155
Tekoah, Yosef 98
The American Council of Judaism 10
The New York Times ix, xiii, 71, 159, 164, 259
The Next Phase 138
The Pledge 103
The Quiet Diplomat 152, 163
The Traveler's Guide to Jewish Landmarks in Europe 17
The Wall Street Journal iv, 290
This Year in Jerusalem Mission xiii, 72, 193
tikkun olam 144
Tisch, Wilma 5
Tishman, Peggy 5
To Give Life xvii
Treblinka viii
"Truth to power" 269, 271, 273
Tucker, Sophie ix
TWA 72

U

UJA Archival Center xvii
U.S. Holocaust Commission 63
U.S. Holocaust Memorial Council xiv, 63, 167, 256
U.S. Point-4 Program 191
United Israel Appeal (UIA) xiii, 120, 291
United Palestine Appeal (UPA) 3, 82, 89, 120, 188
United Way iv, 109, 117
UNRRA 14, 15

V

van der Heuvel, William 259-261
Vanik, Charles 66
Venezky, Julian 85, 91, 100, 101
Vietnam 241
Vinitzky, Chaim 296

W

Waldman, Bernard 206
Waldman, Bernice 206, 301
Walters, Barbara 69
War of Independence 2
War Refugee Board 2
Warburg, Edward M. 80, 82, 83, 91, 120, 122, 151, 190, 202, 298
Warburg, Mrs. Felix M. 202, 203, 301
Washington Post iv
"We Are One" 65, 69, 73, 74, 192, 288
Wechsler, Ralph 8, 19-20, 21
Weiler, Jack D. 5
Weinberg, Barbara 5, 177
Weinberg, Larry 177
Weinberg, Rabbi Dudley 304
Weiner, Sandra 66
Weiss, Eve xiv
Weitz, Ra'anan 174
Weizman, Ezer 157, 240, 241
Weizman, Reuma 240
Weizmann, Chaim 8, 12, 13, 103, 120, 175
Westheimer, Dr. Ruth 181
Wexler, Richard L. 298
Wiener, Barbara K. 302
Wiesel, Elie xiv, 63, 69, 70, 71, 72 , 256–277
works by: "Against Despair" 71, 264, 265
A Beggar in Jerusalem 256
A Jew Today 72, 265, 274
A Passover Haggadah 256
La Nuit [Night] 256

Sages and Dreamers 256
The Fifth Son 256
The Forgotten 256
The Testament 256
Tous les fleuves vont à la mer [All Rivers Run to the Sea] 256
Zalman, or The Madness of God 70, 264–266
Wiesel, Marion 257
Wiesel, Shlomo Elisha 257
Wingate, Mrs. Orde 12
Winik, Elaine K. 5, 170, 173, 204, 301
Wise, Rabbi Jonah B. xii, 4, 298
Wiseman, Joseph 70, 265
Women's Division 5, 166–184, 202, 203, 204, 205, 206
World Gathering of Holocaust Survivors xiv, 193
World Zionist Organization 36, 119

Y

Yadin, Carmela 175
Yadin, Orly 175
Yadin, Yigael iii, xviii, 24–34, 42, 43, 44, 46, 47, 175, 206
Yariv, General Aharon 250
Yavneh 37
Yeshiva University vii, xiv, 109, 294
Yishuv 3, 15, 24, 27, 102, 207
Yom Kippur War iv, 65, 72, 91, 98, 104, 105, 140, 173, 250, 265
Young Leadership xiii, xiii, 72, 97, 163, 218, 247
Young, Theodore A. 302
Youth Aliyah 13

Z

Zacks, Gordon 39, 302
Zahala 252
Zahler, Eric J. 303
Zedek, Rabbi Michael R. 304
Zimern, Emily F. 303
Zimmerman, Harriet 301
Zuckerman, Paul 63, 91, 92, 98, 104, 298